MW01484771

Tough Man,
Tender Chicken

Business & Life Lessons
from
Frank Perdue

Enjoy!

Mitzi Perdue

By
Mitzi Perdue

All photos courtesy of Perdue Farms, Inc. records,
Franklin P. Perdue Museum of Business
and Entrepreneurship,
Salisbury University, Salisbury, Maryland.

ISBN: 978-1-884108-09-9

Second Edition
Published June 2015
R. J. Myers Publishing Co. , Washington, D.C.

Book Design:
Initial Design & Media

DEDICATION

To the staff and volunteers of the Cal Ripken, Sr. Foundation. The good that they do cannot be calculated. Their signature program, *Badges for Baseball*, was created in collaboration with the U.S. Department of Justice, as a juvenile crime prevention initiative. Using baseball as a hook, law enforcement officers are paired with kids and through this program, underserved and at-risk youngsters are not only mentored by men and women in law enforcement, the kids learn important lessons about teamwork, communication, respect, healthy lifestyle, work ethic and leadership. The lessons are important not only on the baseball field, but also in life. More than one million youngsters have been impacted by Foundation programs since its inception in 2003.

TABLE OF CONTENTS

TABLE OF CONTENTS

TABLE OF CONTENTS

PREFACE

I've read that the first necessity for a biographer is "to kill the widow." To no one's great surprise, I consider this a remarkably bad idea.

But even so, I'm aware that the reason the phrase gained popularity is because there's so much truth to it. After all, how could a wife not be biased? In my case, defending myself against the charge is somewhat difficult because I labor under two related disadvantages: a) it's true, and b) I'm guilty.

In view of which, why do as I, as Frank's widow, dare write about his life?

The answer is, even though the source–me– is totally suspect, I still think that if you'll come along with me and see what it took to build a family business that started with a father and son, and grew into a company that today employs 19,000 men and women, and that sells its products in more than 100 different countries, you'll find the story entertaining, inspirational, and if you're a business school student or future entrepreneur, helpful for your career. In fact, I believe that a lot of his lessons were life lessons as well as business lessons.

Frank Perdue was an epic person. People who knew him well often speak of him as being larger than life. He had insights, courage, values, and a work ethic that, when combined, virtually guaranteed that he was going to make his mark.

He was demanding, occasionally difficult (one man I interviewed told me that he carried a bottle of Tums whenever he knew he was going to be seeing Frank), and Frank, honestly, was probably as tough as they make them. But he also inspired loyalty, and a stunning percentage of the people I talked with worked for him their whole lives and wouldn't have had it any other way.

Others, who didn't stay with the company, told me that working for him meant some of the best times of their lives, and the reason was that being with him was like going to one of the world's best educational institutions: Perdue University. (Much as I love the institution, I am not referring to Indiana's Purdue University).

Frank Perdue's "chicken university" could be difficult and there were the equivalent of exams, but you learned more and grew more than at any other time in your life. You always felt that he was challenging you to be all that you could be. Many of the people I interviewed said that they loved being on a winning team and were excited to come to work. They also liked that Frank Perdue specialized in developing and rewarding talent.

Were there detractors? You bet. I've included them, too, not because I want to, but because it gives a fuller picture, and also because I actually am sensitive to the I'm-really-really-really-biased problem.

There's also another aspect of the widow bias problem: I know that people talking to a man's widow are probably going to censor their stories. That means I can't promise you a fair and balanced view, but I do promise to tell things as they appeared to me or were told to me and to do it as honestly as I can.

Something else I can promise you: this was written by me, not a ghostwriter. I've been a writer all my life, including a couple of decades as a syndicated columnist, first for Capitol News and then for Scripps Howard. What you read here, pretty much every word of it, is mine. As far as having people change my work, I think the economist Thomas Sowell had it just right when he famously said that he's living proof the death penalty is a deterrent; he hasn't yet murdered an editor!

When I was first thinking about writing a biography of Frank, my goal was to write something that might be useful for business school students. I was hoping for part road map, part inspiration, and part simply a sense of Frank's reaching across the decades to show what it takes to accomplish big things. He was a mentor to many, and maybe through this book, I could continue that tradition. My original title for this book was "Business Lessons from Frank Perdue."

I think Frank would have liked the idea of still being involved in teaching, given that to his core he was a teacher. Students were always a major focus for Frank. He cared enough about transmitting knowledge that would be helpful to business school students that he founded a business school.

There are a lot of ways he could have spent his philanthropic money, but he chose creating a business school because of his commitment both to young people and to education. He wanted to make things just a little easier for them. Business school courses today teach many things that he had to learn through trial and error.

Well, that's the book I intended to write, but as I got further along in it, I realized that a lot of his story might interest people who grew up watching his TV ads. I can't count the number of people who've told me that they felt that they knew him, and that in a funny TV-kind of way, he was almost a family member. People I've met often seem hungry to know more what he was really like. So, with that in mind, this book grew in scope.

There's another group – I assume a much, much smaller one – who might be interested in how the chicken industry works. I'm guessing this group exists because I know, when I meet people, they're often curious about my family's industry. I'm not a certified expert, but I'll share what I've seen and learned after being closely associated with it for a quarter of a century.

It's a fascinating story to see how things get done in a big organization, and also to see how much of a role personnel and personality play. I have a master's degree in public administration, and I'm always amazed at how much more complex things are in real life, compared to the theories we studied. An idea can sound good and make sense, but what it takes to talk about it versus what it takes actually to implement it is the difference between a paper airplane and a massive rocket ship to the outer solar system. In this book, I wanted to show some of this complexity. For people who haven't seen a large and complex company up close and personal, I'd like to show that things don't happen just because someone at the top said, "Let it be so!"

So, whoever you are and whatever your interests, come along with me, and take a behind-the-scenes look at the life of a self-made man: an entrepreneur, a businessman, an advertising genius, and a man who on top of this had the folksy wisdom of a Will Rogers, and loved to encourage young people. The story of Frank Perdue isn't just about business lessons: it's also about life lessons. Enjoy!

INTRODUCTION

SUCCESS is a puzzle that has fascinated me since childhood. The curiosity started because of my father, who in the hotel business was known as a genius for having co-founded the Sheraton hotels. As a child, I tried to figure out just what he had that made him a success. But to his growing daughter, he seemed to be exactly like other grown-ups. He wasn't more driven or more energetic, as far as I could see.

The mystery of his success deepened when I was in graduate school studying management. Contrasting what we were taught with what I observed, I came to the same conclusion that an engineer once came to about bumble bees. This long ago engineer calculated that the bumblebee couldn't possibly fly; and I concluded that-if conventional explanations of successful leadership were true – my father couldn't have built Sheraton.

I often talked with him about just what it had taken. He told me that one of his secrets was to try a hundred leads, knowing that only one might pan out. But although that may have been one of the pieces of the puzzle, it certainly didn't account for the whole picture. After all, there are a lot of persistent people who don't build successful companies.

Something else: he was good at inspiring loyalty. People who started working for him usually stayed with him for the rest of their careers. Also, he put tremendous value on getting new information because he felt that "One good idea can change your life."

Other than these few factors, I wasn't quite sure why he was the success he was. Observing him at home, he seemed mild-mannered, laid-back and kind of ordinary.

INTRODUCTION

Frank Perdue's success, on the other hand, doesn't seem mysterious at all. I think there are very few people who would accuse Frank Perdue of being ordinary. His energy level, his intelligence, his persistence, his attention to detail, his dedication, were all on a stratospheric level.

The first time it occurred to me to want to write his biography was a quarter of a century ago, when I had known him less than 24 hours. I heard him talking to an associate on the phone, ("associate" is Perdue-speak for "employee"), and as I listened, I remember thinking, "This man speaks in aphorisms. He's a genius. It's not any accident that this man heads a Fortune 500-size company."

The conversation wasn't any trouble to overhear because Frank was ticked, and the decibel level was impressive. It was clear that something wasn't up to his standard, and he wanted to have whatever it was attended to *at once.*

"We have no right to sell a product that isn't the best we can make it!" he said forcefully. "You say that fewer than one percent of them have this defect? That's not good enough! The housewife doesn't buy averages, *she buys chicken one at a time!*"

The conversation didn't end there. He went on to give remarkably specific directions on what seemed like a half a dozen things that he wanted done immediately. He finished by demanding that, in view of the urgency of the situation, the man call him back with a report in half an hour.

Thwack. Frank set the phone back on the hook.

I can't remember today exactly what steps he had wanted the associate to take to solve whatever problem it was, but I clearly remember thinking that the logic of the steps was brilliant, and that he had an ability to analyze, and an ability to calculate how to get from here to there, that was the most impressive I had ever come across.

In a matter of seconds, Frank changed back to being relaxed, affable and fun, but I was left thinking about what he'd just said, and how he had said it.

x

INTRODUCTION

"Wow!" I marveled to myself, "This is how it's done! This is the kind of effort, commitment and brilliance it took!"

From then on, I made it a point to keep my Bic pen and notepad handy. Whenever we were together, I'd surreptitiously make notes on his conversations, stories and theories. We could even be at a white tablecloth restaurant, maybe sipping a glass of wine, and I'd nevertheless have my notepad on my lap, and there I was, as unobtrusively as I could, taking notes on what he had just said. As I began to meet his friends, I also made notes on what they said to him or about him.

I've sometimes wondered what he and they thought of my doing this. I never asked, and they seemed simply to accept that this is what Mitzi does. Looking back on it, I'm amazed that I got away with it.

During the entire 17 years of our marriage, I was always on the lookout for just what it was that made him such a success. I saw that he was very good at the practicalities of figuring out how to get from wherever he was to wherever he wanted to be. He had drive, endless curiosity, studied whatever it was he wanted to with at least the dedication of a Ph.D. student, but most of all, I thought he had a striking ability to see opportunities that were invisible to others and then to make those opportunities a reality.

For the record, Frank himself never shared my view that he was exceptional. If you asked him, he'd be a little embarrassed and mumble something about being in the right place at the right time. If you pressed him further, he would almost certainly have said something about having the good fortune to work with great people. But if you really, really pressed him and wouldn't let up, he'd repeat a quote that his daughter-in-law Jan Perdue had calligraphed for him and that was displayed prominently behind his desk in his office at home. It was from Alexander Hamilton, and he knew it by heart:

> *Men give me credit for some genius. All the genius I have lies in this; when I have a subject in hand, I study it profoundly. Day and night it is before me. My mind becomes pervaded with it. Then the effort that I have made*

is what people are pleased to call the fruit of genius. It is the fruit of labor and thought.

CHAPTER ONE

CHILDHOOD: WERE THERE CLUES
HE'D BE A SUCCESS?

Frank Perdue's life is like the kind of detective story in which you're told at the beginning what happened. The mystery is the events that led up to what happened. What did it take to build Perdue Farms?

The beginnings were not promising. Frank didn't excel at school and none of his childhood contemporaries guessed that he would get as far as he did. I've talked with dozens of them and the consensus seems to be that he was a normal kid – shy, not academically inclined, and the only really notable thing about him was his dedication to helping his father with the farming chores. According to classmate Georgia Coffin, he didn't participate in after-school events because the minute school was over, "He took off running as hard as he could" for home, which was two miles away.

As a child, he had been helping his father since, as he once told me, he was "so small he had to hold an egg with two hands." The earliest chores of this future captain of industry included collecting eggs, washing them, candling them and crating them.

CHILDHOOD: WERE THERE CLUES
HE'D BE A SUCCESS?

Round-cheeked and ready for winter, young Frank Perdue grew up to be one of America's most successful agricultural leaders.

One Early Clue

However, there was an early clue. In an event that foreshadowed much of Frank's future life, his father gave him fifty laying hens for a 4-H project. The fifty chickens were culls, chosen from the least promising 2.5% of his father's 2,000-hen flock.

You would expect these culls to perform badly, especially in the hands of a ten-year-old child. To an experienced poultry man like Frank's father, there are signs that a hen won't produce well, such as the condition of the feathers, or the appearance of the comb and wattles. The culls that he gave his young son would be predicted, under just about any normal circumstance, to produce very few eggs.

Surprisingly (if not amazingly), Frank's fifty culls far out-produced and out-performed the better birds. Frank explained this unexpected outcome by saying he gave his birds more individual care and that they had good genetics.

His unexpected success with the unpromising birds was a tip-off as to what he would accomplish later in life. This extra care plus the energy and commitment it required are among the secrets of his future success.

CHILDHOOD: WERE THERE CLUES
HE'D BE A SUCCESS?

The regular little boy with his dog and wagon from the Eastern Shore of Maryland would grow up to revolutionize an industry.

Frugality

Frugality always played an important part in Frank's career, and the ethic of being frugal and not wasting is an important part of Perdue Farms' culture today. This ethic had its roots in his father's example.

"My father used to save shoe leather from old shoes to make the hinges for the small doors of the chicken houses," Frank said. "He'd drive the three miles to town only once a week because the gas for the pickup, by his standards, was expensive. Trips to town had to coincide with the egg deliveries for shipment by train to the city markets. If you wanted something from town, you waited for that day."

CHILDHOOD: WERE THERE CLUES
HE'D BE A SUCCESS?

Hard Work

Taking care of the chickens and cleaning and packing the eggs all had to be done' without respite, seven days a week. Frank once told me, "No one was more negative to the chicken business than I was as a high-school student."

When Frank entered Salisbury State Teachers' College as a freshman in 1937, he had no plans to continue in the chicken business. But he wasn't sure what else he wanted to do either, and meanwhile, in between his college classes, he still had chores at home. "I used to mix feed at night," he remembered, "and then I'd get up at 5:00 a.m. to take care of the baby chicks. Part of my job was to empty the ashes and then fill each stove with fresh coal."

Frank Perdue's early dream was to play professional ball. He didn't have the necessary talent to be a player but, eventually became Co-Owner of three minor league teams in Eastern Maryland

Although Frank didn't engage in many extracurricular activities, the one exception was baseball. He loved baseball, and to the end of his days, Frank talked about how he would have liked to be a professional ball player. The problem was he couldn't hit the ball. He wasn't much good at catching it either. "I remember one day trying for a ball as an outfielder, and I backed up, backed up, backed up, reaching for the ball and confident that I was going to catch it. But I missed it. The batter got a triple."

CHILDHOOD: WERE THERE CLUES
HE'D BE A SUCCESS?

Drifting Into His Career

In June 1939, Frank left Salisbury State and returned to work for his father full time, two years short of completing his degree. "I didn't have any dreams of grandeur," he said. "It was more a question of drifting into it."

Nevertheless, the economics of the business proved to be a powerful lure. "I got my first flock of 800 New Hampshire Red breeders at that time," he said. "I soon found I could make as much as $40 a week selling hatching eggs."

The hatching eggs, by the way, are a different segment of the chicken industry from the breakfast eggs you eat. Frank's flock of breeding hens would produce hatching eggs, which he'd sell to the local hatchery. The hatchery would then hatch the eggs and sell the newly hatched chickens to farmers. The farmers, in turn, would raise the males for meat and the females for producing the breakfast eggs that we consumers eat.

Frank Perdue and Madeline Godfrey, his popular and athletic classmate at Salisbury State Teachers' College, married in 1941. The young couple worked seven days a week, packing the eggs from 10,000 hens at night after supper, and then still later, mixing the feed. His four children, Sandy, Anne, Beverly and Jim were born in the 1940s.

Frank continued with the farming chores, taking care of the chickens during the day. He was still painfully shy and admired Madeline's outgoing nature because it was such a contrast with his.

A Catastrophe Turns into a Good Fortune

In the early 1940s, something happened that at the time appeared to be a catastrophe for the business. The Perdues' entire flock of 10,000 laying hens was wiped out by fowl typhoid fever. "We lost $12,000," he said. It felt like the end of the world."

It wasn't the end of the world at all. After considerable research, Frank and his father replaced the flock of laying hens with a meat breed that wasn't susceptible to the disease. Because wartime demand for chicken was so great, they were able to sell the resulting broilers at a price that made up for their previous loss.

The sale was just in time. Ten days later, because of the war there was a price freeze, and the price of broilers dropped from 50 cents a pound to 35 cents a pound.

The price freeze ushered in the infamous days of black market chicken. To get around the price controls, unscrupulous buyers would say something like, "I'm not going to pay you one penny above the legal price for your chickens. I'm a law-abiding man. Thirty-five cents a pound and *that's it*. But I wonder, hmmm," and here the would-be buyer would stop and wink, "do you suppose you could jump over that chicken crate? If you can, I'll give you $10,000 to do it – in addition to the 35 cents a pound I'm offering you for your chickens."

Frank didn't engage in this himself. However, he knew that a lot of high-priced broilers were sold in the United States during the price freeze.

Meanwhile, the poultry business was expanding. During the war years, local farmers were anxious to buy Perdue chicks, or any chicks for that matter, because wartime demand insured a ready market for all the broilers the farmers could produce.

During this period, the company hired its first full-time employee, Herman Ruark. "I worked for Frank from Labor Day in 1941until I retired in 1963," said Ruark. "Back then, Frank was just a regular farm boy, interested in chickens and farming. When it came to cleaning out the chicken houses, Frank jumped right in there with us and did as much as we did."

Ruark got $11 a week, plus rent, light, chickens and eggs. The workweek was seven days, from 7:00 AM until 6:30 PM In today's inflation adjusted figures that would be $178 a week.

CHILDHOOD: WERE THERE CLUES
HE'D BE A SUCCESS?

Ruark considered Frank an easy boss. "He never gave me no trouble in his life. I enjoyed every minute of working for him. He never complained about my work, and I enjoyed being with him or around him. It's true, we all had to work fast to get the job done, but most of the people I know stayed with him until they retired."

When asked if the young Frank showed any signs of being the success he ultimately became, Ruark was emphatic. "No sir. He was regular." Other than Frank's energy, Ruark said he had no idea what the future held for his fellow worker.

The Beginning Salesman

The year 1946 marked the beginning of a major change in Frank's career, a change that, over the ensuing decades, would transform him from a shy and introverted farm boy to a world renowned sales and marketing success. The change began when, with his father's encouragement, he began selling commercial chicken feed.

The beginnings weren't promising. Initially Frank was so shy that he'd look at his feet instead of looking at his prospect. However, Frank more than made up for his shyness by his tremendous drive. In fact, he didn't just make up for it, he conquered it. When I asked him later in life which aspect of his entire business career he enjoyed most, his unhesitating answer was "sales and marketing."

It might seem a paradox that someone who was unusually shy would end up liking sales, but Frank had an unusual ability to intuit and appreciate what another person was feeling. With his gift for empathy, when he was calling on a prospect, he was able to transform himself into a trusted advisor, almost an auxiliary employee who fortunately was on someone else's payroll.

"A good salesman doesn't wing it," Frank would often say. "You've got to be impeccably honest and do those things which make you reliable. You've got to be able to say 'no' and you've got to be able to say why you've said no.

CHILDHOOD: WERE THERE CLUES
HE'D BE A SUCCESS?

You've got to take care of the customer. Your business is on the line every time you take an order."

As his fellow seed salesman Walter Johnson told me, Frank was effective because he was so knowledgeable about his product. "He knew which varieties did well, and he could sell the varieties he felt he the farmers should use and how they should use them. The farmers believed him."

By developing a reputation for doing what was best for his customers, Frank eventually became the biggest Beacon feed dealer in the country.

FRANK PERDUE'S LESSONS

YOU DON'T NEED TO START OUT AS A GENIUS– As a child, no one predicted that Frank would be the success he later became.

EXTRA CARE AND EFFORT PAYS OFF– By taking special care of his 50 cull hens, he was able to get better results than others were getting with hens that were predicted to do far better.

THINGS THAT LOOK LIKE A CATASTROPHE CAN TURN INTO GOOD FORTUNE– When a poultry disease wiped out the family's entire flock of egg producing chickens, it forced Frank and his father to convert to meat breeds. Being in the chicken business instead of the egg business turned out to be a tremendous benefit for the company.

LEARN TO TRANSCEND YOUR LIMITATIONS– Frank started out so shy that when it came to sales, he looked at his shoes instead of his customer. Through will and effort, he overcame his shyness and became the most successful Beacon dealer in the country.

CHAPTER TWO
EARLY DAYS: GROWING CHICKENS AND GROWING A FAMILY

By 1950, big changes were happening in the poultry industry, changes that would influence Frank's career. There was a trend among poultry farmers to grow their broilers "under contract." For the farmer, this meant the contractor would provide him with chicks, feed and fuel. The contractor would also shoulder the loss when the market was down or take a portion of the profits when prices were up.

The big advantage for an individual farmer was that with a contract he would be protected against heavy losses; without a contract, he would have to sell his flock to the highest bidder, usually at the local auction, and hope that the price he received would cover his costs. Linwood Shockley, Frank's second cousin and one of his first contract producers, said, "If you were on your own, and you would strike three or four low-priced flocks in a row, you'd lose everything."

For the individual farmer contract growing meant a reliable income stream, and this was (and is) especially important to farmers who are growing other crops. Farmers always have to worry about a drought year or a year when too much rain means they can't plant their fields on time. Having a reliable income from raising chickens can mean the difference between keeping the farm in the family—or losing everything.

The contract system had advantages for the farmers, but it was advantageous for the contractors also. When Frank and his father began contracting with farmers to grow their flocks, they could average the prices they received when selling them, making them less vulnerable to the day-to-day shifts in the market prices.

Early Participants in Contract Growing

Roger Richardson is a chicken farmer and grain grower whose parents were among the first to participate in contract growing. They had been buying baby chicks from the Perdue hatchery since the early 1940s, but one day in early 1950, things changed.

As Richardson tells it, Mr. Arthur (Frank's father) called on Richardson's father explaining that he had a lot of newly hatched chicks and no home for them. Mr. Arthur didn't want to gas his baby chicks and asked Richardson's parents if they could take them.

Richardson's father turned him down. The markets just didn't look good at this point, and it would be too big a risk.

Mr. Arthur countered with a proposal that was one of the forerunners of how most commercial chickens are grown in the United States today. He suggested that if the Richardsons would grow the newly hatched chicks and, if the flock lost money when it came time to sell, he (Mr. Arthur) would take all losses associated with the cost of the baby chicks, plus the fuel and feed that it took to grow the birds.

The Richardsons would lose their time and effort, but they wouldn't be out any money. On the other hand, if they made money on the flock, Mr. Arthur would take a percentage of the profits.

The deal made sense for both sides, and pretty soon other growers wanted to make the same arrangement. Today, although the details aren't quite the same, it's standard practice, at least in the United States, for the farmers to specialize in growing chickens under contract, knowing that except in unusual cases, they'll have a reliable income stream.

EARLY DAYS: GROWING CHICKENS
AND GROWING A FAMILY

Business Relationships Weren't Just about Dollars and Cents

Many of the relationships Frank had with the growers spanned generations. Roger Richardson continued working with Frank until the time of Frank's passing, and they became close social friends as well as business associates.

Carl Wagner's family had a similar experience. His family began producing hatching eggs for the Perdue Company back in 1926.

Carl's most memorable experience with Frank began when the Wagner family was converting from growing the breeding hens that were right for producing breakfast eggs to the kind of birds that would end up as broilers.

Making the change is difficult because it takes a completely different kind of hen to produce meat birds. If your goal is meat, you want a bird with a big breast. If you're after high egg production, a bird that looks almost scrawny by comparison is going to do far better. The serious downside to a breed that produces big-breasted birds is that those birds will produce far fewer eggs. If you're making your living selling eggs to the hatchery, having fewer eggs from each bird is an economic problem.

When converting from breakfast egg hens to broiler hens, Wagner realized that his breeding hens weren't producing enough eggs to pay the feed bill. He mentioned this to Frank while at a social function in Salisbury. Frank was polite but gave no hint that he even really heard what Wagner had just said.

However, Frank had heard. As Wagner told it, "At 10:00 p.m. that night, I heard a knock at the door, and it was Frank. 'I've been thinking about what we were talking about,' Frank said gently, 'and I'd like to sit down and see if we can come up with some solutions.'"

"We sat down and explored the different possibilities," Wagner remembers. "I was impressed by how analytical Frank could be. He never implied that I was a bad manager. We looked at what the alternatives were, and then he pointed out a number of additional resources I could fall back on, including the Federal Land Bank or other sources of credit.

"This was many decades ago, but you don't forget something like that. That personal caring is a big part of his success."

Service Men Become Part of the Mix

Initially with contract growing, Frank or his father would call on the farmers to help them with problems. However, as the contract growing system grew, there were eventually too many growers for Frank or his father to visit personally.

They were replaced by "service men," which may sound like someone serving in the military, but at Perdue, it refers to the representatives from Perdue Farms who would visit the contract chicken growers to see if everything was going well. A service man (or starting in the early 1980s, it could also have been a service woman) would typically call on a farmer once or more a week to check that the feed and water were clean and adequate, and the temperatures right.

The service men were often poultry science graduates, so they were also qualified to check on the health of the chickens. How well the chickens were doing was influenced by how conscientious the growers were. As in any operation with hundreds or thousands of participants, there's a spectrum of growers, from those who are meticulous about doing everything exactly right, to those who, well, aren't so meticulous.

John Munro was one of the very early flock advisors and has a unique view of the early days, before Perdue became big and successful. He got to observe the variation in how well the growers treated their flocks.

John Munro's Story

Frank wanted to hire Munro because Munro had a degree in poultry husbandry from Cornell. Frank offered to pay for Munro's trip from Syracuse to Salisbury, and the trip was to include Munro's wife, Joan.

EARLY DAYS: GROWING CHICKENS
AND GROWING A FAMILY

Munro has vivid memories of Frank's recruiting efforts. "Once we were in Salisbury, Frank took us both for lunch. 'What would be the thing,' Frank asked Joan, 'that would get you and your husband to come down here?'"

"I've always wanted my own house," she said dreamily.

According to Munro, Frank called up a banker that day, left some money in escrow on their behalf, and they ended up with a nice two-bedroom house. "Joan was happy as a lark about this. And as for me, my dream in college had been to be making $5,000 a year and have my own car. I got both with Frank."

Munro's new job was to visit about 50 farmers a week. He'd check on how the flocks were doing, and generally make any suggestions for helping the farmers, based on his poultry husbandry background. The growers often referred to him and his fellow service men as "The Chicken Doctors."

If the growers did everything right, they'd have healthier chickens that would gain weight faster, and they'd make more money. But even so, Munro got to witness a disparity in how well the growers took care of their chickens.

"We had ways of knowing how conscientious a farmer was. One of our little tricks, and we had several, was leaving a penny in the water trough that the chickens used for drinking. The grower was supposed to wash out the trough every day. It was basic hygiene and doing it right meant a healthier flock. However, we service men knew that if the penny was still there the next time we came around, the grower hadn't been diligent about washing out the troughs."

The service men had meetings every Saturday to discuss such things as how to be responsive to grower complaints or figuring out ways to make improvements. But they'd also discuss issues such as what to do about a grower whose chickens weren't healthy and weren't growing well. The guy might swear he was doing everything right, but the service men knew the farmer hadn't cleaned the water trough in a week.

EARLY DAYS: GROWING CHICKENS
AND GROWING A FAMILY

Munro also mentioned how hard Frank's wife Madeline worked. "She was a real fine lady and everyone liked her. She was always busy. She not only did the books for the company, she was the one who drove the chick trucks. These were converted school buses, and she delivered the baby chicks from the hatchery to the growers."

Munro concluded our conversation by saying, "Last night I got to thinking about my experiences with Frank, and I realized that in my 81 years, he had more influence over my life than any other individual except my parents. He was an effect for good. He always did everything he said he would. He was hard working, and even in little things he still has an impact. He once gave me a little notebook and instructed me to take notes, to write everything down. I still do that, even today."

The late Royce White was also one of the people who began working for the company in the 1950s. In his case, he started in 1958 and retired in 1997.

He found Frank a demanding man to work for, but "If you did your job, you were OK. If you didn't, he was hell to work for. I don't think he ever fired anyone, but he could make someone who wasn't doing the job well want to quit."

White's first assignment was working nights at the hatchery, and to his surprise, he found that Frank would frequently stop by at 3:00 a.m. with an unusual request. He'd tell White that he was on his way home, but wanted White to call him at 6:00 a.m.

Eventually, White learned why Frank wanted these calls. White was serving as Frank's alarm clock.

White's final thoughts on Frank were, "He was above all a fair man. He always treated me well. He was a hard man, yet at the same time you could always respect him because he was so smart and so hard-working."

EARLY DAYS: GROWING CHICKENS AND GROWING A FAMILY

Jack Brittingham was yet another of the early service men. He began with Perdue Farms in February 1959 and stayed 38 years.

When he started, there were 90 or so employees, and although he was on salary, his attitude and the attitude of his peers was that you worked until you got your job done. After all, Frank had warned him, "We don't run a country club here!"

Brittingham told me, "You didn't mind working hard because you knew Frank was working harder."

Brittingham has an early memory of this time. Once he got a call at 2:00 a.m. from a man who wanted to know if Brittingham knew where to find an extra truckload of chickens to complete an order. Brittingham could easily solve the man's problem because he had a list of everyone who was working that night and knew where each truck was picking up chickens. No problem.

This, however, wasn't the part that made the evening memorable. The guy who needed the extra truckload was pleased, but he ended the call by saying, "I hope I didn't get you in any trouble."

"No, I don't think so, why would you say that?"

"Well, I needed to get hold of you and I didn't have your number. So I called Frank."

Brittingham knew that he wasn't going to get in trouble over that. He knew Frank was sure to be awake anyway.

View from a Competitor

Although contract chicken growing began in the middle of the last century, it continues today. Things have changed somewhat in those 60 years, but one thing that hasn't changed is competition for good growers. Here's an up-to-date view of it from Mike McCready, a man who currently works for one of our biggest competitors. Up until a couple of years ago, he worked for Frank.

His job today actually includes trying to convince Perdue growers to come grow birds for the company he works for now.

There may be industry people who will be surprised to see McCready's name in a book on Frank, but I don't have any hard feelings for what McCready does. Trying to recruit each other's growers is normal industry practice and for good reason. People in the chicken industry want to get the best growers, and it makes sense to target people who already have a record for producing great chickens.

The high demand for growers has to be good for the growers, and in the end, it's good for the chicken industry because this kind of competition helps make growing chickens an attractive career. The way I look at it, it's a compliment if our growers are so good that others really want them. Um, but on the other hand, I'm not entirely sure that I want this particular compliment. Anyway, I like Mike McCready and I wish he'd come back.

Mike McCready's Story

McCready started with Perdue in 2002 and stayed until 2011. For a good bit of his time with Perdue, he was a flock advisor, and since Frank, in his 80s, loved to accompany the service men on their rounds, McCready got to spend time with Frank.

McCready believes that just as it was back in the 1950s, building chicken houses is usually a good investment for the farmer. If they do a conscientious job, they'll make money on it.

However, McCready can think of a striking exception to that rule, and it was a time when he saw Frank living up to his reputation for being tough. It involved a couple in a small town near Salisbury. The wife had an outside job and the husband took care of the chickens.

EARLY DAYS: GROWING CHICKENS
AND GROWING A FAMILY

As McCready tells it, "The husband was doing a god-awful job. The chickens were so stressed that some of them were actually dying. I drove Frank to see the couple.

"Frank sat down in their kitchen and told them, 'I'm just going to be honest with you. This is not working out.'

"He looked at both of them and then said, 'The only way this is going to work is if you' (he's now looking at the woman), 'come home and take care of the chickens, and you,' he's now looking at the man, 'take your talents elsewhere.'"

To McCready's surprise, it was an ideal solution. The woman turned out to be a really good grower and she was able to improve things dramatically.

McCready was personally familiar with the fact that today, as has always been the case, there's a variety in how conscientious and skilled the growers are. And the service men or women knew this without having to study feed conversion rates or other metrics.

"We service people had a pretty good idea of how good of a job the growers were doing For example, many years ago we sometimes would tie a very thin white cotton thread on the door, and when you opened the door, the thread would tear and look exactly like a cobweb. If that thread was still there unbroken when you came by next time, then you knew the grower hadn't been in the chicken house and was being negligent about growing the chickens."

McCready always hoped he wouldn't find the telltale unbroken thread. But if he did, and if the grower was making excuses for having his chickens not growing well, maybe using the excuse that he had simply gotten a batch of unhealthy chicks from the hatchery, McCready could mention the unbroken thread that showed the grower hadn't even entered the chicken house in days. Or he could mention the coin or other object that he had left in the water trough that was still there that showed the grower wasn't changing the water and scrubbing the trough clean each day.

However, those kinds of tests aren't used today, and McCready is quick to point out that things are entirely different in the modern chicken houses. Computers and automation take care of a lot of the tasks that a grower in the past needed to do.

For instance, computers create the exact temperature conditions under which the birds will flourish. Baby chicks do best at higher temperatures, but by seven weeks of age the birds prefer a cooler environment. As the chickens get older, the computerized controller will drop the temperature each day, sometimes by as little as two-thirds of degree, to correspond to the exact temperatures that poultry scientists say are best for the chickens at each age.

McCready also points out that the water system is different, and today there would be no point to leaving a coin in the water trough. That's because water troughs are no longer used.

"Instead of having open troughs of water that are exposed to dust and that can be a vector for disease," he points out, "the birds now take sips from a closed water system that delivers individual drops of water to each chicken."

The system he's describing is called "nipple drinkers." You have several two-inch PVC pipes that extend the length of the chicken houses. They are three inches off the ground when it's for the baby chicks, and then the pipe get raised farther off the ground as the chickens grow bigger. At intervals of several inches, there are little holes drilled at the bottom of the pipe and a little "nipple" is inserted in the hole. The nipple is stainless steel, and it's engineered so that when a chicken pecks at it, it releases a drop of pure fresh well water.

Somehow the baby chicks know from day one how to peck at the nipples. It's mysterious to me how the baby chicks know to do this because surely there's nothing exactly like this in nature. But still, I've watched newly hatched chicks approach the pipe, peck at the shiny stainless steel nipple, and then when the drop of water follows, they learn to drink from the nipple. Maybe it's as simple as it's instinctive to peck at something shiny.

McCready is proud that the chicken industry has fostered innovations like the nipple drinkers. "These innovations show up in the feed conversion rates, meaning it costs less to grow a chicken. As a result of these and others improvements, the market price per pound that people pay in the supermarket today is much lower than it would be otherwise."

Frank Became an Incubator of Entrepreneurs

The farmers who were part of the contract growing system with Perdue benefitted in an important but little-known way. According to Tim Mescon, founding Dean of the Franklin P. Perdue School of Business and now President of Columbus State University, Frank didn't just incubate chickens; he incubated entrepreneurs. Mescon is referring to Frank's role in enabling farmers, sometimes even hardscrabble, barely-making-it farmers, to become wildly successful "farming entrepreneurs."

For Perdue, the contract growing business has expanded from the single grower, Roger Richardson's father, to today's 5,000 men and women who grow for Perdue. Many of them are second, third or even fourth generation growers. There's also the construction workers who started businesses to build the houses, the 5,000 farmers who grow the grain to feed the chickens, plus the people who provide the propane to heat or cool the houses, not to mention those who sell the woodchips for litter, the computer experts who make the work of running a chicken house easier and more accurate than ever before, and on and on.

In Tim Mescon's view, "By supporting the growers with the low-cost loans that enabled them to build chicken houses, Frank created entrepreneurs. Before this, particularly on the Eastern Shore, a farmer's life was apt to be feast or famine, always vulnerable to withering heat, extensive droughts, or having so much rain that they couldn't plant their crops. However, once they were in the chicken business, they had an alternate source of income. If on a given year they were struggling with their crops, they could still count on a dependable revenue stream from growing chickens."

These men and women all meet the definition of entrepreneurs: Because of the chicken house loans, they were putting their money at risk in order to make money.

Mescon mentions that some have estimated that when you take the growers who became entrepreneurs by investing in chicken houses, and when you take into consideration the ancillary business that these businesses created, Perdue Farms may have made an economic contribution to the lives of more than a million people.

"How many people have made a contribution of that scope and breadth to economic development over such a broad geography?" Mescon asks, and then answering himself: "Not many."

Frank's Three Daughters

While Frank was involved with growing the business, he also enjoyed being a family man, although probably not your average family man. His three daughters, who were teenagers during this period, all have vivid memories of him.

Sandy Spedden

Sandy Spedden, the oldest, remembers her time as a receptionist working at the company office. "When Dad came in, I'd know it was him even if I didn't see him because I'd hear him running up the stairs, taking them three at a time. He was always in a hurry."

Back then she remembered that there were maybe 50 other poultry companies. "I think AW Perdue and Son was so successful because father and son were a team. Dad Perdue was a 'prayer warrior,' and my dad was his hands and feet for his prayers."

EARLY DAYS: GROWING CHICKENS
AND GROWING A FAMILY

Something that impressed Sandy for the rest of her life: "Dad told me once that he and his dad never had an argument in their lives, and I, being married at the time, said, 'That's impossible, nobody can get along that well!'

"He answered simply, 'We did.'"

Anne Oliviero

Daughter Anne, remembering the early days, thinks of Frank as "a happy person. He'd line the three of us up and say, 'Okay, you girls, it's time for you to play baseball,' and then he'd throw us balls for twenty minutes."

One memory from that period still influences her today. From age 14 to 20 she worked for Perdue in an office job during the summers, and also Saturdays during the school year. She is generally a very prompt person, but one day, because a drawbridge was up, she was 15 minutes late to work. She was mortified.

As she takes up the story, "The next week it happened again and this time I was even more mortified because being on time was really important to me.

"But it got worse. Dad called me into his office and said, 'If this happens one more time, you're done.'

"He impressed on us that we were like any employee and there would be no exceptions made for us. 'You're just going to have to leave 20 minutes early in case the bridge goes up.'"

Frank let Anne and her siblings knew that, "Our behavior had to be exemplary as other employees would notice any 'special privileges.'"

Beverly Perdue Jennings

Bev said her father was the most unique person she ever knew. "I thought all fathers worked seven days a week and ten hours a day. Dad could work these hours because he could take catnaps in an instant even standing up in church totally asleep while everyone else was singing."

She remembers that everything he did was fast: eating, walking, retrieving tennis balls on a tennis court between points, or dancing.

"Dad loved to dance and my parents took dancing lessons with a Mrs. Ziegler in town. The only issue with Dad's dancing was again he was going to his own beat, which was always faster than the music's. I could dance with him because he was a good leader but I had to find his rhythm. He always said he liked the way I could keep up with him, and I will always cherish those dancing times we had together."

For Bev, Frank was a father who gave quality time if not quantity. "He would listen to you and be open minded. I knew I could always count on him and he would always be there for me. I was very blessed having him as my Dad."

FRANK PERDUE'S LESSONS

BUSINESS ISN'T JUST ABOUT DOLLARS AND CENTS– Business is about honesty and fairness and going the extra mile, as when he took time to call on Carl Wagner at 10:00 p.m. when Wagner was in a financial bind.

BEING FAIR AND HARD WORKING HELPS CREATE LOYALTY– Many of the people who started with Perdue stayed with him their entire careers. Most of them mentioned that he was a fair man, and they admired that he was hard working.

A GOOD BUSINESS MODEL ENCOURAGES SUCCESS IN OTHERS– By encouraging thousands of men and women to invest in growing chickens, he simultaneously created thousands of entrepreneurs and also thousands of millionaires.

IT'S POSSIBLE TO BE A GOOD BUSINESSMAN AND A GOOD FAMILY MAN– Frank may have been busy with the business, but having a family was a crucial and cherished part of his life.

CHAPTER THREE
CHICKEN FEED: IT ISN'T JUST *CHICKEN FEED*

While the growth of Perdue Farms continued, all the interlocking moving parts that supported that growth still needed to be functioning smoothly. One of those moving parts was the grain supply that made growing the chickens possible.

Frank wanted to control the quality of the grain his chickens consumed. After all, a chicken's health and growth is highly dependent on the quality of its feed. Frank's own research had shown that by controlling the quality of the feed at every step, he could produce feed that was more nutritionally sound than what was available from the commercial feed companies, and this in turn meant healthier chickens.

Building a Feedmill Complex

By the mid-1950s, Frank knew that to achieve the quality he was after, he needed to build a feed mill and soybean crushing plant so he could formulate and produce his own feed. Building the feed mill was to come first.

Before beginning construction, Frank began researching what it would take to build the grain tanks. This, by the way, was something characteristic of Frank throughout his career: When he was starting something new, he lived his favorite Alexander Hamilton quote, "When I have a subject in hand, I study it profoundly. Day and night it is before me. My mind becomes pervaded with it."

23

CHICKEN FEED: IT ISN'T JUST *CHICKEN FEED*

In the case of the feed mill, he started his research by calling an engineer at one of the feed companies, Purina, to ask what kind of steel to use in constructing the tank. "This was somewhat brazen of me," Frank said, "given that I was a competitor, but he told me exactly what I needed to know."

Frank needed this information because when you fill a grain storage tank with a quarter of a million bushels of corn in 100-degree summer weather, and then the tank and its contents contract in zero-degree weather in winter, the steel seams can split. The result is grain spilled all over the ground, meaning both waste and expense.

Poorly constructed grain storage tanks were causing a lot of these kinds of problems back then, and Frank didn't want this to happen in his feed mill complex. Fortunately the Purina engineer shared his expertise on the kind of high-quality, flexible steel needed to avoid the problem.

That was only the beginning of Frank's research for the feed mill and soybean-crushing complex. He contacted countless people asking countless questions. Harold Shockley, who managed the plant almost from the beginning, said, "I toured several plants in other states, and when I'd tell people there who I worked for, they'd say, 'Frank Perdue? That SOB! He must have called me with 150 questions!'

"There wasn't a plant that I ever visited where they didn't know who Frank was because he had called each of them at least several times," Shockley continued. "He called every soybean plant in the country, and he'd ask them every question you can think of, even including 'How much money did you make per bushel last year?'"

Since this was proprietary information, the usual response to Frank was, "None of your business." But that didn't keep Frank from continuing to try, and every once in awhile, it would pay off.

Throughout his life, Frank felt that in terms of time and effort, getting useful information was worth just about any price. In this case, he was amazed by how much proprietary information he could get just by asking.

Frank gave as well as got. When he'd visit a competitor's grain facilities, or for that matter, any other facilities that interested him, he'd always offer to reciprocate and have them tour his operation. It surprised him that out of the hundreds of people he saw over the years, only three or four ever took him up on his offer.

Although Frank was certain he wanted to build the soybean plant, a major obstacle was cost. Building the plant could not be done without a large loan, and he knew that Mr. Arthur had watched his own father struggle with a lifetime of debt. Mr. Arthur believed right down to his core, the maxim that, "If you don't owe money, you can't go broke."

"My dad had never borrowed a dime in his seventy-six years," Frank remembered. The amount Frank wanted to borrow was enormous for the time; $1.5 million at 5.75 percent with a five-year payback.

In the end, Mr. Arthur did sign the loan agreement, and it was a deeply moving day for Frank. His father's willingness to overcome his lifetime aversion to borrowing impressed Frank so much that he still talked about it more than four decades later. Frank was touched that his father believed in him so much.

Success Had a Price

The plant opened in October 1961 and began making money almost immediately. This was of course good news for Frank in view of the debt he was carrying. The bad news was, others, observing the plant's profitability, quickly decided to copy him. A group of his competitors in the chicken business banded together with the goal of building their own competing soybean processing plant.

In October 1962, eleven Delmarva poultry producers applied for a $1.625 million, twenty-five-year loan from what was then the Area Redevelopment Administration (ARA). They were going to do this using a taxpayer-subsidized loan with a five times longer payback period.

The difference between the interest rates on the federally subsidized loan and Frank's bank loan, plus the much longer-term payback schedule, would have given his competitors a $30,000 a year advantage.

Also, whereas Frank was all-in, risking his own funds for his soybean mill, the ARA loan meant that his competitors would be putting only a small percentage of their net worth at risk. The ARA loan would be a virtually no-risk gift because the ARA could waive interest payments if needed, and unlike commercial banks, it rarely foreclosed on delinquent loans.

To get this taxpayer-supported bonanza, Frank's competitors had to prove that they couldn't get the funds on their own under terms that were "reasonable and proper." To his dismay, Frank learned that at the county and state level, the group had already been able to do this. Also, the Eastern Shore's 1st Congressional District representative– Frank's own congressman– and the governor of Maryland backed the loan.

As the company grew, Frank proudly grew his family. Jim sits below his father on the stoop while Frank is surrounded by daughters Anne, Beverly, and Sandy.

Throughout his career, Frank was willing to tackle long odds. In this case, the ARA loan to his competitors, the odds didn't just seem long; the situation looked in every respect like a done deal.

Still, he didn't give up. He began by calling on U.S. Senator John Williams from Delaware, only to learn that the ARA, established by Congress only a year earlier, was actually eager to make the loan. The ARA was looking for loans that would be repaid, and unfortunately for Frank, his competitors were among the few with track records that gave the ARA confidence.

CHICKEN FEED: IT ISN'T JUST *CHICKEN FEED*

"Frank," he remembered the Senator telling him, "you don't have a chance. Don't waste your time."

Discouraging as it was, the talk with Senator Williams revealed some interesting and, in the end, helpful information. The law was written so that if applicants for federal funding could get money from conventional commercial banks, they were ineligible for the taxpayer-subsidized loan.

There was a Catch-22 aspect to this because the ARA was never intended to subsidize the very wealthy, and yet the most attractive applicants for the federal money were those who were "substantial" and had significant assets. In time, Frank was to make use of this information.

Meanwhile, the situation looked grim. Frank sought allies. "I went to the National Soybean Processors' Association and told them about my plight," he recalled. "I said that the government would use federal funds and the taxpayers' money to pay for my competitors' soybean plant. Scott Kramer from Swift & Company said to the other members, 'Look fellows, if it could happen to this man, it could happen to any of us.'"

Kramer wrote to every congressman in Swift's many locations and had them contact the ARA to protest the subsidized loan.

Frank also sought help from his fellow grain dealers, all of whom would have been harmed by unfair competition from a taxpayer-subsidized grain facility. At Frank's direction, Perdue associate Bob Brodey drove around to each of the grain dealers and asked them, in their own self-interest, to write letters on Perdue's behalf.

"I'd tell them to write a letter," said Brodey. "Or I'd tell them 'I'll write it, I'm a typist, I'll type it on your letterhead and I'll even mail it for you.'" Brodey calculated that at least thirty letters on Frank's behalf were written this way.

Meanwhile, Frank was encountering some success. Since he had been able to obtain a bank loan, he wondered how was it that his competitors had not.

Through painstaking research, one day he hit pay dirt. When he was talking with a mid-level bureaucrat at the Department of Commerce, he found out why his competitors hadn't been able to obtain a commercial bank loan. The loans they were asking for were, as Frank's lawyer, Herbert Fenster, would later characterize in testimony before a congressional oversight committee, "unrealistic to the point of being ludicrous." The group was asking the commercial banks for a loan for 84 percent of the total investment (19 percent more than the ARA itself was authorized to loan).

They were, quite simply, asking for terms that no commercial bank would accept for this kind of project. No wonder they had been turned down.

"This abuse galvanized me into action," said Frank. "It made me more determined than ever that this malpractice should be exposed. It was never the intent of the Congress that money should be squandered like this when the proponents were obviously financially able to fund the project themselves." In the days before word processors, Frank wrote a personal letter to every member of Congress, detailing the abuse.

For additional armament in his battle against the subsidized loan, Frank asked his staff hatchery expert, Harry Palmer, to evaluate and price every hatchery owned by the group. Another Perdue expert evaluated the feed mills, and still another studied all the other assets owned by the group.

As a result of these appraisals, Frank knew that the group jointly owned assets worth far in excess of $10 million. The bottom line was that the American taxpayer was being asked to subsidize millionaires.

Influenced by Frank, the Wall Street Journal ran a front-page story, and finally, as a result of the support Frank was generating, the late Congressman Rogers C. B. Morton called a hearing of the oversight committee, which had the power to correct abuses. The soybean battle, after almost a year, was finally coming to a head.

CHICKEN FEED: IT ISN'T JUST *CHICKEN FEED*

The Case Goes to Court

The hearing was called for May 16, 1963. For Paul Phillips, Frank's college classmate who was helping Frank, it was an anxious time. He'd been to see every member of the Congressional committee who had a say in the soybean plant loan with one exception, the most important member – the then Congressman Bob Dole.

"I had to see him before the committee meeting," said Phillips, "but I was never able to get in. It wasn't until twenty minutes before the hearing began that I was able to see him. Dole was standing outside his office, talking with his secretary. I stood there and Dole said, 'Come on in.'

"I began to unravel this story and he became interested. 'Sit down,' he invited, and I finally got a chance to tell him our side." Phillips poured out the story, including the abuses and the injustice, and then entreated the Congressman to ask a few key questions during the hearing.

Frank remembered that in the actual hearing, he was brilliantly represented by Herbert Fenster, who was then only twenty-eight years old. Fenster knew that both he and the opposing lawyer had forty-five minutes each to make their cases.

Both Frank and Fenster listened with glee as the opposing attorney used up half of the allotted time on sheer generalities and never got half of his witnesses on. During the forty-five minutes allocated to Frank's position, Fenster got all his witnesses on and had them make their points succinctly.

When both sides had finished, the Congressmen began asking questions. Frank's side was jubilant because they heard Congressman Dole ask exactly the questions that Phillips had suggested.

According to the transcript that day of the hearing of the Committee on Agriculture of the 88th Congress, Congressman Dole asked one of the proponents of the group, "As a matter of information, what would be the total assets of these eleven incorporators, the total assets?"

". . . maybe it is $10 million," came back the answer.

Congressman Dole then asked why they had not been able to obtain a regular bank loan. According to the transcript, the witness's exact answer was, "We could not raise enough equity out of our own businesses without jeopardizing what we already are doing."

Phillips remembers that everything was silent for a long moment. The conclusions were right there for everyone to draw: Members of the opposing group didn't want to put their own money in jeopardy, and their soybean mill might not be a viable endeavor without the government subsidy. He also remembers Dole's admonishing the group that if the members weren't willing to jeopardize their own money, then the government shouldn't be willing to risk the taxpayers' money.

Phillips said, "You didn't have to be very smart to see that the other side had lost their case right then and there."

The soybean battle touched the lives of the Perdue family. Frank's daughter Anne remembers, "Some people wouldn't speak to us, people who had once been friends."

Phillips said that Frank took this with grace.

"Frank, you're gonna lose some friends," he had warned. "'Well,' Frank answered, 'I guess I'll have to make some new ones.'"

Frank's secretary at the time, Doris Ball, remembers this as the most exhilarating time of her career. "It was a time of fighting in the trenches for something we believed in," she said. "Also it was the best example of why Frank was so successful."

Ball went on to talk about how she's seen that most successful people have the same traits as Frank, such as creativity, good solid values, drive, charm and so on, but very few actually apply the unrelenting labor and thought to a subject that Frank did. She said, "The people who worked closely with him felt that he could have authored the Alexander Hamilton quote himself. It fit him like a tailor-made suit."

The soybean plant battle was a business success for Frank. It was also a personal success because it added to the small case of hero worship his daughter Beverly already felt for her father. "Everyone my age back then admired Kennedy," Beverly said when thinking back over these times. "For me, my own daddy was my Kennedy. Everyone told him that he couldn't possibly win the soybean battle, that it would cost him a lot, and that he would lose. He wouldn't talk about it around the kitchen table, but we all knew the odds." To this day, Beverly is still impressed by her father's strength and courage.

When I once asked Frank to name the single event in his business life that gave him the most satisfaction, Frank answered that it was the congressional decision on the ARA soybean plant loan. In summing up his memories of those times, Frank said, "Democracy will work, but sometimes you have to work like hell to make it work."

Memories of Frank from this Period

The soybean plant battle consumed a lot of Frank's attention, but there was still a company to run. Old timers like Harold Shockley, who began in 1955 and still does consulting for the company almost 60 years later, remembers what Frank was like during this period.

He saw Frank as tough. "His work style meant that the weak people were weeded out, although he never fired more than a couple of people."

One who was fired was a man who worked in the Perdue hatchery. The man had a deal with a local bakery that would privately buy from him the cracked eggs that weren't going to hatch. The problem was there were all of a sudden a lot of cracked eggs.

As Harold Shockley tells it, Frank went up to the man and said, "Lester, have you got a dollar?"

Lester handed Frank a dollar, and then Frank took one of his own dollars from his wallet. With a dollar in each hand, Frank suddenly thrust both of his own hands behind his back, and a moment later brought them out, holding the two dollars in his outstretched hands. He asked Lester, 'Which one is yours?'

"I don't know," the man said, "I can't tell which is which."

"'That's the problem," Frank said. "You don't know what is yours and what is mine."

Perdue Farms is one of the most recognized family businesses in America. Jim Perdue, who heads the company today, is seen here as a child working with his father Frank and Mr. Arthur, his grandfather.

That guy was fired, but usually, when someone was not pulling their weight. they wouldn't be comfortable working for the company and would quit on their own.

When Perdue Farms was still small, Frank had his finger on everything. According to Shockley, when the management report came out on the 15th of the month, by the 16th you'd get a handwritten note asking such things as "Why is this expense higher than last month and what steps are you going to take to change it?"

"He didn't forget it the next month either, he'd notice. He was sharp. He knew exactly what every dollar went for. But then, the other side is if things had gone well, you could bet your sweet butt that you'd get a note from him saying something like, 'Great job!'"

Shockley found Frank's style inspirational. "He had a knack to get things done in a way that once you talked with him you felt, damn it, I'm gonna do it or die trying. You were part of a team and you didn't want to let him down."

Frank allowed people to make decisions on their own, and according to Shockley, a person could fail a couple of times without its being a big deal. "In the end, he wanted results, but you could go your own way as long as we were all going the right direction."

Shockley still remembers a phrase Frank used: "If you don't grow, you should go."

Janet Shockley knew that her husband enjoyed his career and she had an opinion as to why. "Whenever Frank was at a function, he'd give everyone else credit for the company's success. If that doesn't give you a great sense of pride both in yourself and in that person, there's something wrong with you."

Ralph Moore is another Perdue veteran of this era. He started as a service man, but a year and a half into his employment found himself invited to the company headquarters. Moore was puzzled that he was being asked to take all kinds of tests, including one for finger dexterity.

He soon found out that the tests were to determine if an existing company employee would be suited to manage the new soybean processing plant. Moore got the job, but Frank warned him that he was tough to work for.

Moore had an answer. "Frank, hold on, I already know from your reputation that you're the biggest son-of-a-bitch on the Eastern Shore. I had checked you out real good before I even came to Salisbury."

I asked Moore how Frank took this.

"He laughed his head off! I could talk with him like that."

The relationship turned out to be entirely supportive. "He gave me plenty of rope. I remember during my soybean years, he told me, 'You have a blank check to do what you need to get it to work right.' He never took that blank check away."

Al Ball, Doris's husband, also started work during this period. What impressed Al right from the beginning, more than anything else, was that Frank allowed people to make mistakes. It was part of the culture Frank instilled in the company.

Ball learned this when he had an idea that he felt would make things easier. However, being the low man on the totem pole, he was hesitant about even saying something, let alone putting it into action. He did mention it to his supervisor, and a couple of days later, the man asked him if he had gotten it done yet. Al answered that he didn't know if it would work. The answer, which Ball loved, was, "You won't know unless you try it."

"The culture of the company was you were allowed to try something new, and if it didn't work, they were okay with your learning from your mistakes," Ball said. "Some of the ideas we had were hair-brained as all get out, but some paid off wonderfully."

Though Frank was OK with trying new things, he also wasn't eager to be a pioneer. "You know what happens to pioneers?" Frank used to ask. "They get scalped."

For Ball, there's an important point here. When Frank was about to try a new idea, he'd find out every single thing that he could about it. He didn't make a decision until he had thoroughly studied it from all sides. According to Ball, Frank may have been OK with making mistakes, "But he didn't make that many because he put so much effort into thinking about all aspects of a decision before he acted on it."

And he got his people to believe – something else that Ball felt was characteristic of Frank. "He was a master salesman of ideas long before he became a master salesman of chickens."

George Coffin also began working for Perdue Farms during this time. Although he later switched to the company's transportation department, Coffin started out working at night at the grain dryer. Frank used to stop by the dryer to chat with Coffin, often at 2:00 a.m. Coffin wondered if Frank ever slept.

"You could talk to him about anything," remembers Coffin. "He'd take the time to listen. I think he loved the people who worked for him, and he got that from Mr. Arthur."

Coffin once overheard Frank talking with a man who told him, "You must be one of the smartest people in the business." Frank answered, "No, sir, I'm smart enough to surround myself with smart people."

Coffin was impressed that the owner of the company would say this. "He had a humility to him. He'd tell you in a heartbeat that he wasn't the smartest man around, but I thought he was."

Jim Perdue and a Feed Mill Problem

It was around this time that the plant figured in an experience that caused Jim Perdue to gain an increased appreciation for his father's skills.

"After the feed mill had been in operation for awhile," Jim remembers, "more than 600 farmers depended on its production to feed their chickens. There was a huge snowstorm. It snowed-in everything and this was a disaster for the chickens. The chickens have to eat, but the feed trucks couldn't get to the chicken houses with the feed."

Jim, who was in his early teens at this point, accompanied his father to the feed mill. Frank instantly grasped that there were two problems. "First, every producer, whether he had a two days' supply of grain or was down to his last kernel, called in to say that his was an emergency case and he needed feed immediately. It was understandable that an individual producer would claim he was in need – he didn't want to be put at the bottom of the list of those to be supplied."

According to Jim, there were no realistic priorities for who would get the urgently needed feed; feed trucks would go to farms that had feed and miss those that were completely out.

A second problem was that the feed trucks would drive off and get stuck on unplowed roads. The result was chaos.

Probably for the first time, Jim saw his father really take control. Frank assigned the flock supervisors the job of figuring out from past deliveries which farms were truly in need.

He started down the list and in one hour had identified all the farms listed that needed feed, and he had set up a system whereby each truck driver would not deliver feed until he got an okay from the flock supervisor that the road to each of the needy farms on his route was passable.

The flock supervisor had to phone each farmer and check that he had cleared the road with his tractor. It was a coordinated system. Jim to this day remembers being impressed by how decisive his dad was.

More Views of Frank from the 1970s

Benny Vanderwende also got to see this side of Frank's nature from a close vantage point. He began his Perdue career in 1977 working in Grain and Dispatching.

Vanderwende felt the Eastern Shore was lucky that Frank Perdue was in the grain business. The grain tanks enabled local farmers to have a home for their grain, and they no longer needed to ship it outside of the region. It also meant a competitive edge for growing chicken when the grain could be bought and stored locally.

Vanderwende was impressed that Frank wasn't above doing menial work himself. Once, when the company had recently installed a 10,000-bushel-an-hour grain elevator, no one could convince Frank that the elevator couldn't be made to go faster. Frank stood there with a stopwatch as Vanderwende and his colleagues increased the speed. Suddenly vast quantities of soybeans started spewing out all over the basement.

Frank was unrattled. "Since I helped make this mess," he told Vanderwende, "I'll help clean it up." Frank rolled up the sleeves of his dress white shirt, ignored the fact that he was wearing dress pants, and then began energetically shoveling the spilled grain back into the hoppers.

Vanderwende couldn't imagine another CEOs doing that. Also, he couldn't help noticing that Frank had obviously done a lot of it. Frank was shoveling rhythmically, over and over again, the shovel going right where it was supposed to and then Frank would lift the shovel with its contents and accurately heave the contents into the bin. "He really knew how to shovel."

Vanderwende remembered the last time he talked with Frank. "It was in early 2005. I said, 'Good morning, Frank. You're looking good today.'

"You're either blind or a damn good liar," Frank joked, adding, "I don't know which."

"It was just like Frank, always saying something funny or off the wall. It was shortly after that he passed away."

Harry Pearson's Story

By the mid-1970s, the grain side of Perdue Farms was taking hold and becoming an institution for farmers. It was also a totally congenial activity for Frank, since he had a lifelong love of the harvest. After all, he had been a grain farmer himself (an unsuccessful one, as he would tell anyone), and he loved hanging out with the farmers.

Harry Pearson, a grain farmer, had a revealing experience that encapsulates some of Frank's attitude toward the grain growers.

To understand the story, keep in mind that part of what a farmer is paid for his or her grain depends on its moisture content. The tolerances for moisture are tight because if the grain is too dry, it will crack or break. If there's too much moisture, it's likely to spoil. Grain can be dried with fans but it's a fuel-intensive process, and therefore, expensive. For all these reasons, getting the moisture content just right is something everyone strives for.

One day, however, Pearson had an almighty obstacle to delivering his soybeans at the correct moisture level. It was mid corn harvest and at that time all the farmers hauled corn in six-wheeled trucks.

"This particular afternoon," said Pearson, "the trucks were lined up and it began raining – a regular downpour. The men who were doing the moisture sampling stopped working and the line stopped moving. In a short time, the trucks were lined up for a quarter of a mile across Old Ocean City Road, water pouring out the bottoms of the truck bodies."

While the farmers waited, they all knew that they'd be dealing with a high moisture reading when the line reopened, and they were also thinking about how costly this delay was for them, not being able to get back to their fields at the busiest time of year.

"The right lane was totally blocked with trucks when suddenly a big black Oldsmobile sped by in the left lane. One man in our group said, 'That's Frank Perdue. You'll see something happen now!'"

The farmer was right. The line suddenly began moving, even faster than normal. As Pearson drove up to the testing station, he was asked what the moisture reading had been on his previous load. Frank had told the people at the testing station to accept the word of every farmer in the line, since the corn could not be tested fairly in the rain.

"I'm sure that decision cost the Perdue Grain Division a lot of money that day, but the good will it created was immeasurable," Pearson said.

Dick Willey's Story

Dick Willey, President of Perdue AgriBusiness, started with the company in 1986, and he also witnessed the extraordinary lengths Frank would go to in order to look out for the grain farmers. There was one year when large corn plantings combined with phenomenally favorable weather meant such an outsize crop that there was nowhere near enough storage on the Delmarva

Peninsula for all the grain.

This was an excruciating problem for the farmers because after all the time, effort and expense of growing the crop, there was the possibility of not finding a buyer for it. Grain can be stored on the ground, covered with tarpaulins, but for a potential buyer, it's a tremendous risk. Tarpaulins are no protection against a hurricane, and if one came, the buyer could find that the grain he had purchased had been blown across five counties. Naturally, this meant that most grain buyers had no interest in purchasing the grain that they couldn't store in their existing tanks.

However, to help the farmers, Frank was willing to take on that risk. According to Willey, "Frank was out talking to farmers, beaming because he was able to provide a solution for them."

April Cheesman, the Senior Merchandiser in Willey's division also noticed how committed Frank was to the farmers. "My job is to buy grain from farmers. Frank wanted the associates who were in contact with the farmers to be out in the community, talking to the farmers and being available to provide the feed mill services pretty much all the time. During harvest, the elevators would be open late at night, including weekends, to serve the farmers' needs."

Frank put at least as much thought and effort into treating the farmers well as he did in taking care of the customers who bought Perdue chicken.

FRANK PERDUE'S LESSONS

PUT IN THE TIME AND EFFORT– Frank couldn't produce superior chickens if he didn't control the quality of their feed. He put a legendary amount of time and effort into studying the grain business before getting into it.

STAND UP FOR YOURSELF, AND FOR WHAT'S RIGHT– The resulting feed mill and soybean crushing plant was such a success that it quickly inspired competitors. These were millionaires who had lobbied to get a taxpayer-subsidized loan that could have put Frank out of business. He was willing to take on extraordinarily long odds to defeat what had been viewed as a fait accompli.

TAKE RISKS, AND GIVE CREDIT TO THOSE WHO EARN IT– During this period he created a culture where employees were all allowed to try new things, and making mistakes was acceptable. It became a trademark for him always to give his employees credit for Perdue Farms' success.

TRUST AND BE TRUSTED– His dealings with farmers were generous. When a rainstorm threatened to ruin the farmers' truckloads of grain as they waited in line to deliver their grain at the feed mill, he speeded up the line by simply trusting the farmers' word on the quality. He almost certainly lost money that day, but he gained a lifetime of good will.

CHAPTER FOUR

PROCESSING CHICKEN: OPPORTUNITY, AND THE BEGINNINGS OF A FULL-BLOWN OBSESSION

By 1967, the Perdue Company had become one of the biggest producers of live chickens in the country and was supplying 800,000 chickens a week to commercial customers. However, Frank hadn't yet gotten into processing chickens, something he needed to do if he was to control the quality of his chickens at every step.

Still, Frank was reluctant to get into this side of the business. Having a chicken processing plant would mean a large labor force, and he had no experience in this. It also would mean the complicated process of selling the dressed chickens to multiple buyers in urban markets, as opposed to the relatively simple process of taking live chickens to the local poultry auction.

Also, there was an economic factor that had kept him from getting into processing. During most of the 1960s, the average poultry processing plant was making just $60,000 a year, and economically it made more sense for him to invest in building more grain storage.

Actually, at this point the company was doing so well that Frank briefly considered building an impressive office building to replace the ramshackle wooden structure the company was then occupying–and would continue to occupy for the next 30 years. He had plans drawn up for a modern, $800,000 headquarters. But then he decided against it.

Commenting on Frank's decision, Tim Mescon, former Dean of the Perdue School of Business at Salisbury State University, said, "For a company as large and successful as Perdue Farms, you might expect a fifty-story glistening palace over the horizon. But with Perdue, the ultimate emphasis and the ultimate worth is in the final product, not on monuments."

Besides, as Frank once confided to his friend Shirley Phillips, monuments weren't important to him. "I don't want those things. I don't need them. I love to work and I love people, and the rest doesn't mean a thing to me."

There was still another factor in his not building the impressive office building. I, who have observed his attitude on spending throughout his life, think his attitude can be reduced to two simple equations: *Investment = Wonderful; Consumption = Suspect.* The office building, in his mind, was consumption.

It was fortunate that he didn't build the impressive headquarters because in short order, he had a better and more urgent use for the money. Up until this period, Frank had been selling his chickens at the local auction in Selbyville, Delaware. However, in 1966 and 1967, there was a glut of chickens in

relation to the number of existing processing plants. In those two years he lost close to $3 million. During this same period, the processors who bought those chickens were making extraordinary profits.

Frank and his dad, Mr. Arthur. Mr. Arthur believed right down to his core that, "If you don't owe money, you can't go broke."

PROCESSING CHICKEN: OPPORTUNITY, AND THE BEGINNINGS OF A FULL-BLOWN OBSESSION

An Opportunity Presents Itself

By the fall of 1967, the company's unprecedented losses guaranteed that Frank was reconsidering his position on processing. At just this moment, a chicken processing plant in Salisbury closed.

Don Mabe, who later became President and CEO of Perdue Farms, vividly remembers the events that followed. "It all happened suddenly, and we didn't have much time to think about it. I remember we flew to Chicago, bought it for about $300,000, and returned that night."

Between October and the end of February when the rehabbed plant re-opened, Mabe remembers that Frank would call him every single morning between 1:00 a.m. and 2:00 a.m. The strange hours didn't seem strange to Frank. And it doesn't seem to have occurred to Mabe to question this unusual procedure, either.

Mabe would just wake up, talk with Frank, and then go back to sleep. "Frank would tell me what he had learned about such things as the kind of crate the buyers wanted, what kind of liner, what kind of tags to use on the chickens, who the best truckers were, and what buyers were paying for chickens." Mabe in turn would tell Frank about what had been going with the plant renovation that day.

While Mabe was working on updating the plant and all its equipment, Frank was working in the Northeast, making sure there were markets for the dressed chickens that they would soon be selling.

"By the way," Mabe said recently, "the late night phone calls didn't bother me. This was partly because I'd take a nap before he'd call and partly because I was glad to tell him what we had done that day and glad to hear what he had been doing."

PROCESSING CHICKEN: OPPORTUNITY, AND THE BEGINNINGS OF A FULL-BLOWN OBSESSION

The Chickens Will Need to Be Sold

From the time the company bought the processing facility in October 1967 until the plant opened on February 29, 1968, Frank had only a limited time to line up buyers for his chickens. The plant would soon be processing 12,000 chickens an hour, and he urgently needed to secure a market for them.

To do so, he visited potential customers in Baltimore, Philadelphia, New York, Providence, Boston and as far away as Chicago and Pittsburgh. He quickly narrowed his focus to New York City.

"If you want the biggest Maine lobster, you don't buy it in Maine, you buy it in New York," he reasoned, "and if you want the best Kansas City beef, you won't find it there, you'll find it in Manhattan." Since he was selling a premium product, it was logical for him to concentrate on the area that wanted – and was willing to pay for – the best.

Having settled on New York City, he narrowed the focus further by aiming at the butcher shops, all 3,000 of them at the time. It was a clever approach because supermarket chains were hurting the butcher shops by selling chicken as loss leaders.

However, Frank understood that the butcher shops' niche was providing a better product than was available in the chain stores. By offering a superior chicken, he could give the butchers just what they most needed: a means of attracting customers back to their shops.

Frank also needed to line up the poultry distributors, that is, the people who would take a truckload of Frank's chickens and then break the load down to distribute to smaller trucks, which in turn would make deliveries to butchers and other retail outlets.

Frank talked with eighty distributors, asking them a list of twenty-five questions, and then, in his microscopic handwriting, he recorded their answers in a notebook. The notebook, by the way, still exists.

As a sample of the details that interested him, here are the actual questions he asked, in his own words:

1. Future of ice pack versus frozen or chill pak?

2. Appearance=crate; luggage tag; type wing tag; staple liner; stenciled name; packing procedure, our label.

3. How much more will you pay for wing tagged versus the lesser grade?

4. Would you accept birds in corrugated boxes?

5. How much cut-up do you handle?

6. How do you want the cut-up packaged?

7. How many heavy fowl (5-6 pound) do you want per week?

8. Do you want fowl fresh or frozen?

9. How do you feel that we should spend our advertising dollar?

10. Do you feel that we would gain much of the market as a result of radio advertising?

11. What plants do you buy from on the Shore?

12. Who has top quality that you buy from? (Rate in order)

13. About how many loads do you buy each week: how many from the Shore?

14. When do you pay for poultry?

15. If we were beginning operations next week, could I interest you in a load of poultry?

16. Your favorite sales manager

17. Parts prices

18. Parts Formula and price

19. The number of delivery trucks you have: - percent you haul versus percent picked up by your customers.

20. Unload When. (How long hold up our trucks.)

21. Day of week you Price and Buy.

22. Field Man. (Do we need one?)

23. How to start selling

24. On our delivering for the distributor (Where')

25. Do you prefer wing tagged birds?

Questions 9 and 10 are interesting. They indicate that he was thinking about advertising before ever processing a single chicken.

The last question, No. 25, was a Perdue innovation that did for chickens what Chiquita did for bananas and what the Lacoste crocodile did for sports shirts. Hanging a wing tag bearing the Perdue name was a watershed in the beginnings of branded chicken.

Besides the above questions, he also took notes on what the distributors said apart from answering the set questions, and compiled that information into a supplemental 100-page notebook. These included comments about who was a good salesman, who might be good to recruit, whose judgment could be trusted, and so on.

Allen Kosofsky and his father, Ben, were two of the distributors Frank called on at that time. They ended up becoming good friends, but Allen remembers that to the sophisticated New Yorkers, Frank looked "very countrified." To Kosofsky, "It seemed as if he was wearing high-button shoes and a straw hat."

PROCESSING CHICKEN: OPPORTUNITY, AND THE BEGINNINGS OF A FULL-BLOWN OBSESSION

Walter Myslinski Sr. was another distributor Frank contacted. "He came up to Brooklyn and we sat down and talked," remembers Myslinski. "Frank was very good at picking everyone's brain. Whenever the thought came to him, he'd call, even at 2:00 a.m. He'd ask things like, 'Well, do you think we should go ahead and change the color on the boxes? Is it yellow enough? Are the customers satisfied with this?'

Myslinski recalls that Frank wanted to make sure that what he sold was the finest available and he had to know that no one else could beat him. "Most CEOs would delegate this responsibility. But he was in the field more than his sales reps."

Myslinski's strongest memory of Frank is that "He didn't like you to schmooze him. He liked total honesty. If you told him when he did something wrong, he appreciated it."

By the opening day of the newly renovated Salisbury processing plant, Frank had the needed buyers and distributors lined up. Now the job was to produce the superior quality chickens.

Frank had always cared about quality in both the feed business and the chicken business. But when he got into the processing business, quality became a full-blown obsession. To the end of his days, Frank would shudder at the memory of his first day of processing chickens.

The First Day is a Trauma

That first day there were two absolutely intolerable defects. The grease on the old overhead conveyor belt, which was not part of the pre-opening renovations, would drip down onto the chickens, and the steel shavings from the badly fitting new screw conveyors would fall on the freshly processed birds.

Frank was traumatized. "My God," he thought, "our first day and we're ruining the Perdue name."

47

PROCESSING CHICKEN: OPPORTUNITY, AND THE BEGINNINGS OF A FULL-BLOWN OBSESSION

Of course he didn't sell a single Perdue chicken until the problems were fixed. Meanwhile, it was an agonizing experience.

Ellis Wainwright, who became a Perdue Supervisor of Grading for the next 23 years, also had vivid memories of the plant start-up. He had been a government grading inspector when Frank had initially bought the plant and remembers that for the first few days, none of the chickens were good enough even to consider for the Perdue label.

Frank had told him that the standards he wanted were higher than the Government Grade A standard. By the third day, the problems were mostly fixed and Wainwright started his grading. "We graded all morning," said Wainwright, "and I found only five boxes that passed what I took to be Frank's standards.

Frank's standards literally were higher than the government's. According to Wainwright, you could have torn skin on a Grade A chicken, but not with Perdue; or you could have a discolored wing, but not with Perdue. A small bruise the size of pencil eraser wasn't acceptable to Frank even though this was acceptable by government standards.

Wainwright was afraid Frank was going to raise Cain that he had accepted so few. Then, to Wainwright's surprise, Frank came through and rejected half of the ones that Wainwright had approved.

The rejects weren't a loss and could be sold at commodity prices, but they couldn't be marked Perdue. Of the 10,000 chickens processed that day, most passed the USDA standards, but only sixty of them met Frank's criteria for quality. Sixty chickens were not enough to sell separately, so they, too, were sold unlabeled at commodity prices.

Part of the reason for so many rejects was that people hadn't learned to use the feather- picking machines well, and they were knocking the yellow pigmentation off. "Frank wasn't upset or angry," Wainwright remembered. "He just said, 'Ellis, we've got to be better than anyone else. We want to put out the best quality that can be put out.'"

Within a couple of days, Don Mabe had fixed the picking machine problems, and the company was finally able to produce chickens good enough for Frank to be willing to have the Perdue name on them.

From the beginning, Frank instituted quality controls. Alan Culver, who later became Vice President of Quality Assurance, was the quality control czar. His job was to determine whether the Perdue product was worse than, better than, or the same as the quality of the competitors.

"Quality was the backbone of the success of our company since its inception," Frank said, and then referring to this period, "Every two weeks, the company had a team of people who anonymously would check Perdue products and the competition's. The product is coded so the checkers do not know which is which and therefore can't be biased by the name."

According to a plan instituted by Frank and Culver, the competitors' product samples, together with Perdue samples, were brought back every two weeks from the marketplace. In checking fifty-seven factors (bruises, hair, feathers, breast width, etc.), Perdue associates checked what the consumer sees and what the first receiver gets, and also what the chain stores and the distributors who distribute to the small chains and butcher shops get.

For the distributor or chain receiver, Perdue associates checked box quality, so the bottom box didn't collapse and have everything fall to the floor. Markings on the box had to be legible. The processing date had to be visible so that rotation schedules could be effective. The amount of ice had to be adequate.

"In the fifty-seven quality checks," Frank said, "we never lost in comparison to our competitors. We always come in first."

As Garland Eutsler, who later became the Plant Superintendent at the Accomac processing plant, and who was with Perdue since the early

PROCESSING CHICKEN: OPPORTUNITY, AND THE BEGINNINGS OF A FULL-BLOWN OBSESSION

processing days, said, "From the first day I met Frank, he never stopped talking quality. His memory of the tiniest details was amazing and he had the greatest foresight of any human being I ever met. Ninety-nine times out of 100, he would come up with the right answer. It's as if he could foresee the future."

Larry Taylor continued the Perdue efforts at maintaining high quality. His title was Quality Assurance Division Manager, and though he retired in 2013, he still talks about his somewhat traumatic first encounter with Frank.

Taylor had just begun working for Perdue, back in December of 1975 and was having a coffee in the cafeteria at the Salisbury, Maryland processing plant. From where he was sitting in a corner of the cafeteria, he could see Frank in the middle of the cafeteria, talking with the cafeteria manager. Taylor was impressed that the big boss was in the employee cafeteria, hanging out where the hourly workers ate.

Taylor's thoughts were interrupted when moments later he realized that Frank was looking at him, and was now striding over to where Taylor was sitting. Taylor was a new hire, he was in his early 20s, and he had expected to be invisible. Suddenly here was Frank demanding, "Who are you?"

The Salisbury plant had more than 500 employees, and Taylor never expected Frank to recognize that there was someone new in the plant. Taylor had assumed he was wearing a cloak of invisibility.

"I'm Larry Taylor," he managed to blurt out.

Frank scrutinized him for a moment and then demanded, "What do you do?"

"I'm going to be managing the Grading Department," the nervous new hire responded.

And then, as Taylor remembers it, everything changed. Frank cocked his head to one side and his face brightened with interest. He immediately sat

PROCESSING CHICKEN: OPPORTUNITY, AND THE BEGINNINGS OF A FULL-BLOWN OBSESSION

down at Taylor's table and talked with him for an entire 30 minutes. The conversations was about how important the job of a grader was and how Frank was counting on Taylor to make sure that every chicken that had the Perdue name on the package would not only be better than the competition, but it would have to exceed the USDA requirements. If there were chickens going through the processing plant that weren't achieving that standard, Taylor had the authority to slow down the line until it got straightened out.

Ralph Moore, whose career included being a service man and manager of the soybean plant, was tapped to manage the new processing plant. Moore noticed that, "Persistence was a real strong point with Frank. He'd get on a subject and he'd learn everything there was to know about it. If it took a week or a month, that's what he did."

Conversations between Moore and Frank would often begin at midnight and could last two or three hours. "I'd be in bed when he called," said Moore, "so I'd tuck the phone under my head, and I'd just talk and grunt, while my wife slept right on through."

"One time when Frank called, Moore knew Frank was traveling, but even so they were having a lengthy phone conversation. "Where are you Frank?" he asked.

"I'm in a hotel in New York."

"But Frank, that's long distance, it's going to cost you $2,000!" (Forty years ago, for you younger readers, even a call between Salisbury, Maryland, and New York was long distance –and expensive.)

"Don't worry," Frank answered, "this is information, and information is worth the price."

Moore felt that Frank had a knack for motivating people. "He let you be freehanded and make decisions, like you're part of the family. He was tough and expected a lot out of you, but he never gave you more than you could

51

do. People wanted to do their best for him."

Frank Wood, a friend and employee, marveled at Frank's collegial relations with the men and women who worked at the Salisbury Plant. "It was like working with him rather than for him. It was obvious that he enjoyed being with us. He was good at making us feel important."

FRANK PERDUE'S LESSONS

PREFER INVESTMENT TO CONSUMPTION– Frank could have built an ego-satisfying headquarters tower, but that would have been consumption. Not building the impressive headquarters, meant he had the funds available when the opportunity came to buy a chicken processing plant.

WHEN BEGINNING A NEW VENTURE, FIGURE OUT THE SKILLS NEEDED FOR SUCCESS, AND THEN LEARN THOSE SKILLS– Producing the chickens meant Frank would need a market for them. He visited 80 of the poultry distributors and a large number of the 3,000 butcher shops in New York. As a farm boy, New York was almost foreign territory for him, but he made the effort to learn the new culture and was able to have buyers lined up for his premium-branded chicken by the time the plant opened five months later.

DON'T COMPROMISE ON QUALITY– Although the initial production from the plant was good enough for USDA standards, he refused to put his name on the first three days' production and instead sold it at commodity prices. His marketing vision called for a superior product, and he wouldn't accept less, because "Quality was the backbone of the success of the company since its inception."

CREATE A TEAM– He treated his employees with so much respect that many felt as if they were working *with* him, not *for* him. He excelled at making employees feel important and valued, and in return, many were willing to give their all to making the effort a success.

CHAPTER FIVE

MARKETING: STUDYING IT, PRACTICING IT, EXCELLING AT IT

With the Salisbury plant producing 12,000 broilers an hour, the company had finally achieved complete integration. Perdue Farms hatched the eggs, delivered them to contract producers, picked up the mature birds for processing, put the dressed chicken on ice, and delivered them overnight to New York.

Selling his chickens wasn't a problem, but selling them at a price that would justify the extra cost of producing a superior product required marketing expertise. Frank realized that he needed to study marketing if he was to make this happen.

Studying Marketing and Putting It Into Practice

Frank became a major success as a marketer–some say that by the 1970s he was the most successful marketer in the country–but even though he had good instincts for marketing, these instincts were only part of the story. According to Professor Frank Shipper from the Perdue School of Business, what really counted was both how thoroughly he studied marketing and then how brilliantly he put into practice what he had learned.

"When he was learning about marketing," said Shipper, "he'd talk with marketing professors at major universities as well as reading and studying marketing books and journals. Then, after he'd talked with the experts, he'd say, 'Who else should I talk with? What else should I read?' And then he would interview the additional people and do the additional reading."

53

MARKETING: STUDYING IT, PRACTICING IT, EXCELLING AT IT

When putting this knowledge into practice, Frank's efforts focused on what the consumer wanted or needed, and importantly, what the consumer might want or need in the future. With this information, Frank could tailor what he was offering to what would best meet those wants and needs.

Four Marketing Targets

Frank's marketing efforts were not directed solely toward consumers. As you'll see, to be a success he had to be aware of and market to at least four distinct customers: the distributors, the butchers' union, the retail stores and the buying public.

The distributors were a critical group for Frank if his chickens were to reach grocery shoppers. To take New York City as an example, when a truckload of

He became one of the most successful marketers in America.

Perdue chicken arrived in New York, it didn't go directly to the stores; it went to an intermediary, the distributor. The distributor received the chicken, inventoried it, and then sent it out in smaller trucks to the butcher shops and retail stores. Frank needed to have the distributors want to carry Perdue products or his chickens would never reach the stores.

In addition, it was critical to get buy-in for cut-up, prepackaged chicken from members of the butchers or meat cutters union. Initially, they strongly opposed this on the grounds that pre-cut chicken would cost them jobs.

The marketing efforts also had to target the retail stores. If they weren't pleased, if they didn't want to carry the product, Perdue chicken wouldn't reach the consumer. And of course he also needed to market to grocery shoppers.

Frank's marketing efforts had to be successful with all four groups, and his efforts to woo all of them were intense and unprecedented. Associates still remember how he'd start his market research meetings at 7:00 a.m. and would come in with "19,000 memos," and his executive assistant, Elaine Barnes, would be there "with 120 items on the agenda."

A Virtual Sixth Sense

The source of those memos and agenda items was the dreaded marketing reports, an intelligence-gathering institution Frank created to learn about customer wants and needs. At the end of each day, each marketing rep in each city was required to dictate a report on the roughly ten stores and distributors that he or she had called on that day.

As Frank told me, "We had more people in the field at the retail level than any other company. Our marketing reports were unique, and we started them as an effort to get in writing every day what happened."

The report included what customers had liked and not liked, problems such as leaky bags or product not stored right, information on what the competition was doing, and how satisfied the customers were. Every item of information was designed to understand better what customers wanted and didn't want.

Frank was so assiduous in studying these reports that even on our honeymoon he was reading them. I used to joke that on our wedding night, Frank didn't touch me but was instead reading marketing reports. That's technically true, but it's not exactly the whole story. The fact is, that night we were on a flight to Rome. Since it was a night flight, I slept through a good bit of it, but occasionally I'd wake up and notice that he alone among the plane's passengers had his light on. He was studying the marketing reports. He liked reading these reports even on an overnight flight to Rome because they provided him with a virtual sixth sense, allowing him to see what was going on in the different markets in ways that were invisible to his competitors.

Finding and Developing Good Marketing Reps

Recruiting, hiring, and training the marketing representatives was an example of the effort it took to become an outstanding marketer. To use a phrase that you've seen before in this book, Frank didn't just say, "Let it be so," and the marketing reps magically appeared.

His first efforts in selecting marketing people were a failure. In the early 1970s, he had reasoned that the best marketers would be the broiler service men. After all, they knew firsthand the efforts the company put into growing cleaner, healthier, meatier chickens. They could explain the company better than anyone else because of their personal knowledge and experience, plus they had a track record of hard work, responsibility and problem solving.

The problem with that theory was that when he was first trying to carry it out, none of the broiler service men whom Frank initially tapped for marketing lasted more than a single day in New York. To a man, they felt overwhelmed by the crowds, the noise, the traffic and the city itself.

Having failed at that, Frank tried the opposite approach. He'd get a city person with a degree in marketing and try to teach him about what it took to grow good chickens. The person he found was Michael Ottomanelli.

Ottomanelli had just finished college with a marketing degree. After being interviewed by Frank and accepting the job, he was amazed to find that a half hour later, a courier arrived with tickets for him to fly to Salisbury. He found himself starting work the next day.

Once there, Ottomanelli remembers Frank's telling him, "Forget about your marketing degree: you've got to learn about all the parts of the chicken business, starting with the processing plant, after that the feed mill, and then you'll ride with the service men visiting the farms."

Ottomanelli also remembers that, "Frank was a really good teacher. He appreciated and believed in young people, and he liked to get you young, before you were set in your ways."

Under Frank's direction, Ottomanelli spent months learning different aspects of what it took to grow good chickens. "Frank would be questioning me all the time, checking if I had learned what I needed to be learning. Then one day he told me, 'Now I want you to move back to New York and be my eyes and ears there.'"

Ottomanelli had been watching Frank on the production side of the company, but now he also got to see Frank interacting with the distributors, the buyers in the stores, and the retail customers. Many of the interactions he got to witness involved Frank's doing market research.

"He always kept little pieces of paper in his breast pocket," remembered Ottomanelli, "and when there was some new piece of information, he'd write it down in his little tiny handwriting."

Ottomanelli describes how a grandmotherly woman might come up to Frank and say, "I really like your chickens."

"Why's that?" Frank would pleasantly inquire, his whole manner indicating that he was genuinely interested in what she had to say.

"Well, because they're fresh," she might say.

"What does fresh mean to you?" he'd gently ask, paying total attention to her, as if for the moment, nothing else in the world mattered to him.

Collecting, and More Important, Using Information

Whatever her answer, Frank would reach into his shirt pocket for one of the little pieces of paper – they were each about the size and shape of a playing card – and make a note of it. At any one moment, Frank might have 25 pieces of paper with notes on them in his breast pocket, and each might have seven or eight notes on it. When Frank had in one way or another dealt with a note, he'd cross it off. Each paper stayed in his breast pocket until he had drawn a line through all of the notes written on it.

The point is, Frank didn't just gather information; instead, with the help of those notes, he translated the information into knowledge, and then the knowledge into action

As an example of this process, Frank learned from talking with customers in the stores that often people who were used to whole birds weren't sure how to deal with the innovation of cut-up chicken. These individuals might know how to roast or stew a whole chicken, but they just weren't familiar with how to cook chicken parts.

In response, he proposed to have recipe cards in each package of cut-up chicken. This idea, of course, came up in the marketing meetings. The response of the Perdue finance people, according to Ottomanelli, was, 'It's going to cost two cents a pound, where are we going to get the money?'

Although almost everyone opposed it, Frank pushed ahead and got it done anyway. Ottomanelli watched in fascination as this innovation increased demand so much that in the end it was worth 7 cents a pound.

"He was a true marketing genius," said Ottomanelli. "He represented the difference between sales and marketing. With sales, there's a tendency to see only as far as your nose, while marketing involves being able to see around the block."

Paying for Improved Packaging

In his quest for information, Frank instructed his marketing reps not to ask, "What are we doing right?" He felt he could only correct problems if he knew about them and he didn't want to use up scarce time on good news since good news generally didn't require action.

Instead, the appropriate question for the marketing rep to ask was, "What's wrong that we can do better?" Or, equally good, "What problems can we solve?"

In the case of the distributors, one of the problems that this kind of question rapidly revealed was that the boxes that everyone's chicken was shipped in were too flimsy. The owner of a typical chicken processing company would see nice handsome boxes leaving the processing plant, and without having marketing reps at the unloading docks in the cities, he or she didn't know how grungy and unattractive the crushed leaking boxes were at the end of the trip. Frank's marketing reps made sure Frank knew.

In response, Frank got his top people together and told them, "I want a box that's going to last for at least a week without collapsing." Top management answered that doing that would be prohibitively expensive. "We can't afford it," they sternly informed him.

"I don't care what it costs. *We can't afford not to*," he countered.

Since his marketing efforts were centered on being better than everybody else, solving the collapsing box problem wasn't an expense. Instead, it turned out to be a heaven-sent opportunity.

Gus LeBois, one of the early marketing reps, said, "Frank was so right about this because once we figured out how to make crushproof shipping boxes, the industry took a whole year to copy us. During this time they had their heads handed to them. Today in the industry, good boxes are standard, but it stuck with me ever since that it doesn't matter what it costs if that's what the customer wants. They'll come back to you if you take care of them."

Improving Service through Reliable Delivery Times

Broken or crushed boxes weren't the only opportunity cleverly disguised as a problem. As LeBois remembered, "Often the trucks that were delivering the product weren't cleaned out sufficiently. I could see the deliveries coming in

---

from competitors, and the delivery trucks were beat up and dirty. When the distributors opened the back of the truck to get out the product, there would be volumes of bloody water everywhere."

And if that weren't enough of a problem, LeBois noticed that, "Frequently there would also be broken pallets, something that's a real headache for the receiver because it's hard to get a forklift underneath to pick up the pallet."

Frank approached solving these kinds of problems with a number of innovations. One of the first things he did was give the distributors his own personal phone number. He told them they could call him in the middle of the night if there were a problem, and he'd get it straightened out.

Being willing to take the calls was itself superb marketing. How better to signal to a distributor that Frank truly valued the relationship? And on a more practical level, it also meant that when there was a problem, the distributors had someone to go to who could solve the problem. None of Frank's competitors back then matched this level of service.

By the way, the distributors did call Frank. LeBois knows this very well, because if someone called Frank at 2:30 a.m., Frank was sure to be on the phone with LeBois at 2:35 a.m., working to get the problem solved. This happened countless times.

Frank's next steps had to do with on-time deliveries, and again, he put immense personal effort into it. Another of the early marketing reps, Ted Cook, said, "I was involved with getting trucks to the distributors on time. The problem was, trucks which should have been at Hunt's Point in New York by 5:00 a.m., sometimes wouldn't arrive until 10:00 a.m.

"Frank had me go to Hunt's Point, where we had five distributors. 'Keep your ears to the ground,' he told me. 'I want to know what's going on!'"

Cook had to be at Hunt's Point by 4:30 a.m. each morning to find out why deliveries were so often late. As part of his investigation, he initiated a system whereby, immediately after arriving at Hunt's Point, he'd call the Perdue Transportation Department back in Salisbury to check if a particular driver had left on time.

To Cook's intense surprise, he found that at the beginning of this research the guy answering the phone back in Salisbury was Frank Perdue himself. "Frank was in the trenches, staying on top of things," marvels Cook. He noticed that Frank kept this up for two weeks until he got his answers about what was going on and could plan what to do about the problems.

"You don't see other CEOs like that," stresses Cook. "He was hands-on. He set an example."

Cook was impressed not only with Frank's dedication, but also that he encouraged action. "Cook," he told the young man one day, "The greatest sin is to do nothing. If there's a problem and you didn't address it, then you are the bigger problem. Try a solution, and if it doesn't work, I won't get mad at you."

According to Ted Cook, "Frank wanted us to keep in mind that 'The buyer has plenty of headaches, and our job is to make sure we aren't one of them.' And, 'The more we solve his problems, the more business we'll get.'"

It worked. With that kind of attitude, Perdue often had as much as 70 percent of the chicken in the poultry shelf space in a store, and at some stores, 100 percent.

As the processing business began to take hold, Frank made use of some of the information he had developed when interviewing butchers and distributors in New York. He began offering cut-up chicken to national or ethnic groups in the form that they preferred. Did Puerto Rican cuisine require small chickens? Perdue was there to provide them. And Cuban recipes used bigger legs? Perdue had them.

MARKETING: STUDYING IT, PRACTICING IT, EXCELLING AT IT

The Chinese wanted roaster breasts in particular, and after breasts, they wanted legs and wings. "It was a boon for everyone involved," remembered Allen Kosofsky, a distributor. "Everyone loved it because they got what they want. Chinatown people loved him, and even those who barely spoke English, they all knew 'Perdue, Perdue, Perdue.'"

Kosofsky had an additional observation on what set Frank apart. "One thing that he was very good at which makes the company successful: he'd get right on the phone and say, 'What in the hell is going on here?' and fix it. No other company in the business would do this. Nobody else paid attention to complaints like him."

Frank knew from his market research that the buying public wanted cut-up chicken in trays. It was ideal to be able to give people a choice, but before these pre-pack cut up trays could appear in the grocery shelves, there was another constituency that had to approve: the butchers.

Initially, they didn't.

Getting Union Buy-in

There was strong opposition from the butchers' union because on the face of it, it looked as if cut-up chicken would be costing them jobs. However, Frank's research had convinced him that cut-up chicken would be an immense benefit to them, and he made a major effort to demonstrate this.

The underlying fact that Frank had to work with is that for the butcher, cutting chicken is his least profitable activity. Chicken itself is a low-profit item, and before pre-packaged, cut-up chicken, the butchers had to spend valuable time sanitizing their equipment when moving between chicken, beef and pork.

Instead, with pre-pak, they could be spending their time where it was best compensated, which was with meat. When they were busy cutting up expensive, profitable cuts of meat and the chicken case was low, all they had to do was open a carton of chicken packages, put on a price sticker, and slide the packages into the refrigerated case. They no longer had to devote the time to cleaning their equipment between shifting from chicken to other meats.

To sell the butchers and meat managers on this idea, Frank had Gus LeBois bring 30 planeloads of them to the processing plant in Accomac, Virginia, with the goal of showing them how tray-pack would work for them. Over a period of more than a year, 1,000 meat managers and butchers came to Accomac to see for themselves how all this worked and why tray-pack would be a benefit.

Given the cost of the chartered planes from New York, plus the time of top management, and the cost of a nice lunch at the Elk's Club, this was an expensive thing to do. Incidentally (or should I say not incidentally) the cost of these trips was a constant battle between Frank and the rest of top management.

They'd say this was all too expensive, especially the nice lunch at the Elks Lodge. People in top management generally didn't want anything to do with it because of the cost.

Frank's response was to point out that we needed the meat managers and butchers on our side. We were never going to be successful unless they actively embraced what we were doing.

This, by the way, is an example of one of the factors that made Frank a success. He could see how to get from here to there, and was willing to invest the time, energy and money to do it. He needed the butchers if tray-pak was to take hold, and he worked hard to get their buy-in.

His marketing to the union members and meat managers went way beyond the simple and objective facts of how pre-pak would benefit them in both money and convenience. He went to the added trouble of the nice lunch, and as a personal touch, he'd pose with each person for an 8 by 10 photograph.

He'd sign each photograph with a personal message to the individual, and then a marketing rep in the field would hand-deliver the photo. Gus LeBois, who was a witness to all of this, said, "To this day these signed pictures adorn the offices and meat rooms and homes of all those fortunate enough to have been able to attend. It was another way that Frank earned the trust and loyalty of the very tough bunch of meat people in a very tough market in the NYC area. And some of the original customers that Frank started with back then are still with us today. They're still very loyal."

Gus LeBois sums it up by saying, "With innovations like these, Frank changed the industry. It gave us a phenomenal marketing advantage for years, until everyone else wised up. The resulting growth was incredible."

Teaching by Questioning

In addition to marketing to the distributors and the unions, there remained still another marketing target before getting to the retail consumer: the supermarkets and grocery chains. Frank wanted to make a product that not only the customers wanted, and that the distributors and butchers wanted to handle, but he also needed to persuade the supermarkets and chains that they were better off carrying Perdue.

Charlie Carpenter is now the Perdue Director of Breeders and Hatcheries, but his career with Perdue included marketing during the 1970s. He got to see firsthand Frank's approach to marketing to the chains and supermarkets.

"He was a great teacher," remembered Carpenter, "and he taught by asking questions. Interestingly, he always knew the answers himself. When I was in marketing from 1976-1977, the kinds of questions he'd ask me about just one supermarket might include:

"Who are the decision makers?"

"Who is on the buying committee?"

"What days do they have to make the decision to buy ads?"

MARKETING: STUDYING IT, PRACTICING IT, EXCELLING AT IT

"What does it take to get our chicken in their ads?"

"How much of a discount did we need to offer to get a feature?"

Frank would keep asking questions until Carpenter reached the point where he didn't know the answers. Frank would then ask additional questions. Carpenter kept a notebook to write down what those questions were. He'd make sure to find the answers in the next 24 hours.

"It was all about learning," said Carpenter. "He wanted to drive product sales by being the best, and Frank felt that knowing what was going on was an essential ingredient in this."

Pre-Marketing Marketing and Quality Control

Kory Hooker, another of the early marketing reps, valued Frank's giving young people a lot of opportunity. Hooker was 23 years old when he was given responsibility for the Virginia Market, and by the time he was 30, he was responsible for most of the southeast markets in the United States.

Hooker was impressed by the effectiveness of the marketing reports, but he also participated in another reality check for how well Perdue was meeting its promise of being the best. In the Accomac plant, Frank had created a packaging report room. He'd have samples of Perdue products and competitor's products from all over the country, and on a weekly basis, people at Accomac had the job of checking how Perdue was doing in relation to the competition.

The information would be funneled into the quarterly pre-marketing marketing and quality control meetings. "At these meetings," remembered Hooker, "we'd typically start at 7:00 a.m., and we'd go through every note that Frank had written that wasn't yet resolved. There could be a stack of these two feet high, and sometimes we didn't finish until 12 hours later."

For Hooker, the job was never really done. "When you went to bed in the evening, you'd keep a piece of paper and a pen on the bed stand because if

Frank had something on his mind, he'd call at 2:00 or 3:00 a.m. and it was a good idea to write notes so you'd remember the next day."

How did Hooker feel about getting called at 2:00 a.m.? "I was in my mid-20s, and Frank was my mentor figure. I used to think, if he's 60 and he's got that that much drive and energy, then who am I to complain?"

One of Hooker's favorite sayings from Frank relates to Frank's perseverance. "Just because it's hard doesn't mean you don't pursue it. It may not work, but you don't know unless you try."

Developing and Nurturing Personal Relationships

Frank's marketing efforts were centered on being the best, but he also put a lot of effort into personal relationships. For instance, because of his celebrity, he was in a perfect position to do the meat directors in the stores a favor by attending the grand openings of supermarkets.

According to Ted Cook, if Frank attended one of these store openings it could guarantee success, because there would always be long lines of people attending, all of them there for the chance to meet Frank Perdue.

Meanwhile, Frank was making the meat director who had invited him look really, really good. It was a personal favor, and it meant a personal relationship that the meat directors appreciated.

Frank also had a gift for making each of them feel important. He'd give them his home number and they had the bragging rights of being able to tell people, "I can talk to Frank Perdue any time I want!"

Having these personal relationships made life easier for the marketers. Often if the meat manager needed a favor, such as they were short of something that was on sale, the marketers could help them out. But it also worked the other way when Perdue was long on something. As an example – one of many that Cook remembers – is he'd call his friend Clayton Sheppard at Pathmark.

MARKETING: STUDYING IT,
PRACTICING IT, EXCELLING AT IT

"We're really long on chicken legs and could use some help," he'd say.

Minutes later, Sheppard would be calling back with an order for three trailer loads of legs that he'd be putting on sale at Pathmark. These kinds of relationships made life easier for all concerned.

Bryan Hurst, who started out as a flock supervisor in 1982 and is today Vice President of Sales for the Specialty Foods Channel also remembers Frank's emphasis on the personal side of sales. "One of the best lessons Frank taught me was the importance of being humble in front of a customer. You were not going to have any air of arrogance, as far as Frank was concerned. Our job was to find out what the customer needed and to fill those needs.

Hurst also noticed that Frank put the effort into learning people's names. "He had a phenomenal memory and was well known for recognizing people he hadn't seen in a long time. At a store, he'd know the director and the buyer, and as rarely happened, if he happened not to know, he'd made sure to find out."

Going at It on All Fronts

Although Frank worked hard to develop relationships at all levels, his relationship with his marketing teams was, to use a word that I heard from one of them (and that I take to be a euphemism), "challenging."

For Ted Cook, on the one hand it was inspiring to be working with the best marketing man in the country. On the other, working for Frank was not easy. "Today, Perdue veterans from back then joke that we would all have been dead if Frank had had a cell phone because he'd be calling us ten times a day."

Cook still remembers what a day with Frank Perdue would be like. Cook would drive to New York's Pierre Hotel in his "Perduemobile" (it was actually a Chevrolet Impala) to pick up Frank. Cook's car would be surrounded with Rolls Royces and Mercedes while he waited.

MARKETING: STUDYING IT, PRACTICING IT, EXCELLING AT IT

That part may have been awesome, but as soon as Frank was in the car, he'd start driving Cook crazy. It would start out with a rapid-fire series of statements such as, "Cook, I don't have any time for red lights! If you time it right, you won't get any." "Go this way, turn left, avoid the 59th Street Bridge, don't allow more than six feet between you and the car in front of you or someone could come in between."

Frank wanted to cover as much ground as possible, and being with him wasn't exactly a relaxing experience. "By the end of a day driving with Frank," remembers Cook, "I was ready for two stiff drinks."

Jonathan Poole today works for Eastern Poultry Distributors, Inc. in West Hills, California, but he worked for Frank in marketing from 1984 to 1988, and he also has found Frank the marketer to be challenging.

"Of all the people I've been in business with, he is the one you love to hate. He did things that drove me crazy and irritated the hell out of me, but it all came from the drive and motivation to do things right and make sure everything was going as it should. The problem with Frank was he didn't consider your personal time. If he wanted to talk with you, he picked up the phone no matter what time it was."

Poole felt that Frank was like a horse with blinders on when he was going after something. He simply kept at it until he had it done. "He had high expectations, he was impatient, and he wanted things done yesterday."

On the other hand, that kind of drive and impatience paid off. As Poole remembered, "In marketing, he knew how to cultivate people. If a buyer mentioned a Yankees game to him, the next thing would be Frank calling me saying, 'Hey Jon, did you know he likes the Yankees?'

"'No, Frank.'

"'Get the best tickets to a Yankees game that you can and take him to it!'"

If a buyer or distributor had an interest, Frank would be grilling Poole about it, whether it was flying in hot air balloons, or supporting the Bronx Zoo, or whatever. The relationships Frank wanted had to be more than a buy-sell contractual kind of thing. He understood that personal relationships play a big role in who you want to do business with.

Poole found himself wondering, "How many businessmen go at it on all fronts like Frank did?"

Poole also recalls that Frank always wanted to know the bad news rather than the good news. A typical conversation might start with Frank's asking, "How's it going with Pathmark?"

"We've been doing well, no complaints, and on-time deliveries," Poole would answer.

That was not the kind of answer Frank was looking for.

"Tell me what's wrong," he'd insist.

"Nothing that I know of."

"There's gotta be something wrong, I can't work on what's right."

Doing What You Say You're Going to Do

Gene Buckley worked for Perdue Farms from 1979 until his retirement in 1996. His job was Perdue's New England Marketing Representative. He and Frank had a bond because they both had competitive natures, and for both of them work wasn't work; it was fun.

"Frank told me right at the beginning," said Buckley, "that as someone in my mid-thirties, I was not the age that he normally was looking for. He liked to get people right out of college and train them in the Perdue way."

"I answered him, 'But I don't have any bad habits, hire me anyway!'"

The hiring turned out to be a major success. Buckley brought to the table something that Frank valued highly, and that was relationships with all the major New England chains. Buckley could get Frank in to see the key people.

"Once he got in, they loved him," said Buckley. "He wasn't a high-powered salesman and he wasn't a BS-er, but instead you could tell that he was honest and people quickly discovered that he'd do what he said he was going to do."

Buckley remembers that meeting Frank was a whole new experience for the buyers. They weren't used to finding someone who knew so much about chickens and who was so concerned about what they, the buyers, needed.

As he did in other areas, Frank also went out of his way to help the New England buyers by accepting invitations to attend store grand openings. "What's interesting," said Buckley, "is he would go no matter how small the store was. Also, understand that these grand openings would be on the weekends when the most people could come, so it meant his giving up a lot of weekends. Not many people who are as successful and famous as he was would do that."

Today, Buckley still remembers Frank fondly. "The best part of my job was knowing Frank. We weren't boss-employer; we were buddies."

Pricing and Shelf-Space

Jack Tatem began his Perdue career in 1974, working in one of the hatcheries, but rapidly transitioned into sales. He retired 39 years later as the Vice President of Wholesale/Industrial Sales.

Tatem saw firsthand that an important part of Frank's marketing efforts involved making sure that Perdue chicken was the first chicken consumers would see as they cycled through a store.

"To help with this goal," said Tatem, "we had a Perdue Planagram, in which we figured out the traffic pattern for each store so we could track if we were in the desired location."

Tatem thought that Frank's handling of pricing was brilliant. Frank's strategy was to price Perdue chicken 7 cents per pound above what the competition did, and the store would charge 10 cents per pound more for the product at retail, thus promoting a higher gross markup for the meat department. This had the effect of enlisting the meat manager as a Perdue partner.

In Tatem's view, when this pricing strategy was coupled with advertising, "The effect was incredible. For the first 10 years in sales, I don't think I really had to sell anything, I had to allocate product, and by that I mean I had more orders than product to fill the orders."

In short, it was a salesman's dream. But that wasn't the part that Tatem most admired.

"We were worth the extra cost because we had a better product, and we had to charge more because it cost us more to make it. But the most important part of this story is, we could have charged a lot more than the 7 cents a pound we were charging, but Frank had a tremendous insight about this. 'Never get so greedy with your profitability that you invite competition. If you're making too much on something,' he'd tell us, 'it won't be long before someone comes in to undercut you.'"

Frank was a skilled marketer, but he also knew how to be supportive of his marketers. As Tatem tells it, his elderly mother had seen Frank in TV commercials and one day asked if she could meet him.

"I doubt it," Tatem answered and didn't give it much thought until a couple of years later Frank asked out of the blue, "Jack, is there anything I can do for you?"

"If you ever get through Pocomoke City, Maryland, would you stop by and see my mother?" Tatem asked.

About a year later, Tatem's mother called and told him that Frank had just stopped by and spent 30 minutes visiting with her. She was thrilled.

MARKETING: STUDYING IT, PRACTICING IT, EXCELLING AT IT

"This," said Tatem, "is the Frank Perdue I admire equally as much as Frank Perdue the marketer. Down deep he cared about everything!"

Tatem is retired now, but in thinking over his life and his experiences with Frank, he has a thought to share with young people. "One of the best pieces of advice I can give to people just starting work is, 'Shut up and listen.' Most kids I run into today seem to think they already know it all. Frank was a one-of-a-kind genius, but even as successful as he was, he was always listening."

Calling on Customers Regardless of Size

Stew Leonard was one of Frank's closest friends and a fellow marketing visionary. Like Frank, Leonard built a large business almost from scratch and he did it with a total commitment to excellence. The Guinness Book of World Records cites Stew Leonard's as the food store in the United States with the greatest sales per unit area.

One day Frank called on him at his store in Norwalk, Connecticut. Frank had never met Leonard, but made the trip because he had read about Leonard in one of the grocery trade magazines. It was a cold call and Frank didn't even have an appointment.

Leonard's secretary, Ann Ainsworth, buzzed him to say that Frank Perdue himself was in the waiting room. It was a surprise to Leonard, but soon the two men were talking about Leonard's carrying Perdue chicken. After some sparring on price, they came to an agreement, but Frank insisted on what, from Leonard's point of view, was an unusual condition.

Frank wanted to check the refrigerated room where his chicken would be stored. "This was odd," remembered Leonard. "He was after my business, but here he was sort of interrogating me about the way I would handle his chicken. I was his customer and he's going on about how he had to know we'd be handling his chicken right."

MARKETING: STUDYING IT, PRACTICING IT, EXCELLING AT IT

Leonard took him to the store's big walk-in refrigerator. Frank took a little thermometer from his breast pocket and measured the temperature of the refrigerator.

"This will never do," Frank said. "I can't supply you with my chickens if you're going to store them here. Thirty-six degrees might be okay for milk, but it's not cold enough for my chickens. If you want to store my chickens in here, you'll have to drop the temperature down to 33 degrees and maintain it there twenty-four hours a day."

Leonard couldn't believe his ears. Seeing Leonard's surprise, Frank said, "Look, Stew, either you drop the temperature to 33 degrees or it's no deal. My fresh chickens require a lower temperature, period."

For Leonard, it was a revelation: Frank really was a tough man and a quality fanatic.

"We did end up buying his chicken, and according to Frank, we sold more Perdue chicken than any other single store in the country. Big chains with 50 stores were selling more than we did, but on a single-store basis we were his biggest customer."

For Leonard, the most important thing he took away from this story was Frank's constant perseverance: At that time, Leonard had only one location, and yet Frank was willing to make the time to come from Maryland to Connecticut to call on a guy who had just one store. Frank was never too busy to call on a customer.

Leonard had another memory of Frank, and it was when Frank was trying to sell chicken hot dogs. "His marketing was brilliant," said Leonard. "Ed McCabe, his advertising copywriter, had made lifelike rubber masks of Frank, and these were given to the New York hot dog vendors, so there the vendors would be, wearing the masks and hawking Perdue hotdogs. It was an amazing thing."

But that wasn't the part that impressed Leonard most. About a month after Frank started selling the hot dogs Leonard asked him, "Frank, how're the chicken hot dogs going?"

"Too early to tell."

"What do you mean?"

"I haven't yet been able to find my Mr. Hot Dog."

"'What do you mean, your 'Mr. Hot Dog?'"

"That's a guy who goes to bed thinking chicken hot dogs, and then the first thing he thinks of when he wakes up is chicken hot dogs."

"I understood what Frank meant because that's the way I was with my own business," Leonard said.

Frank knew that in marketing, the chicken hot dogs weren't going to make it unless he found someone with a passion for marketing them, since Frank couldn't do it alone.

As far as I know, Frank didn't find his Mr. or Ms. Hot Dog, and although we sell millions of pounds of chicken hot dogs each year overseas, they never caught on in the United States.

Leonard wanted to add a personal note to his comments on Frank. Since they were such good friends, I'm including it, especially since it reveals more about Frank as a person.

"On January 1, 1989," Leonard said, "we lost one of our grandchildren to a drowning accident in St. Martin. Frank who was vacationing there at the time, was the one who broke the devastating news to Marianne and me. I remember how emotional Frank was and how sensitive he was to my situation. That's what good friends do for each other. They're there for each other. Frank was a really good friend."

MARKETING: STUDYING IT, PRACTICING IT, EXCELLING AT IT

FRANK PERDUE'S LESSONS

DON'T JUST STUDY MARKETING PRINCIPLES, PUT THEM INTO PRACTICE– A lot went into Frank's earning his reputation as the best marketer in the country. It was a combination of first understanding the need for marketing, then taking the time to study it (reading the top books and journals on marketing and then interviewing academic experts), and finally, it took putting into practice all he had learned.

RESEARCH WHAT THE CONSUMER WANTS AND WILL WANT– In addition to his own research, Frank hired dozens of marketing reps who each day would be his "eyes and ears," as to what his different customers wanted. These kinds of marketing efforts meant that Frank had an unmatched understanding of the wants and needs of his prospective customers.

TRANSLATE INFORMATION INTO ACTION- On a daily basis, Frank was translating information into action. This meant collecting the information through the marketing reports and then having a structured way of assigning responsibility for responding to the information.

THERE'S MORE TO A SALE THAN PRICE– Frank put great effort into service, reliability, and nurturing personal relationships. He developed a reputation for doing what he said he would be doing, he'd go out of his way to do favors for the meat managers by attending store openings, and he made sure to know the personal side of buyers, such as their hobbies and passions.

THE MORE YOU SOLVE YOUR CUTOMER'S PROBLEMS, THE MORE BUSINESS YOU'LL GET– By encouraging the sales reps to ask, "What can we do better?" and "What problems can we solve?" he was often able to be a buyer's first choice when the customer was deciding whom to do business with.

CHAPTER SIX
ADVERTISING: RE-WRITING THE RULES

In 1971, Frank Perdue simultaneously helped pioneer the art of turning a commodity into a brand while also becoming one of the first CEOs to appear in his own commercials.

His tag line, "It takes a tough man to make a tender chicken," was lauded as one of the iconic advertising campaigns of the 1970s, and it helped him grow what had once been a father-and-son egg business into a multi-billion dollar international poultry company with 19,000 associates and sales in more than 100 countries.

It's incongruous that a small town, basically shy chicken farmer was able to transform himself into a sophisticated marketing man and his commodity into an international brand. It happened because, given the high cost of producing a premium chicken, he needed to charge more for it, and that meant communicating with potential buyers why his product was worth more.

Since he was not only monitoring how his chickens were grown and fed, and he was also using genetics to create broader-breasted, meatier birds, and then processing them using standards higher than the U.S. Department of Agriculture mandated, Frank believed that there was a lot more difference in the quality of superior versus average chickens than there was between brands of soap or beer. If you could advertise soap or beer, he reasoned, why not advertise his superior chickens?

Frank decided to do what no chicken farmer had done before. He took ten weeks off from running his company, travelled to New York and began a total immersion, full-time study of the theory and practice of advertising. However, his initial investigations on the subject were not promising. Had he followed the advice of the people he spoke with first, Perdue chicken would never be the household brand it is today.

One of the first people he went to for advice when he was starting was the head of advertising at Best Foods. The man asked Frank, "What percentage of the New York consumers can find a Perdue chicken where they shop?"

When Frank answered, "Maybe 3 percent," his advisor said, "Best Foods would not advertise until we had 50 percent of the stores, so don't waste your money."

Frank proceeded with an advertising program anyway. In 1968 and 1969, the company invested $50,000 and $80,000 respectively for radio. Then he went to that original agency and suggested some TV advertising. The agency owner said it would be a waste of money. Frank said, "Since I don't think Procter & Gamble is a bunch of dummies, I'm going to do it anyhow," and added $80,000 in TV money to the $80,000 already being spent in radio.

In just three months, the premium for Perdue chickens increased to exactly three times what it had achieved in twenty-four months of radio advertising, going from an average of 28/100ths of a cent per pound to 84/100ths of a cent per pound. This was during a period when the market price for chicken was averaging 25 cents per pound.

Searching for an Ad Agency

However, Frank concluded that the agency he was dealing with didn't match one of the basic Perdue tenets: "The people you deal with should be as good at what they do as you are at what you do."

That decision to change ad agencies set off a storm of activity on Frank's part. The thoroughness and persistence with which he investigated the different agencies is almost legendary. And in the process of selecting the agency, Frank learned more about advertising than any poultry man had before him.

Having expertise in advertising enabled Frank to transform a commodity into a branded item, and catapulted his company into the ranks of the top poultry producers in the country.

While studying advertising, he read books and papers on advertising, talked to the sales managers of every newspaper, radio and television station in the New York area, and consulted experts and interviewed agencies. He also joined the Association of National Advertisers for the express purpose of accessing their extensive library. He remembered that during this period he ignored all the papers accumulating on his desk and thought of nothing but the problem at hand.

After investigating 66 agencies, and personally interviewing officials at 48 of them, he finally had the selection narrowed down to three. "The finalists had billings of $19 million, $15 million, and $12 million. "I didn't go to any of the big ones," he told me, "because I figured I wouldn't be important to them."

Frank's intuitive advertising sense went against received wisdom but, proved successful as sales soared

He began systematically calling the clients of the three finalists to find out what kind of experiences they had had with the agencies. In the middle of this process, he got an angry phone call. "Why are you calling my clients?" demanded the president of one of the agencies, his voice bristling with irritation.

"Because," Frank answered coolly, "I can't tell by looking in your eyes whether you are a priest or a crook." With a certain relish, Frank continued his phone calls to the rest of the man's clients.

Even today, Ed McCabe, the copywriter who eventually made Frank famous, still remembers exactly how many agencies Frank studied and how many finalists there were. "I know this for certain," McCabe said recently, "because we all spoke to and commiserated with one another on a regular basis about the hoops Frank was putting us through."

In that same conversation, McCabe told me he had said to Frank, "I'm not even sure I want your account any more because you're such a pain in the ass."

Unperturbed, Frank agreed with McCabe's judgment and went right on asking more questions.

Barbara Hunter, a friend from Hunter MacKenzie Cooper, Inc., public relations, was one of his sounding boards at the time. She remembers the progress of the search, and looking back on it, marveled, "I've never ever seen anyone so thorough. The amazing thing is he did all the research himself, rather than delegating it to someone."

On April 2, 1971, he and Don Mabe (who was at that time running the Accomac Plant), plus two former associates, Tom Robinson and Doris Ball, announced that they'd selected the advertising firm, Scali, McCabe, and Sloves. The agency had been in business five years and had total billings of $12 million. Marvin Sloves, the agency's president, wrote to Frank, "If you spend as much time inspecting your chickens as you have our agency, you've got to have the best chickens in the world."

Creating an Uncopiable Advertising Campaign

Ed McCabe was to be the copywriter. The initial problem the advertising agency faced was that with chickens, whatever selling point the copywriters came up with, a competitor could quickly copy it in their own advertisements. Perdue chickens are yellow? A competitor could say his chickens were yellow. Perdue chickens are fresh? The competitors could emphasize freshness.

What McCabe was looking for was something a competitor couldn't steal. "Nobody had ever advertised a brand-name chicken before," McCabe said, "and just looking at Perdue and listening to him was a new experience, too. He looked a little like a chicken himself, and he sounded a little like one, and he squawked a lot."Thinking about how Frank looked and sounded like a chicken, McCabe said it just clicked: "Here's the answer: Frank Perdue himself should be the spokesman." Frank, he rightly decided, could give the campaign a unique identity that couldn't be copied by a competitor.

Initially Frank resisted the idea. It may be surprising to learn, given how famous Frank later became, that he was a basically shy man who hadn't even appeared in a school play. Nevertheless, McCabe wanted to convince Frank that having Frank Perdue himself was the best way to solve the imitator problem.

Frank's Decision to Appear in the Ads

Tom Robinson, who was in poultry sales at the time, witnessed how it was a close call whether Frank would appear in the ads as McCabe wanted. The agency's first recommendation, once they were hired, was that Frank star in the commercials. Robinson remembers a group of five sitting around a table, including Frank, Doris Ball, Don Mabe, Connie Littleton (now Connie Littleton Messick) and himself, helping make the decision about whether Frank should be in the spots.

Frank hadn't made a decision, but half of the people there wanted Frank to do it, and half were strongly against it. Those who were totally against it, Robinson remembers, reasoned that since no other head of a company had done it, there was probably a reason that businesses didn't have their CEOs as spokespersons.

Robinson knew that Frank had spent days thinking about this and he hated making the decision. Breaking the tie was going to be Frank's call. Ed McCabe pushed Frank hard to be the spokesperson, and Frank reluctantly agreed.

Even then, things didn't go smoothly. Daughter Bev witnessed what was going on behind the scenes before the first commercial was shot.

"I was home then and he was about to shoot it in the Salisbury Park. He would practice the lines and insisted that I sit through many recitals. What impressed me was how much practice he put into getting the expression and believability just right."

Robinson takes up the story. "I remember shooting the first commercial in the park in his hometown of Salisbury. It was in front of a body of water with a white wooden bridge in the background and Frank was sitting on the ground as if he was about to have a picnic. The problem was, having to talk into a video camera was really hard for him because he was a shy man.

"I can't act like you want me to do," he complained to McCabe. "I can't remember the lines, and I just don't feel I can do a good job at it."

"Just be yourself," McCabe directed. "Tell us why your chicken is good."

During the shoot, Frank talked about how his chickens eat better than people do, and then at the end, he was supposed to be enthusiastic about a drumstick. He kept flubbing his lines, but finally, when the shoot was apparently over and the cameras off, someone handed Frank a fresh, hot, chicken drumstick.

The drumsticks used in the actual shoot had all been cold by the time he was supposed to bite into them. Suddenly tasting a hot, fresh drumstick, Frank said with surprise and spontaneous enthusiasm, "That's really good!"

The cameras were off, but the sound happened to be on, and a microphone captured his genuine appreciation. The director used Frank's unscripted comment as a voice-over for the tough man slogan that appears on screen at the end.

According to Robinson, "They had to shoot two hours of film to get 30 seconds that they could use, but the end result was he turned out to be believable and likable."

Frank's friend, Allen Kosofsky, the distributor from Interstate Poultry, will never forget the initial previews of the ads. "Frank picked out a restaurant and showed us this thing that said 'It takes a tough man to make a tender chicken.' We thought it was awful. In fact, we thought it was terrible. We thought he had flipped. We thought it would bomb. But. . . it took the country by storm."

Others who attended the preview were also sure that Frank had lost his mind. They were astonished when a couple of weeks later it seemed as if everyone in New York was talking about the ads.

One of the reasons that prudent men thought Frank had flipped was that up until then, the conventional wisdom was that you never advertise a commodity. The idea of pouring money into the chicken business, with its small profit margins, seemed dumb to just about everyone.

It Begins to Pay Off

However, Frank's vision paid off. In 1970, after two years of radio advertising at a budget ranging from $50,000 to $160,000, sales were $50 million. By 1972, after a year of "It takes a tough man to make a tender chicken," sales had leapfrogged to $80 million. The advertising budget for the first year with Scali, McCabe and Sloves was $200,000.

According to a July 13, 1971, column on advertising that appeared in *The New York Times*, the campaign was off to a flying start soon after Scali, McCabe and Sloves got the account. "In some New York area shops at least, quotations from Mr. Perdue will become far better known than those of Chairman Mao. Examples: 'Freeze my chickens? I'd sooner eat beef!' 'My fresh young chicken is cheaper than hamburger. Good for you, bad for me.' 'Everybody's chickens are approved by the government, but only my chickens are approved by me.'"

In 1972, one out of every six chickens eaten in New York was a Perdue chicken. Fifty-one percent of New Yorkers recognized the Perdue label. The ads also achieved critical acclaim. In the first year of the campaign, the Copy

Club of New York ranked a Perdue ad the best television commercial of less than 60 seconds. Advertising Age called it "the best trade campaign of the year."

A major reason for the success of the ads was Frank's believability. As Alan Pesky, a Scali, McCabe partner, said in a *New Yorker* interview, "Frank is a very believable person. . . the TV viewers feel that Frank is on their side." McCabe added, "This was advertising in which Perdue had a personality that lent credibility to the product. If Frank Perdue didn't look and sound like chicken, he wouldn't be in the commercials. There's nothing straight-out spokesman about him. He always appeared a little bit off the wall, a little bit irregular."

The *New Yorker* expanded on what McCabe meant about Frank's looking and sounding like a chicken. "Certainly Perdue in his commercial appearances has made a memorable impression on large numbers of viewers. His features – a mostly bald pate, a corrugated brow, shrewdly intent eyes, a beaked nose, and a thin neck, together with a notably squawky voice–impart an avian suggestion to his appearance."

Connie Littleton, was Director of Advertising and Marketing Services at Perdue, and calculated that one of the greatest ingredients in his success was that he meant what he said and people knew it. "I remember when we were doing a commercial that included something on building grow-out houses. One line in it talked about a bank giving you a loan. But he couldn't say 'give you' a loan, he couldn't get the words out. He didn't believe in them because, as he explained, 'the blankety-blank bank doesn't *give* you anything.' We had to change the line to 'make you' a loan."

Beverly Perdue Jennings is convinced that her father's success as a television personality comes simply from the fact that "The commercials reflect the real man, and the real man connects with each viewer."

The advertisements mixed humor and information. Often they focused on the care his chickens received. Perdue chickens weren't just mass-produced bottles of pop or some other inanimate factory-produced object. Frank's tender young chickens lived a soft life in $60,000 houses, got eight hours sleep, drank pure, fresh well water, ate a balanced diet including marigold petals, and finished with cookies for dessert. Frank's chickens "eat better than you do."

Sometimes the commercials were suggestive. In one, he said confidentially, "I've got a problem here that you can help me with. My breasts aren't moving as fast as my legs. We've got to get this breast problem straightened out or there'll be no end of grief. Now, I'm not one to complain about having a few extra breasts on my hands. But I'm on the brink of a major leg shortage. You're just going to have to start buying more Perdue chicken breasts or I'm going to have to start coming up with a three-legged chicken."

His most famous commercial, known as "Guests for Dinner," began with a shot of Frank coming home and putting four Perdue Cornish Game Hens in the oven. Next, the viewer sees Frank showering, shaving, chilling a bottle of champagne, sniffing a pot on the stove, adjusting his bow tie, and setting the cooked hens on a serving platter. At that point, the doorbell rings and in walk three incredibly gorgeous young women. "Try Perdue Fresh Cornish Game Hens and spend more time with your guests," the voice-over tells the viewers. On screen, Frank looks into the camera and gives an engaging wink.

"I had some problems with the commercial," Frank once told me. "We sell chickens in the Bible belt, and I worried that having three women in the script would bother some people."

McCabe convinced Frank that it was more attention getting to have three and that the story would instantly lose its punch if the number were reduced. The script stayed as it was.

Consumer complaints were nonexistent. Chris Whaley, Public Relations Coordinator, said that "Guests for Dinner" sparked more favorable letters than any other advertisement the company ever did.

ADVERTISING: RE-WRITING THE RULES

That ad and others like it have been so successful that, speaking in a 1988 issue *of Farm Futures,* McCabe said, "We have a ton of research on awareness and attitudes and perceptions of Frank among the public. It's record shattering. Every measurement –awareness, share of market, sales – is just breathtaking. We've got nearly 100 percent brand awareness and close to 100 percent advertising awareness. The perception is that the product is the best in the category far and away."

Frank had his own view as to why the ad campaign was so successful. As he told a Rotary audience in Charlotte, North Carolina, in March of 1989, "Advertising has been a tremendous marketing tool for Perdue, not because I've done the ads for eighteen years, but, rather, the product met the promise of the advertising and was far superior to the competition. Two great sayings tell it all: 'Nothing will destroy a poor product as quickly as good advertising,' and 'A gifted product is mightier than a gifted pen!'"

Context for Advertising a Brand

Ken Roman a former CEO of Ogilvy & Mather Worldwide and a man some people describe as one of the prototypes for the TV series, *Mad Men,* had some insights on Frank's decision to advertise a commodity.

"Frank Perdue was a symbol of that era," said Roman. It had to do with what had been going on in branding beginning in the 1950s.

As Roman observed, "Before the 1950s, people were served by grocers who took products from their shelves for their customers – and sometimes suggested one product over another."

Things changed when the supermarkets introduced self-service. Since the grocer wasn't there to tell people what to buy, it fell to advertising – especially on TV – to take over the role of adviser. More important, advertising helped build brands so consumers could know which products to buy. As Lily Tomlin cracked, "Without advertising, people would wander aimlessly up and down supermarket aisles."

Typically, the branded products came in packages – hence, "packaged goods." Advertising touted the merits of Crest or Tide, and established them as unique brands. "What Frank and his copywriter Ed McCabe at the Scali McCabe Sloves agency did," said Roman, "was the next big development – to brand a non-packaged good. In this case, a chicken."

According to Roman, having Frank appear in the commercials was perfect casting. "Frank had a skinny chicken-like neck and a raspy, memorable voice. He was completely convincing when he talked about how he fed and cared for his chickens, and why they were superior to any other chicken."

The consumers loved the ads and, for that matter, so did the supermarkets – which could charge more for a premium product.

Roman was struck by the fact that Frank wasn't a marketing man – he was a farmer. But he had an inquiring mind and was wise enough to decide to learn about advertising even before he spoke to an agency.

"The commercials established the Perdue brand. They were also entertaining, so viewers liked to watch them. The combination was a great business success– in that order," said Roman.

Roman concluded by stating, "Some people go through life doing the best they can, but others seek out better answers by talking with successful people or reading books. Frank didn't have a great formal education, but he learned from everything, he read everything, and he sought out successful people so he could ask how they did it."

Genesis of the Slogan, "It takes a tough man..."

Although Ed McCabe was the copywriter for the Perdue account, he also became one of Frank's best friends. Years after they were no longer working together, they would still visit each other.

In McCabe's eyes, the basis of their relationship was that they were both fanatics. "I was as fanatical about my product, advertising, as he was about his product, chicken. It's not about doing a few things in your field well, it's about doing everything well."

McCabe saw Frank's search to find an advertising agency as an example of his wanting to do everything well. While a typical company finds a search consultant whose specialty is searching out ad agencies, Frank, in contrast, made the effort to study the subject himself from top to bottom.

"I think the secret to Frank's success was he did an unbelievably comprehensive amount of research to back up his instincts. He'd start with an instinct, such as that advertising would help his company, and then he'd explore it with tomes and tomes of research."

"He was aggressive about it. Before we had the Perdue contract, he'd barge into my office as part of his research, and I'd say 'What are you doing here? Get the hell out, you don't have an appointment!' That didn't even slow him down."

A perplexed McCabe soon enough found Frank barging in again, unannounced, which was when McCabe rather famously told him. "I don't know if I even want your account you're such a pain in the ass'"

Frank answered, "I'm like that in everything, but once I make up my mind, you'll find that I'm more reasonable."

Interestingly, McCabe said that the inspiration for the ad campaign, "It takes a tough man to make a tender chicken," started with those moments when Frank would barge into his office. After his agency landed the Perdue account and McCabe was visiting Frank in Salisbury, he saw exactly the same kind of behavior at the Perdue headquarters. Frank wouldn't pick up the phone and make an appointment. Instead, he'd just barge in. McCabe started to realize, "This guy is a fanatic on quality and every detail that goes into achieving it. He has no time for formalities or pleasantries or obstacles."

McCabe's understanding that there was a reason the product was good formed the germ of the ad campaign. Also, McCabe felt that Frank's being a spokesman worked because he was both visually and vocally connected to the product. Lee Iacocca had no relation to a car, except by title, but Frank reminded people of a chicken. "He had that screechy, squawky voice. Also, he had personality, which is the one thing most CEOs who want to be in their own ads don't have. He had a strong and unique personality that immediately related to the product he was selling."

I asked McCabe how he dared choose Frank to star in the commercials, given that McCabe knew Frank was a shy person who didn't like public speaking. McCabe answered that after watching Frank in action, he had total confidence that Frank was so success-oriented that he would do whatever it took to learn how to appear on camera.

During the first few shoots, Frank knew that he was supposed to "give" to the camera and not hold back the way a shy person might be inclined to do. McCabe said that he had to tell Frank to "dial back," in order to get the right amount of energy.

The McCabe-Perdue professional relationship worked out well for 20 years. "Working together that long is unheard of in the advertising world," said McCabe. "The average creative person's burnout time on any particular account is about three years. Our 20 years and also the 20 years that I worked on the Volvo account is like some kind of world record."

Besides their professional success, McCabe felt that they each opened up parts of their individual worlds to the other.

"Other than chicken, one of Frank's favorite foods was Maryland hard-shell crabs. I'll never forget the night he took Sam Scali and me to Phillip's Crab House in Ocean City, Maryland, just after our first three Perdue Chicken commercials had been shot.

"I had never seen one of these critters before. I looked down at the placemat, full of diagrams and instructions for how to go about opening and eating one. I said, 'I don't know Frank. This looks pretty complicated.'"

Frank then left the table without a word, only to return to the table a few minutes later with the proprietress of the restaurant, Shirley Phillips. She gave McCabe and his colleagues some one-on-one crab opening and eating instructions.

"That was Frank. In a crab-shell," said McCabe. "As brusque and as pointed as he could sometimes be, he was also tremendously thoughtful and generous."

McCabe felt that he played a role in Frank's becoming more sophisticated. "He had all the instincts, but I also think, for example that with his dressing, his association with me had an impact. We did a lot of wardrobe work with him for commercials and he'd end up liking what had been selected, and was influenced by it. The relationship was very rewarding for both of us."

Frank Could Be Demanding and Difficult

Connie Littleton Messick played a large role in Perdue's advertising and consumer relations efforts. She got that role partly because her initial job of keeping track of the roughly 1,500 time cards at the Salisbury Plant didn't keep her busy. The man who had previously held the position used to take 80 hours to get the job done, but Messick found she could do it in only 21 hours. She asked her boss, Don Mabe for more work.

Mabe gave her an intriguing assignment. He had stacks and stacks of invoices from the advertising agency, Scali, McCabe, and Sloves, and he didn't want to approve them without knowing what they were.

Suddenly the Salisbury Plant Time Keeper was becoming an expert on advertising bills. She ended up being in continuing contact with the ad agency, tracking down all the information on how the shop was spending Perdue's money.

In short order, she knew more than anyone else at Perdue about the nuts and bolts of the agency. This brought her into Frank's orbit, giving her a ringside seat on what it was like working with Frank on advertising.

Messick has her own vantage point of how Frank came to star in his own commercials. "Frank initially rejected the ad agency's suggestion that he be in the ads. He rejected it on its face because he figured that Scali was only playing to his ego. There was also the problem that Frank didn't like public speaking."

According to Messick, Frank never became really comfortable doing the ads. In fact, in the shoots Messick was associated with, she'd watch Frank change from being the good Dr. Jekyll into a monstrous Mr. Hyde. She'd ride with him to a TV shoot, and in the taxi they'd be pleasantly chatting about the weather, or if the Red Sox had a chance in that night's game. However, "The minute we walked through the studio door, he turned into a raging maniac." Messick knew it was nerves.

He'd complain to her about the commercial's having cost $75,000. By that time she knew what the gaffer and the mixer cost, and a hundred other details, but even so, under normal circumstances, she knew he was right, the $75,000 didn't quite make sense.

But she also knew that if he wanted to have the quality he was looking for, he had to pay for it. It would have been possible to shave $2,000 off the price, but it would mean losing the skill and talent of the best people.

"I was the point person in all of this," recalled Messick. "I could see him across the studio, both hands thrust in his pockets, striding towards me. Then, hands out of his pockets, he'd have his left palm out, fingers spread, and with his right pointer finger, he'd start ticking off the fingers of his other hand, one by one, the things he was seeing that were bothering him."

An example of the kind of thing Messick would have to cope with back then, was it was standard practice to have two microphones. One would be a boom microphone that someone would be holding in front of Frank out of view of the camera, and another microphone would be overhead, hung from the ceiling, again out of view of the camera. Both were needed because when you go to mix the sound, you may still be able to have good quality even if something went wrong with one of the mikes, such as someone in the back of the studio coughed.

Frank didn't know that. "Why in the hell do I need two people on two microphones," he'd complain, ticking off that point on one of his fingers. "By the way," said Messick, "I don't think he really wanted to know himself; he just wanted to make sure that somebody was on top of what was going on.

"Frank and I had many moments of difficulty, but one thing he'd always tell me afterwards, and he meant it, was, 'Don't take it personal.'"

Messick found that Frank would be adamant and determined that whatever he wanted done was done right, but significantly, for Frank, "right" didn't have to be what Frank initially wanted. "He was flexible as long as you could convince him of your side."

Messick knew that you weren't going to convince him because he liked you, or because you were a nice guy. What would convince him were facts, and it helped if you had a good track record.

"He was good about giving you the opportunity to make your points. You might have to yell to get his attention, but if you were right, you were right. The thing is, he might yell, but he would also listen."

People might wonder why Messick put up with Frank's difficult side. I did, and I asked her.

Her answer was, "Back then, a lot of us felt a certain pride in being able to take the pressure. But I think the thing that really propelled people with Frank is he was not an ivory tower boss. Maybe the company collected a pint of blood from you every third Tuesday, but you knew that Frank was working harder than you.

"We were also proud of the company. It was breathtaking to live through it. When many of us started, we weren't working for a famous name company, like Ford or Campbell Soup, basically we were working for a chicken farm. But then came the success. Most of us who were working there back then weren't accustomed to so much fame. We were deeply proud of the recognition that was coming the company's way."

The ads were a big part of that. In spite of all the naysayers who thought that Frank was wasting time and money on advertising a commodity, the ads were an extraordinary success. "As part of our market research," said Messick, "we'd check the tracking studies which measure awareness of your company name. Within six months, 90 percent of the people within range of the TV commercials would name Perdue if asked to name a brand of chicken. That kind of marketing success was unprecedented."

It led to a whole new job responsibility for her. The ads included a money-back guarantee, and soon, that meant that the company needed a consumer relations department. Messick created it, but not without effort. "If you don't think convincing 'the boys' to spend bucks on the system was tough—well, giving birth to twin Arabian race horses sounds like more fun."

Messick arranged for the letters to the consumers to be personalized, so it wasn't just a form letter. If Sally Smith wrote in, she was addressed personally as "Ms. Smith," and what she had written about was specifically addressed. If the chicken was too yellow, reasons for the skin color were explained to Ms. Smith. Consumer relations turned out to be an excellent opportunity to complement the company's "voice."

The letters had an impact. In one case, Messick learned that a random customer had saved one of these personalized company letters for five years. Messick found this out when she was calling on a public relations agency, and one of the employees took her aside to show a Perdue response letter she had kept all these years.

Messick would get 40,000 pieces of correspondence a year back in those days, and she felt that almost no one abused the money-back guarantee. A lot of the correspondence was people asking for recipes, and only some of the correspondence was about the guarantee.

"We had a system in place to check for fraud, and the way it worked was if Suzy Smith wanted her money back three times, we'd suspect that we were dealing with an operator. But this kind of thing would only happen three or four times a year out of 40,000 letters. Most people are honest."

Messick sums up her feelings about Frank saying, "He was an individual who had the most extensive range of personality that I've ever known. He could be completely charming, but he could also be extremely demanding and difficult. A day of working with him could leave me exhausted and feeling like crawling into a fetal position. But it could also leave me exhilarated."

FRANK PERDUE'S LESSONS

HAVE THE COURAGE OF YOUR CONVICTIONS– Advertising a commodity meant going against all the received wisdom about how advertising should be done. In spite of being universally told that it was foolish, Frank chose to advertise his chickens anyway, and ended up becoming one of the most successful brands in the country.

BUTTRESS YOUR CONVICTIONS WITH RESEARCH– Frank spent ten weeks doing nothing but studying the theory and practice of advertising. This included reading books and papers on advertising, talking to the sales managers of every newspaper, and radio and television station in the New York area, consulting experts and interviewing agencies. His success in advertising was built on a foundation of knowledge.

BE WILLING TO GO OUTSIDE YOUR COMFORT ZONE– Frank, with his background as a country farmer, plunged into big city advertising, which was a way of life that was entirely foreign to him. He overcame his reluctance to do public speaking and forced himself to learn the necessary on-camera presence.

CHAPTER SEVEN
PUBLIC RELATIONS AND GOVERNMENT AFFAIRS, THE FRANK TOUCH

The advertising's success meant that Frank Perdue was becoming a household name and his company was becoming one of the largest poultry companies in the country. The scale of his fame and the size of Perdue Farms dictated that he would need professional support for interacting with the media and with government. Perdue Farms needed to hire a governmental affairs consultant, as well as a public relations consultant.

Public Relations

Connie Littleton Messick remembers that back in 1980, the search for a public relations expert was as thorough as the search for an advertising agency had been ten years before.

"When we were looking for a PR agency," she recalled, "I thought Frank would drive me crazy. Yet, hard as he was driving me, I could see that he was driving himself still harder."

By the time of the final selection, then-Connie Littleton had, at Frank's direction, spent eight months interviewing twenty-nine different agencies. In January 1981, Perdue Farms hired Richard Auletta's firm. However, before settling on Auletta, Frank or Littleton interviewed every one of Auletta's twenty or so clients. Even then, Frank wasn't satisfied, so he called all of Auletta's former clients as well. Auletta was left with the feeling that Frank Perdue knew more about Auletta's own company than Auletta himself did.

To this day, Auletta is in awe of those research efforts. Auletta remembers that Frank was particularly interested in people who for one reason or another had fired Auletta, and even after he had Littleton interview all of them, Frank still wasn't satisfied.

94

PUBLIC RELATIONS AND GOVERNMENT AFFAIRS, THE FRANK TOUCH

"Auletta," Littleton asked him one day, "where are the bodies buried? The people we called have all confirmed the reasons you said they let you go, but they all said they like you. There have got to be people who don't like you!'

"Call Mr. X,"Auletta answered. "He borrowed money from me, didn't pay me back, and I put him into personal bankruptcy." Auletta also gave her the name of another guy who had an equal reason to badmouth him. As Auletta learned later, Frank called both men. After all of that research, Perdue finally hired Auletta.

Richard Auletta and his firm, R.C. Auletta and Company, handled Perdue public relations for the next two decades. In the years of this relationship, one of Auletta's biggest impressions of Frank was his ability to go without sleep. Auletta remembers landing with Frank at an airport at 2:00 a.m. and Frank's getting up in time for a meeting at 5:30 a.m. "The marketing guys all told me afterwards that he was alert as could be," marveled Auletta.

His relationship with Frank was at times stormy, and it's proof that my dear late husband didn't miss his calling when he didn't choose to have a career in diplomacy. As an example, according to Auletta, Frank called one day and asked to stop by his office in New York. Once there, Frank announced, "I want you to know that I don't like you."

To which Auletta, ever the professional answered, "Well I like you most of the time, but most important, I hope you respect me."

Frank came back with, "I respect you, but I'm not sure I like you."

To my mind, the problem was Frank didn't like the premise of public relations. His whole personality was about being authentic, an I-am-who-I-am kind of approach. You always knew where you stood with him and he didn't sugar-coat things or soften them. But on the other hand, he obviously realized that he needed Auletta because they worked together for 20 years. Oh, and one more thing, I actually know that Frank not only respected Auletta, he liked him a lot.

95

PUBLIC RELATIONS AND GOVERNMENT AFFAIRS, THE FRANK TOUCH

Auletta found that Frank could be impossible to deal with at times, and yet Frank regularly brought forth extraordinary loyalty. "There was almost a Southern charm and a little boy quality," remembered Auletta. "People put up with the impossible part of him because they accepted, even if only subconsciously, that they were in the presence of someone extraordinary."

Auletta observed that part of Frank's being extraordinary had to do with his ferocious attention to detail. For instance, it used to drive Frank crazy when he'd get complaints about the little hairs that you'd find on chickens that hadn't been perfectly plucked. Frank hated that the company hadn't been able to solve this problem.

"One day," remembered Auletta, "when Frank was drying his hands in the blow-drying machine in a restroom, in an 'ah-ha' moment, he observed that because of the blower, the now-dry hairs on his hands were standing up. He called his head of Quality Assurance, Alan Culver, and asked if this principle could work for making the chicken hairs stand up."

"'Yes,' came back the response from Culver, after he had studied the matter, 'but to have enough power to get the job done would take a $50,000 jet engine.' Frank immediately bought two of them."

Auletta saw that Frank could be decisive when he had all the information, but when he didn't have enough, Frank had a problem with what Auletta called "pulling the trigger." Frank wanted to do enough research to be virtually 100 percent certain before taking action.

This got him and Auletta into a world of trouble and anxiety over a TV interview Auletta had set up for *The Regis Philbin Show*. This happened during the time the company was introducing Perdue chicken nuggets.

The plan was that on-air Regis would give Frank some unmarked chicken nuggets, one of which would be a Perdue nugget and three would be from his competitors. Frank was 95% sure that he could distinguish his nuggets from the competition, but he didn't want to be embarrassed.

PUBLIC RELATIONS AND GOVERNMENT AFFAIRS, THE FRANK TOUCH

They were in the studio green room, minutes before they were to go on the air, when Frank, being a shy man anyway, had a terrible attack of stage fright. "I'm not going to do this!" he wailed to Auletta.

Auletta tried to talk him into it, and meanwhile the producer, who had a show to put on, was getting more and more anxious. Finally the producer angrily told Auletta, "You either get him on the set in one minute or get him out of the studio, I don't care which!"

The end of that story was Frank did go on and had absolutely no trouble telling his product from the competitors'. But as Auletta said, "That's just the way he was, he wanted certainty."

His need for certainty may have made Frank a pain in the neck, but there was another aspect that Auletta valued highly. Like many before him, Auletta found Frank to be unusually fair. Auletta saw an example of this when he realized that he had done vastly more work for Perdue Farms than his contract called for.

For 14 months, Frank and Auletta went round and round over the issue of whether Auletta should be paid significantly more than what was called for in the original contract. When at last they came to an agreement, Auletta expected that from that point on the future checks would reflect the increase.

However, the next check Auletta received was for the increase, times 14. "He didn't have to, but here he was paying me for the 14 months that had been in dispute. He was a penny pincher but he had a sense of fairness that was unique."

Auletta found Frank to be "without a doubt one of the most stubborn people I've ever met," but even so, there were exceptions. The naming process for *Perdue Done It!*, a new product line, was one of them. Before that name became official, people at Perdue had decided that it would be good to have a company-wide contest, which yielded a different name.

PUBLIC RELATIONS AND GOVERNMENT AFFAIRS, THE FRANK TOUCH

Auletta was at a meeting with the ad company, and Frank asked the ad people, 'What do you think of the name we came up with in our contest?'

Auletta recalled that copywriter Ed McCabe went ballistic. "What the blankety blank do you want to call it?" McCabe said as if he couldn't believe it, and then added, "I told you what I think we should call it, and that's *Perdue Done It!*"

Both men were unrelenting. McCabe wanted the name he thought was best, and Frank wanted the name the associates had chosen. Both men were screaming and cursing at each other. Finally McCabe said, "Name it whatever you want, but it should be *Perdue Done It!*'

Frank answered, "I may be stubborn, but I'm not stupid," and McCabe got his way.

"Actually," said Auletta, "McCabe was right, you don't leave naming a national brand to an employee contest. The situation did call for a professional."

About this time, the marketing people at the company decided it would be a good idea to have a hardcover Perdue cookbook. Auletta negotiated a deal with a publisher, but after he was about to begin working on it, he told Connie Littleton Messick that he didn't want to do it. "Connie, I've got a problem. I've got a lovely family and I'm too young too die, and dealing with all the minutiae that Frank is going to get into is going to kill me. The cookbook is off."

(By the way, there's a p.s. to the cookbook story. I wrote *The Perdue Chicken Cookbook* in 2000, and I thought that dealing with Frank about it was a breeze. I had written four cookbooks before, including *The Farmer's Cookbook* series, so I was familiar with what it takes to write a cookbook. I tried out every recipe on Frank, and he loved the whole project. He had his likes and dislikes, but I thought it was really cool to have a world expert on chicken advising me.)

PUBLIC RELATIONS AND GOVERNMENT AFFAIRS, THE FRANK TOUCH

For Auletta, every day was interesting and every day was a challenge. There were problems, but also there were the upbeat things like little acknowledgements that Frank thought he was doing a good job. Auletta also enjoyed seeing the respect that people in the community had for Frank.

"Most of the people in the community loved him. There's a story I heard from one of the baggage people in the airport, that someone who worked for the company was sick and dying and Frank went to the hospital every day

and sat with the guy. People who knew him well knew he did things like that."

Or another example: He and Frank had exchanged some harsh words, but a few weeks later, Auletta's father died. It was a dreary, rainy, cold night in November, and suddenly Auletta sees Frank Perdue striding into the funeral parlor in Brooklyn. Frank had heard about Auletta's father's passing, and he

Frank with his close friend and fellow entrepreneur Stew Leonard.

had gone to the trouble of chartering a single-engine airplane from Salisbury on a stormy night just so he could come to pay his respects.

"He was an American original," said Auletta, "and you cannot judge people like that by conventional standards. He could be a courtly Southern gentleman and in the next breath an irascible, bullying, unreasonable, profane human being. Still, I look back at that time in my life with pleasure. It was never dull, always interesting, definitely challenging, and most of the time a lot of fun."

Governmental Affairs

As Perdue Farms grew, Washington's impact on the company grew. Frank recognized that as the company established a larger and larger footprint, he would need to be up on governmental affairs and that meant hiring someone with expertise in this area.

After the usual amount of Perdue research, Jack Kelly was hired as a consultant for Perdue Farms in 1989. He remains the principal adviser for public policy and government affairs today.

When Kelly first started representing Frank in D.C., Frank told him, "You know, Jack, I don't care about all the political stuff; what I care about is policies that affect the price per pound of chicken."

That attitude stuck with Kelly. "In my business, people can get very emotional about politics or what's in the press or what people are saying about them, but Frank could see through to what was important. Because of Frank, I ask the people I'm representing to focus on how whatever-it-is affects their business and their ability to make money. The insight of 'focus on what's important' has helped me no end in my professional life."

Kelly knew they had a good relationship, but even so, from the beginning, Frank's initial reactions to his suggestions were often negative. "The good thing," Kelly said, "is I never had any problem telling him that the emperor has no clothes. 'You own the business,' I'd tell him, 'and we'll do what you want to do, but you're wrong.'"

Kelly found that if he took a deep breath and waited a couple of hours, and then told him, "Frank why don't we look at this way," he'd hem and haw and then he'd change his mind. "I don't recall his ever admitting he was wrong, but he would go ahead and do what I had recommended."

Something surprising to Kelly was that "Frank was a very shy man. He could turn the switch and activate and motivate himself to be outgoing and sociable when there was a reason, but he would never go out of his way to socialize with bigwigs just for the sake of doing it. However, if I told him, 'Frank there's a reason we need to do this,' he'd do whatever mingling was required."

PUBLIC RELATIONS AND GOVERNMENT AFFAIRS, THE FRANK TOUCH

Kelly worked for Frank for almost 20 years without a formal detailed contract. Their engagement was based on a handshake. Literally. "That's something that just doesn't happen in my profession. No way. But one thing about Frank, he was honest."

"He could be cantankerous, but underneath, he had a total heart of gold. Something he didn't talk about and something I don't think he ever let people know about happened when a hurricane barreled through Eastern North Carolina. There were terrible floods and some of the Perdue chicken growers were badly flooded. Frank called me up, and said, 'Get down to Salisbury, *now!*'

"When I arrived from Washington, three hours away, he handed me a packet of envelopes with the names of the 70 farmers who had been flooded. In each packet were crisp $100 bills.

"'Jack, you go down to North Carolina and get this money to each of the people whose names are on the envelopes. Don't say where it came from or how you got it, I don't want anyone to know.'

"'Got it, Frank,' and that's just what I did."

There's an element to this story that Jack Kelly didn't know. I know and Elaine Barnes knows that the envelopes also included a $1,000 check to each grower. That meant every grower who had been damaged by the flood got a personal check for $1,000 from Frank's own money, plus some amount (I'm not sure how much) in cash.

For Frank, the immediate cash was important because the $1000 checks wouldn't arrive in North Carolina before the banks closed. It was Friday, and Frank wanted the families to have the cash needed to help them get through the weekend.

By the way, Frank was told in my hearing that if he'd just wait a week or two to send the checks, there were IRS-approved ways that the gifts could be tax deductible. Frank's answer was "I don't care about tax deductions. The time people need help is right now, not a week or two from now. Write the checks and get the cash to them now."

FRANK PERDUE'S LESSONS

PUT OVER-THE-TOP EFFORT INTO FINDING THE RIGHT CONSULTANTS– Frank's research into finding the right public relations and governmental affairs advice, like his search for an ad agency, was time-consuming, thorough, and involved checking large numbers of references. Doing this extensive research paid immense dividends in the form of long-lasting and productive professional relationships. In all three cases, the relationships lasted for roughly two decades.

LISTEN TO YOUR ADVISORS– Richard Auletta saw Frank as one of the most stubborn people he ever met, but even though stubborn, he would give in when convinced. In governmental affairs, Jack Kelly was impressed that he could tell Frank that the emperor wore no clothes, and that Frank could be flexible enough to change his initial opinions.

CHAPTER EIGHT
PACKAGING: SURPRISINGLY IMPORTANT

Frank put extraordinary effort into getting his packaging right. His interest extended not just to what the consumer would pick up in the grocery story, but also the large boxes used to transport the packages of chicken from the processing facilities to the distributors. He knew he needed to protect his products to ensure the chicken remained uncompromised at all stages of distribution until opened by the consumer. Packaging was important for food safety as well as consumer appeal.

A Professional Packaging Firm

For the retail packaging that the consumer sees, Frank decided that it was just as important to have a great professional packaging firm as it was to have great advertising, public relations and governmental affairs firms. Since there were 200 kinds of packages back then, any design change was going to be a major operation.

The package design firm finally selected was headed by Dick Gerstman, and as Connie Littleton said at the time, "I will guarantee you, Gerstman never had a client like Frank Perdue in his life."

Gerstman himself heartily agreed with Littleton's assessment. "The day of our presentation, someone from the company came in an hour early and asked if we'd had our drinks yet.

"'Be prepared,' the man warned, 'you're going to need them.'"

For Gerstman, the first meeting was rough because Frank disliked listening to the background material that formed an integral part of Gerstman's usual presentation. Frank instead wanted to jump right in and get to the point.

PACKAGING: SURPRISINGLY IMPORTANT

He challenged Gerstman constantly. "How do you know that red is a good color?" "How can you be sure of this?" At one point, someone else from Perdue interrupted to ask, "Why are we paying you to tell us what we already know?"

The Perdue approach was totally different from that of Nabisco, Pillsbury, Heinz, Johnson & Johnson, Lipton or any of Gerstman's other clients. Further, there were about twelve people from Perdue at the meeting, compared to the five or so that another company might send.

The questioning seemed adversarial and unrelenting. At the end, Gerstman felt that he'd never been through such a rough meeting.

Yet, as people were filing out the door, someone from the ad agency leaned over towards him and whispered, "Terrific meeting!" Gerstman discovered later, to his astonishment, that the meeting had been a success.

Gerstman quickly learned that Frank liked to get to the bottom line; he didn't like puffery; he wanted back-up for whatever was said; and he wanted everything very specifically related to that subject. Interacting with Frank at first was a shock, but as Gerstman got to know him and the company culture, he grew to like the total honesty and felt "a tremendous amount of respect for Frank."

Tim Mescon had a special reason to remember Frank's involvement with the packaging. The day Mescon was introduced to Frank at the Business School, Frank had spent the morning on the telephone talking to vendors in Italy. Mescon learned that Frank had been working through two translators as he tried to get exactly the right colors for the packaging materials.

Why Italy? According to Mescon, because Frank had researched the matter, and had become convinced that the Italians produced the best, most vivid colors.

Mescon was impressed that Frank, in spite of the hassle of transatlantic phone calls and translators, was getting into such detail. "There's a zeal there, a drivenness, a ferocity. It's what makes him forge ahead when others would say it's not worth the effort. It is," Mescon said, "the difference between winners and runners up."

Leakproof Packages

Although Frank cared deeply about the appearance of the packaging, it also had to be functional. Brian Lipinski, whose specialty at Perdue is packaging, got to witness Frank's obsession with this.

According to Lipinski, when Frank introduced the cut-up tray pack chicken, the tray packs were new and innovative, and there were seriously annoying problems associated with them. In the past, people who bought whole chickens were used to going to the butcher's and having the whole bird swathed in plastic wrap and then butcher paper.

There would still be blood and drippings when an individual brought the package home, but people were used to it and expected to deal with the problem. What was different with the cut-up, tray pack chicken was if it leaked, the retail buyers would be getting their hands or clothes dirty while still in the store.

Solving the problem wasn't easy. According to Lipinski, the initial approach of just putting Saran Wrap around the cut-up chicken meant that in a high percentage of cases, there would be leaks.

Lipinski and his colleagues learned to seal the plastic packaging, which meant far fewer cases of leakage, but occasionally the integrity of a seal wouldn't hold, and we'd still get a leaky package. That could happen, say, once in 10,000 times, but Frank's goal was zero leakage.

"Frank didn't care about averages or statistics," explained Lipinski. "He wanted every package going out the door to be perfect."

Frank would tell Lipinski and everyone else who had anything to do with packaging, "A housewife buys one chicken at a time, and every chicken has to be right." Or another version of this that I used to hear him say, "A housewife doesn't buy statistics, she buys chickens one at a time."

Frank also felt that for each person who took the trouble to let us know that he or she was dissatisfied, there were hundreds or maybe even thousands of individual who didn't make the call, but instead just walked away dissatisfied.

Lipinski remembers seeing a cartoon drawing of Frank saying, not in anger but in simple puzzlement, "If we can put a man on the moon, why can't we make a package that doesn't leak?"

"For us," said Lipinski, "it was un-imaginable to tell him no, so we simply worked until we finally solved it."

The company invested in new machinery, new technology and new materials that would create a much stronger seal. "We were the pioneers in this," said Lipinski. "Nothing quite like it had existed before. We worked with a machinery and material manufacturer, and together developed new kinds of equipment that automated the process of creating a packaging seal for tray pack chicken."

What Lipinski and his fellow Perdue associates had done was create a whole new approach to packaging chicken parts. Their solutions to leak-free packages are standard throughout the industry today, but they were the pioneers.

Lipinski has a comment on what it was like working for Frank. "At that point in my career I was a peon. But even so, Frank would talk with me very frankly and I could talk with him the same way. He had no airs about him. It was the same throughout my career. You just talked with him and he'd sit there and listen. He was never looking at his watch as if he were wondering what time it would be over. He'd ask good questions, intuitive questions, and was really involved."

Sturdy, Functional Packaging

Although attractive and leak-proof packages were a priority for Frank, so were sturdy boxes for transporting chicken from the processing plants to the distributors. The Director of Packaging for Perdue Farms, Owen Schweers, got to see firsthand Frank's emphasis on good packaging.

Although Schweers' specialty was and is packaging, there was such a large intersection between packaging and marketing that Schweers was required to attend the dreaded Quarterly Marketing Meetings. "These were a medieval torture chamber that Frank personally invented," stated Schweers.

The marketing meetings lasted five days, and the breadth of people represented at these meetings impressed Schweers. "Representatives from just about every part of the company would be there, including the reps from Boston, New York, Philadelphia and elsewhere, plus the people in charge of seeing that the chickens were grown well (the 'grow out' people), the marketing people, people from the plants, quality control people, and technical services."

Schweers' role was to listen to and respond to complaints or ideas about packaging, and also to brainstorm about what improvements they could make. "It was actually tremendous for morale. We all felt pumped up because we were on a team that was working so hard to be the best."

Another time-consuming activity for Schweers was frequently traveling to Hunts' Point in New York to check how well the packages of chickens were holding up when they arrived at the distributors. Schweers had to meet the Perdue truckers, usually between 1:00 a.m. and 4:00 a.m.

There was a huge advantage to being there personally, because not only could he use his professional expertise to assess how the Perdue packages were holding up, he could also check how the competitors were doing.

The receivers allowed him to do this because, "They liked what we were doing and it made their lives easier when they didn't have to cope with crushed or leaking boxes."

One of the ideas that came from Schweers' research was a box that would hold the same weight of chicken, but because it was shorter in height and longer in length, was a better fit for the configuration of the delivery trucks. This meant Perdue could fit more boxes of chicken in a truck, which in turn meant savings on fuel costs.

It didn't work out as Schweers hoped. "There are all kinds of economies that come with having a truck loaded optimally, but we ran into a problem. When it came time for the roll-out of our newly designed boxes, which by the way included expensive and tedious redesigning of the machines that made the boxes, I started by doing a trial run using roaster parts."

The trial run was to take place in New York's Chinatown because Perdue roasters had proven to be a favorite there. Unfortunately, although the 40 pounds of chicken inside the box was still the same, the different dimensions caused confusion.

The first man Schweers showed the newly styled box to found it suspicious. This happened almost 40 years ago, but Schweers still remembers clearly what the man told him in somewhat broken English: "You come from big company, you know something we don't know, you figure out some way cheat us!"

At exactly this time, Frank, who was on the other side of town, called Schweers and said that people where he was were also suspicious about the new boxes. "That's it," said Frank, "'We're out of this, change the box back!'"

"We could have saved money with the new configuration," said Schweers, "but Frank, with his deep belief that the customer is always right, wasn't going to do it."

There is a p.s. to this story. Frank, together with the entire Board of Directors, knew that Schweers had invested a lot of work, and heart as well, into designing and making the boxes. The Board has only once in its history given out a *Great Failed Project Award,* and it was to Schweers. They wanted to cheer him up, given that he had put so much thought and effort into the project.

Schweers enjoyed working for Perdue. "People say that Frank was hard to work for and demanded a lot, and that's true. He'd talk with me like a Jewish mother: 'What are you doing! You're tearing my company apart!' Nobody likes to be challenged, but it went with the territory, and you liked knowing you were on a winning team."

FRANK PERDUE'S LESSONS

PAY ATTENTION TO DETAILS– When trying to get the right colors for his packaging, he communicated through two translators on a trans-Atlantic phone call. The Italian vendor he was working with had the best colors for what he needed, and he was willing to invest this kind of time and effort to get it right. Attention to detail hallmarks the difference between winners and runners-up.

EACH CUSTOMER COUNTS– His view that the customer doesn't buy statistics but buys chickens one at a time meant an insistence on zero defects in packaging. This emphasis on zero defects led to the development of new methods and new equipment and greatly increased customer satisfaction.

MAKE THE COMPANY GRATIFYING TO WORK FOR– When an associate put many months of effort and expertise into developing a better shipping box but it bombed in the marketplace, Frank had empathy for the individual's disappointment. Frank, along with his Board of Directors, gave the man the *Great Failed Project Award*. Frank understood the small human touches that engender loyalty.

CHAPTER NINE
OVEN STUFFER® ROASTERS: THE WORLD'S FIRST PROPRIETARY COMMERCIAL CHICKEN

The next landmark in the company's growth was the 1974 introduction of the *Oven Stuffer® Roaster*. This was the first proprietary commercial breed in chicken history, and it was the result of Frank's directive to Perdue's geneticists to breed a broader-breasted, meatier chicken.

Oven Stuffer® Roasters were the result. Interestingly, they're noticeably more flavorful.

It may surprise you, but the biggest factor in their being more flavorful has to do with the age of the bird. Because of the way flavor chemistry works, older, bigger birds have a more intense chicken flavor than younger, smaller birds.

Roasters are typically marketed when they're around seven pounds, as opposed to broilers, which are typically in the five-pound range. The taste aspect comes about because as chickens get older, they produce more of the chemical compounds that give them what we recognize as chicken flavor.

These are the same flavor compounds that you taste in a younger chicken, but by the time a chicken has reached seven or so pounds, it has vastly more of these compounds and the compounds are more concentrated. The resulting flavor tastes much more "chickeny" to us.

For Frank, the *Oven Stuffer® Roaster* had many advantages over what was currently available on the market. However, he immediately encountered a major obstacle to commercial success. Because of its size, the *Oven Stuffer®*

OVEN STUFFER® ROASTERS: THE WORLD'S FIRST PROPRIETARY COMMERCIAL CHICKEN

Roaster was a new product category, and in spite of its many advantages, initially there was no market for it.

There were a number of Perdue associates who were telling him at this point (or at least thinking it), "I told you so!" From the time Frank had the idea of breeding a better bird until the time it proved a commercial success, there was tremendous resistance to the idea.

Many in the company resisted so fiercely that old-timers speak of the early 70s period as "The War of the Roasters." Part of the problem was a natural tendency to resist what costs a lot.

From the first time Frank began suggesting the idea, others in the company were calculating that the expenditures for genetics, re-tooling the processing plants, marketing and advertising would be somewhere between substantial and prohibitive.

Frank believed in the roasters enough to push the program through anyway. He surprised even his colleagues by his determined support for these innovative birds. One associate commented wryly that a man who would hang onto old shoes for the sake of saving $50 would without a qualm spend millions on advertising when he believed in a product.

Frank had started by giving the company genetics department the assignment of breeding the broadest-breasted roaster in the business. Fortunately, they were able to score a genetic bull's-eye. The birds that resulted were healthy, vigorous, and had dramatically broader breasts than any competitive birds.

The next problem was to develop a market for them. Jim Perdue remembered how single-minded his father was on the subject. "When he latched onto something like the roasters, if you saw him four times in the next week, he'd bring it up four times. For example, you're talking about a baseball game, and that suddenly would make him think of a way to get the roaster volume up."

Even so, it took years for the roasters to take hold and fulfill their potential. Frank held onto his vision that the roaster was a great program and a great bird. In the meantime the advertising costs were high, and the product had to be sold at a low price to get the product into the stores and keep it moving. However, once consumers tried a Perdue Farms *Oven Stuffer® Roaster,* they loved it.

When the *Oven Stuffer®Roaster* eventually became popular, competitors naturally enough tried to imitate it. However, they weren't as fortunate with their breeding program as Perdue had been. One competitor's birds had a tendency to develop unsightly blisters on their breasts. Others had the catastrophic problem of having legs that weren't strong enough to support the birds' heavy bodies.

Still others had programs that wouldn't provide a sufficient percent of Grade A whole birds. That meant having to sell too many of their roasters in a cut-up form at commodity prices.

The Perdue genetics department had won the lottery when it came to producing a healthy, strong, fast-growing and tasty chicken. Even so, there was a problem with them, which is they were somewhat seasonal.

In winter, people with families might enjoy putting an *Oven Stuffer®* in the oven, but in summer they are less eager to spend time in a hot kitchen. Enter Terry Ashby.

Thin-Sliced Roaster Breasts

Terry Ashby started with Perdue in 1979 and quickly become the roaster sales manager. He remembers an interaction from back then that was just pure, typical Frank.

For Ashby, it began when he came across a retailer in Long Island who was making thin-sliced boneless chicken breasts. Since the company needed to sell more *Oven Stuffer®* breasts in the summer, having thin-sliced Roaster breasts seemed like a great new item that could be sold during the warmer season.

However, as Ashby quickly experienced, there are a lot of steps between wanting to sell a new product and actually doing it. For a start, the retail butcher was slicing the chicken breasts by hand, and getting the same result using mass production in a plant environment is an entirely different problem.

"We started with a potato chip slicer," explained Ashby, "but the sizes of the slices weren't right. We eventually used Hobart slicing machines, and much later as this item grew in popularity, we found poultry equipment manufacturers who were willing to develop equipment specific for just this application."

Frank played a somewhat negative role in this, at least from Ashby's point of view. "When I started working on the project," Ashby said, "I asked everyone who was working on it to keep this to ourselves and get it done quietly. I knew that as soon as Frank got wind of it, he'd be calling us every day, asking why we hadn't shipped product already."

Of course, pretty soon Frank did hear about it, and of course he wanted to know why Ashby hadn't said anything to him. Ashby told Frank, "I didn't tell you, Frank, because I knew you'd start calling me every day, asking why it's taking so long."

"Yup," Frank answered, "you've got that exactly right!" According to Ashby, Frank took it with good humor, and said that being quiet about it had been a smart thing to do.

"Still," Ashby added, "from then on, things turned out just as I had predicted. There were the daily phone calls, wanting to know why we didn't have it in the marketplace already. Frank Perdue was nothing if not tenacious. But still, he could be good-humored about it."

Ashby remembered that Frank had an interesting way of teaching. "He had memorable sayings, and many of us remember them to this day. 'You've got

113

to be better than the competition.' 'The consumer is not an idiot.' 'The quality of our product and the value to the consumer are what drives everything.'"

Another thing Ashby observed about Frank: "He always thought long term. One of his favorite sayings said it all: 'If you make an excellent product, the profits and volume will follow.'"

Steve Evans began working for Perdue in 1985, and by the time he left in 2013, he was Vice President of Optimization, Food Service, and International Sales. He watched how Frank's detail-mindedness helped make the Roaster program a success.

One of the things that surprised Evans was he could pretty much expect a phone call from Frank calling every single day to check on flock weights and ages. "Can you imagine the CEO of other large companies calling like this?" Evans asked.

I wondered if getting into this much detail might be excessive, but Evans answered, "At that time, it was a good thing. The industry was growing rapidly, and it was important to make sure that there was a process in place to get the weights right."

For Evans, the point of this story was that Frank was creating and reinforcing a culture of expecting people to know the details. "Frank did this by continually asking you questions," said Evans. "I can remember before computers, people would bring five-inch binders to meetings with Frank because they knew Frank was going to be asking them questions, and they'd better be on top of things. I think one of the reasons Perdue was so successful is because everybody knew the details."

But there was another crucial part. Knowing the details was the necessary prelude to action, something that in Evans' view the company excels at. "His assistant Elaine Barnes spent many hours following up on Frank's notes to you. If you didn't answer promptly, you'd soon enough hear from Elaine with a second notice. You didn't want to get many second notices."

There was a yin and a yang to this, though. "He was also very good about sending personal notes of appreciation. He wrote me more than 20 of those during my time at Perdue and I've kept them all."

One of these read, "Congratulations on a fact-based, detailed presentation! It assists us in making better decisions. Many thanks, Frank." For Evans, "There was nothing like those notes of appreciation for motivation."

Although the Roasters turned into a major success for the company, and had the superlative advantage of being genetically very difficult to copy, there was another side to this coin.

Every Roaster Male Has a Cornish Sister

Every roaster is a male, and the females of this breed are called Cornish. They not only grow more slowly than the male, they also need more feed if they're to be grown to the seven or so pound weight of a roaster. Because of this, when a female hatches, it is generally destined to be processed at two pounds.

Cornish hens are typically sold for individual servings, and since the people from the Sales Department believed there wasn't enough demand for individual servings, they wanted to destroy all female roasters as soon as they hatched.

In fact, almost no one wanted to get into the Cornish hen business. They generally thought Cornish hens were a guaranteed money loser.

Jack Tatem has vivid memories of Frank and his efforts to get Don Mabe and the sales people to support selling the Cornish hens. One instance that Tatem particularly remembers happened when Frank had assembled a meeting with six sales people whom Frank, for unknown reasons, had nicknamed, "the Whores and the Booger Bears."

This group was in a small room with the sales people sitting along the sides of the conference table, and Don Made – the company president at the time –

at one end and Frank Perdue at the other.

According to Tatem, Frank and Mabe had been fighting like cats and dogs all day long about whether to scrap the Cornish program. The company culture at the time tolerated and perhaps even encouraged vigorous debate, but this was, at least for someone new to Perdue, astonishing.

As Tatem tells it, "Don got so mad that he took his glasses off, threw them down hard on the table – the glasses bounced once and ended up hitting Frank square in the chest!"

For Tatem, it was all so intense that it seemed to be happening in slow motion. He was even having trouble catching his breath. "Damn it, Frank," Tatem remembered Mabe yelling at Frank, "Why don't you get a hobby like sailing a boat or flying an airplane! Cornish are just going to lose you money!"

Tatem remembers that Frank picked up Don's reading glasses, calmly handed them to the guy next to him, who handed them to the guy next to him until the glasses got back to Mabe, as meanwhile the argument continued to rage.

"You'd think an incident like that would rupture their relationship," said Tatem, "but when the meeting ended, and they were leaving, I watched as Don and Frank were chatting amiably with each other as if the incident I just described had never happened."

Frank won that day's argument, but hard as it was to convince the Perdue associates to have a Cornish program, it was even harder to convince the distributors.

The problem was that Perdue Farms wanted to stay with its tradition of selling fresh chicken, but Cornish was a high-priced, low-volume item and therefore had a greater risk of going out of condition in the meat department.

The low volume wouldn't be an insurmountable problem for a frozen product, but with a fresh product, if chickens didn't move and the retailer lost even a few Cornish hens out of a twelve-hen box, he wouldn't want to see another box of Cornish ever again.

The problem was to create enough demand to insure rapid turnover. Advertising solved it, particularly Frank's most famous ad, the one in which he serves individual Cornish hens to three beautiful guests. However, before the advertising could be effective, Frank had to convince the distributors to carry the Cornish hens.

According to Michael Ottomanelli, Frank visited every major chain in New York and while there, Frank would do his own personal version of what looked to Ottomanelli like the comedy routine: *-Mother-in-Law-Delivering-Maximum-Guilt.* Frank would tell the meat buyers, "My sales manager wants to gas my baby roasters! It's killing me! You're killing me! *Help!*"

Ottomanelli felt that Frank's unique and disarming brand of charm paid off. In the end, it resulted in enough sales to support growing the female roasters to the two-pound weight appropriate for individual servings. What made it work was Frank's taking the time for all the visits, and his willingness to use humor when nothing else seemed to work.

Even though Frank could now sell the Cornish, there remained the formidable problem of making them profitable. For Darrel Keck, who began in Distribution in 1981 and was Cornish Hen Marketing Manager by 1983, Cornish started out as an almost undiluted headache. Because of the higher costs associated with producing a smaller bird, any plant that ran Cornish was going to fare less well in the company's benchmarked performance standards.

Frank wanted him to improve the Cornish performance, and Keck was able to pull it off, but not without stress for him and his team. In the end, "We found a way to grow and keep the line profitable while adding secondary brands and developing more aggressive cross-merchandizing plans." For Keck, rewards for his efforts were, first, two or three handwritten paragraphs from Frank that appeared in one of the marketing reports, giving him and his team a public accolade, and second, a promotion.

FRANK PERDUE'S LESSONS

IF YOU BELIEVE IN YOUR PRODUCT, WORK TO CONVINCE THE PEOPLE WHO ARE RESISTING– What became Perdue's most successful niche product, the *Roaster*, was initially opposed by people in the company, resisted by the distributors, and ignored by the public. Frank spent years influencing all three groups, and since the Roasters did end up being a success, they proved one of Frank's favorite sayings: "If you make an excellent product, the profits and volume will follow."

STRONG, VOCAL DISAGREEMENTS ARE OK, AS LONG AS THEY'RE NOT TAKEN PERSONALLY– The company culture tolerated huge, in-your-face arguments when a decision was at stake, but the culture also expected that after the opinions had been forcefully expressed, that individuals would be friends again and that disagreements were not to be taken personally. The culture of strongly expressed opinions meant many sides of an issue could be aired and explored.

MAKE THE EFFORT TO OVERCOME OBSTACLES– When Frank needed to sell his smaller Cornish hens, he made the effort to call personally on every distributor, and then when using logical arguments wasn't enough, he could also use humor and sheer personality and charm to make the sale.

CHAPTER TEN
HR: GROWING THE COMPANY FROM 3,000 TO 19,000 ASSOCIATES

Frank believed that effective recruitment is one of the key elements of Perdue Farms' success. He liked to tell how Andrew Carnegie, on being asked if he could build his steel empire over again, answered, "You could take away my steel plants, and I could do it. But if you took away the people who helped me build this steel empire, I could never do it again."

The Andrew Carnegie story is a true reflection of Frank's beliefs. He knew that he didn't do it alone.

Frank was always tremendously interested in hiring and personnel. Even when he was in his 80s, this was still a frequent topic of conversation between us. By the way, I had very little to contribute to these conversations, other than being an eager and interested sounding board.

He'd talk about a potential new hire and how much promise the individual had, even if it was someone in his or her 20s. He also would sometimes talk about how good workers seem to run in families, and that if an associate had been raised with a strong work ethic, it often happened that his or her siblings would also be a good fit for Perdue. Actually, I've seen how this played out in practice because I've talked with associates who had as many as five siblings working for Perdue.

Frank always made a point of entertaining the 50 or so summer interns at our house each year. He enjoyed meeting them and talking with him, and my guess is that these events were equally enjoyable for them and him.

119

HR: GROWING THE COMPANY FROM
3,000 TO 19,000 ASSOCIATES

We'd have five 10-foot-long tables and folding chairs set up in our patio area, and we'd put on a crab feast along with fried chicken, corn on the cob, beaten biscuits and plenty of beer. It would be a time for Frank and the interns to get to know each other informally, and in particular, it was a time for them to ask Frank questions.

He'd be sitting at one of the middle seats at one of the tables, and the interns at his table would ask him questions about work in general, or the chicken industry, or their future careers. Oftentimes when he'd answer, the people at the table would be silent, leaning towards him to catch every word. He was in his element when surrounded by young people asking him questions. He genuinely enjoyed sharing what he knew.

He'd dispense wisdom, such as, "When you're in your 20s, don't be influenced by the size of your paycheck when exploring what job to take. Later on in life you may be married and have children to support, and you'll never again have the latitude that you have right now to discover what you really like and are good at."

He'd often tell them, "In your 20s, you learn. In your 30s, you earn."

I was impressed that in his 80s, he was as concerned with recruiting as he had been when I first knew him when he was in his 60s. The fact is, he was helping to recruit people who would be there long after he was gone, and he knew it. Awareness of this didn't slow him down or dim his enthusiasm.

Finding and Hiring the Future Leaders

Frank cared deeply about human resources, and the person he relied on for heading the HR department while I was there was Rob Heflin. Joining the company in 1977, Heflin got to witness the company's growth from 3,000 associates to what it is today, 19,000.

Heflin came in contact with Frank a fair amount during his career, partly because his office was located close to Frank's and party because, as Heflin put it, "Frank was absolutely avid about insuring we were hiring the best talent available, because they would be the future leaders of Perdue."

To get the best talent, Frank used to insist that Heflin and his colleagues check at least ten references for any managerial candidate they were considering. As Heflin delicately put it, "Frank was not fun to be around" if you told him you had a finalist candidate and hadn't yet done the required amount of reference checking.

Frank talked with me about his reason for wanting ten references. "When a person gives five references, he or she has chosen people who will line up like mynah birds to give the story he or she wants told. Instead, ask the references who else knows the applicant, and then talk with the individuals the applicant hasn't already coached on what to say."

Besides being unusual in his insistence on ten references, Frank was also innovative in his college recruitment efforts. Frank instituted the most extensive college recruiting program in the industry, and he started doing college recruiting a decade before his competitors.

According to Heflin, company representatives would visit between 15-20 college campuses annually, and Frank would sometimes come along. "He was always the greatest hit with the college kids, partly because of his celebrity status, partly because of being such a successful entrepreneur, and partly because of his great personality and persona around the college folks."

Heflin admired that Frank, as well as Don Mabe "cared tremendously about every associate in the company, including our hourly production folks." For Heflin, as a human resources practitioner, "It is most unusual to have senior executives at the President and/or CEO level be this visible to the hourly workforce."

Heflin has an all-time favorite memory of Frank. They were flying on the company plane on their way to the Cromwell, Kentucky plant. Frank had been on vacation, attending the tennis matches at Wimbledon, which we did every year.

"It was early morning and still dark in the plane," Heflin recalled. "Frank was sitting right next to me. He had this large black satchel that he had carried with him for decades, and he began pulling papers out of it. I noticed that as he began reading the papers, he was mumbling to himself.

"'Damn,' he's say, and then he'd flip the page to get to the next one. 'Damn!' he'd say again."

"After several repetitions of this, I was getting curious. 'Frank, what's going on?'"

"'I'm reading these production reports," he said, "and obviously I've taken my eye off the ball. It's clear I need to talk with our manager at Cromwell about what's been going on since I've been gone.'

"'In fact, I think I ought to fire myself!'"

For Heflin, that was something you don't often see: a CEO who believes he ought to fire himself if things aren't going as they should!

Another person with insight into Frank and Human Resources is Jim McCauley, Director of Safety and Security from 1979 to 2000.

Moral Hazard

You might not expect Frank McCauley, Director of Safety and Security to appear in a chapter on HR, but as you'll read, Frank had a lot of insight on anything involving personnel and company culture.

McCauley, who worked for Perdue from 1979 to 2000, believed that padlocks aren't about keeping crooks out. Instead, they're there to help keep honest people honest. An organization that is lax about such issues as discrimination or theft risks undermining itself. Frank Perdue endorsed this view, believing that a culture that is strong, vibrant and a source of pride required a foundation of integrity.

HR: GROWING THE COMPANY FROM 3,000 TO 19,000 ASSOCIATES

"Frank was a man of principal," McCauley said as he began our conversation. "If I investigated a long-term employee, I had to convince Frank beyond any reasonable doubt that the guy had violated company policy. He was very protective of his employees."

On the other hand, McCauley witnessed that Frank did not tolerate employees stealing products or supplies, or other violations of company policy, and in those cases, he would go along with a termination. If it was serious enough, it could also include prosecution.

By the way, McCauley wouldn't be involved if the value was less than $500. For situations involving less than $500, the plant manager would handle it.

The cases McCauley would get involved with were when there was a significant loss of inventory. An example that he particularly remembers involved a Perdue associate who was a relative of a high-profile local official in Salisbury. McCauley's investigation revealed that the associate had stolen more than $10,000 in equipment and tools and was intending to use these materials to open up his own repair shop.

McCauley worked with the sheriff to help get the material back. McCauley actually knew exactly where the stolen material was located, but it took law enforcement to be able legally to make the recovery possible.

At this point, Frank began getting phone calls from the high-level local government official. Since the official who was telling Frank to drop the charges was in a position to cause Frank a lot of trouble, there was an implied threat behind the calls.

The phone calls became increasingly worrisome. Frank asked McCauley's opinion.

"I told him, 'Frank, you sign my paycheck but remember, I was hired to protect the company. If you want to send the wrong message to the other associates, if you want to send a message that this kind of action has no consequences, than don't prosecute.'"

Frank's answered with one word: "Prosecute!"

McCauley went on to say, "In a company it's important to have strict rules. The person who starts by simply stealing nickels and dimes begins to think, 'That doesn't get me in trouble, maybe I'll take just a little bit more,' and the amount he or she takes starts growing, and then it grows some more until you're dealing with large numbers.

"A lot of times a manager can't believe that a longtime trusted individual would steal, with the result that the problem can get larger and larger, and the employee, when finally caught, is in very serious trouble with the law. It would have been so much better if the manager had set policies in place and enforced them, and the employee hadn't gradually turned into a crook."

McCauley respected Frank for understanding this kind of moral hazard. Frank had come up through the ranks and he was aware that temptation exists. "He had common sense as well as knowledge," said McCauley. "He understood that you need padlocks because people need to know they're there, and they need to know not to start down that road."

McCauley respected the fact that Frank had an open door policy, and if, for example, someone had a work discrimination case, he or she could contact Frank. When this happened, Frank would call on McCauley to conduct the investigation.

"If I found that the grievance was justified," said McCauley, "the person would be reinstated with back pay. Frank wasn't afraid to be wrong and he wasn't afraid to admit that he was wrong, and he wasn't afraid to take corrective action."

FRANK PERDUE'S LESSONS

PERSONNEL IS CRITICAL TO THE FUTURE OF A COMPANY, AND IT'S WORTH MAKING THE EFFORT TO GET IT RIGHT– Frank was heavily involved in human resources and particularly in recruitment. He enjoyed recruiting on campuses and went out of his way to spend time with and get to know the summer interns. He also made it a practice to interview ten references before offering a candidate a job, and he insisted on the multiplicity of interviews with the idea that you don't just talk with the people the applicant has already lined up and coached on what to say.

BE REALISTIC ABOUT MORAL HAZARD– Frank understood moral hazards and knew that while padlocks may not keep the crook out, they can help keep the honest person from temptation.

CHAPTER ELEVEN
LOGISTICS: TRYING TO UNSCRAMBLE AN EGG

By the late 1970s, the major moving pieces of the company were in place, including the hatcheries, the feed mills, the chicken growing and processing, transportation, sales and marketing, advertising, and public relations. This period saw a continuation of the growth and innovation that characterized the previous decades. Frank's energy continued unabated.

A widely circulated joke about that energy was, "Frank Perdue is the only man who can enter a revolving door in the compartment behind you and leave it ahead of you." (A less flattering description of his drive was "He doesn't get ulcers–but he's a carrier!")

Frank had always expected to differentiate Perdue Farms through quality, service and reliability. As the advertising took hold, the demand for Perdue chicken increased. But having a desirable product and interested buyers was not enough. If the product was to be a success, getting the logistics right became ever more important.

Interestingly, the need for on-time delivery played into one of Frank's most notable characteristics: attention to time. The whole concept of time seemed to occupy a different place in his brain than it does for the rest of us. It very much affected how Frank earned a reputation for on-time deliveries with the distributors.

An example of Frank's unusual relationship with time comes from Roger Brown, who started with Perdue in 1976. Today he's the fleet warranty administrator for the 5,000 vehicles that Perdue Farms owns, and he once told me that Frank was the only person he ever met who would call him and tell him when to meet, and – here's the surprising part – the time would be expressed to the nearest half minute. That kind of precision seemed dumbfounding to Brown, or at least it was dumbfounding the first time Brown heard it.

Brown still vividly remembers that first time. "I happened to be in Frank's office talking with his executive assistant, Elaine Barnes, when I got a call from Frank. He told me, 'I'll be there in seven and a half minutes.'

"I turned to Barnes and said, 'He's kidding, right? Nobody's that exact!'

"'You watch,' Barnes answered. 'He'll do it.'"

Brown looked at his watch, paying careful attention to the second hand. "Sure enough, I saw Frank striding through the door exactly seven minutes and thirty seconds later."

No Excuses On-Time Deliveries

The attitude Roger Brown just described reached its great flaming apogee when it came to on-time deliveries. Frank had been struggling with the problem of late deliveries since the early 1970s, but by the late 1970s, it became clear that to solve it, as opposed to simply making it less bad, he would need to take drastic steps. The steps Frank took to guarantee on-time delivery ended up influencing the entire trucking industry.

To explain how this happened and why, let me give a little context, courtesy of Herb McCoun, who's been with the company since 1982. Today he's Perdue's Director of Supply Planning. Here's how the system worked, or at least was supposed to work.

Imagine you're a trucker with a load of chicken and you've arrived at the distributor's loading dock for you scheduled 3:00 a.m. delivery. A flurry of activity then goes on as forklifts unload your truck, workers put the boxes in a cooler, and then they break the shipment down to individual boxes destined for different grocery stores or butchers.

Logistics from Perdue headquarters would have already called the night before with a breakdown of the day's deliveries. As the truck left the plant, Logistics would also have called the customer and told him or her what was actually shipped, so from a paperwork point of view, the customer was able to pre-receive the product.

However, if a truck were four or five hours late, which often happened back in the early days, this delay would ripple through the supply chain, and at every level, there would be disappointed, irritated, and/or angry people.

Since late delivery problems and the headaches that always went with them were endemic, Frank took a deep dive into trying to figure out what could be done to solve this problem permanently. He realized that although late deliveries were a problem, they were also a tremendous opportunity: whoever could be the most reliable seller would have a compelling advantage over all other competitors.

McCoun remembers Frank's telling him, "Every distributor's life is full of problems and our goal is to be the least of his problems. We want to have our product in the right place at the right time. It's how we are going to differentiate ourselves."

Frank figured that if he could solve the problem of on-time, reliable delivery, the distributors would have Perdue on their speed dial when they wanted more product.

Getting into the Trucking Business

How did Frank solve this?

For one thing, he didn't just set a goal and say, "Let it be so!" Instead, let's take a look at what it took to become the most reliable supplier. A hint: it took time, money, effort and brainpower. Oh, and maybe being a bit stubborn and cantankerous along the way.

Frank's first task was to figure out what was causing late and unreliable deliveries. He already knew that following the usual chicken industry practices at the time, you could rent a truck for $1,000 and make the run from the Salisbury processing plant to the New York metro area to supply its 20 or more meat and or poultry distributors.

However, the situation could and did arise where a trucker might have his $1,000 contract to deliver chicken, but a strawberry grower might be so desperate to get his strawberries to market before they spoiled that he'd offer the same trucker $2,000 for the same trip.

People being human, the trucker might take the $2,000 and ignore his chicken delivery obligation. Perdue officials would be stuck at the last minute, scrambling to find another truck and driver. The delivery would now be many hours late.

Another problem was the drives were sometimes gypsy truckers, that is freelancers with no oversight organization to assure that standards were met. Sometimes an alcohol or a drug problem caused one of these freelance drivers to be half a day late, and while you could make sure never to hire that individual again, you might well come across the same problem with the next freelance trucker you hired.

To deal with the twin issues of occasionally unreliable drivers and trucks that might, in effect, be hijacked by one-off offers of higher prices, Frank took a bold and radical step; he got into the trucking business. He bought trucks and rented additional ones, and then he hired truckers to drive the trucks, truckers who would be on his payroll and whose professionalism he could ensure.

It was something he didn't want to do, had no background in, and the whole proposition must have seemed unreasonably expensive, especially given that he was spending his own money to do it. Still, he calculated that without the ability to control the supply chain, he couldn't achieve his goal of being the most reliable producer.

Ray Hall remembers those early days, once Frank had gotten into the trucking business. Hall began with Perdue in 1965, and at the time of his retirement in 2011, was Director of Transportation and Fleet Maintenance. He saw that even when it came to trucks, Frank was detail-minded and demanding. Frank had arranged for the trucks, including rented trucks, to have the Perdue logo on them, knowing it would be good advertising.

The downside of this in Frank's mind was that if one of his trucks were dirty, people might wonder if what was inside was clean. In response, according to Hall, "We had wash people at every garage that we had, and the drivers knew to get their tractors cleaned at least once a week."

Even the rental trucks had to be clean. "If Frank saw a dirty truck on the highway," said Hall, "he'd give me the truck's number and tell me that I'd better get this in and get it clean. His attitude was cleanliness was next to Godliness."

It turned out that owning or renting the large rigs and being able to screen each trucker in advance of hiring was actually only the beginning of Frank's efforts to have timely deliveries.

Michael Ottomanelli's Story

There were endless problems to be dealt with and one of them, as Michael Ottomanelli, Frank's first marketing representative, remembers, was the gas shortage caused by the Iranian crisis in 1979.

When the Shah of Iran was overthrown, oil exports were halted, and even when they resumed the supply was spotty. Because of tightened supplies, the U.S. was enduring a full-blown energy crisis. Still, Frank's goal was to be a "no-excuses" company, so the Perdue trucks had to get through and on time, no matter what.

As Ottomanelli tells it, "It was a time when gas lines dotted the roads, and to deal with this, Frank had a Perdue fuel truck follow a convoy of northbound Perdue eighteen-wheelers. At the Delaware Memorial Bridge, in Delaware, the convoy would top off, guaranteeing a safe, timely delivery for Perdue product headed to the Northeast."

That was a one-off emergency to be handled. But Frank was also committed to creating a system and a culture that supported on-time deliveries. Ottomanelli remembers that "Frank was a student of time and motions studies, and he was always searching for a better way to perform each part of the tasks involved in the delivery chain."

Ottomanelli has an interesting example of Frank's efforts to change the culture in the early days when the company trucking system was getting established. He was with Frank at a distributor's complex on 14th Street in Manhattan.

The two men were standing near the delivery bay where the trucks pull up to be unloaded. In this particular case, the distributor needed a load of chicken that would be delivered at 5:00 a.m. As Ottomanelli remembers it, that day a Perdue driver pulled his rig in five minutes ahead of the 5:00 a.m. deadline.

Very likely the man was astonished to find the head of the company, Frank Perdue himself, standing there. According to Ottomanelli, Frank greeted the driver and then said, "Let me ask you a question. What time was your appointment?"

"5:00 o'clock, Sir."

"How long does it take you drive here from Salisbury?" Frank asked.

"Five hours. I picked the load up at midnight and then left in time to arrive here at 5:00 a.m."

At that moment, Ottomanelli was sure the guy was being set up for something. It had been too straightforward so far.

"How long does it take you to fix a flat tire?" Frank probed.

The question was entirely unexpected, but after the man thought a moment, he answered "Usually about an hour."

"If you're going to work for me," Frank said, looking him dead in the eye, "you're going to leave an hour early. If you get a flat, you can fix it and still make your appointment."

It was a tough position for Frank to take, but it was worth it. By being a "no excuses" on-time delivery company, the distributors were motivated to buy from him, which resulted in more market share, which meant growth for the company, which meant that everyone who worked for the Perdue company got the satisfaction of being on a winning team.

Today, the transportation side of the business has grown so large that just to supply the grain side takes alone 1,700 rail cars. Sharon Clark, one of Perdue's Senior Vice Presidents, specializes in transportation, and last year was responsible for dispatching 140,000 grain trucks. Frank's almost accidental interest in trucking back in the late 1960s ended up having huge results. For Clark, the growth was not an accident. "He was on top of everything."

FRANK PERDUE'S LESSONS

TO BE A RELIABLE SUPPLIER, CONTROL THE SUPPLY CHAIN– When Frank was getting started selling chickens, the industry was plagued with late deliveries. Sensing an opportunity to differentiate himself from the competition, Frank bought his own trucks and hired his own truckers to ensure control of his supply chain. He knew that "Every distributor's life is full of problems and our goal is to be the least of his problems."

CREATE A CULTURE THAT SUPPORTS YOUR ORGANIZATION'S GOALS– In order to create a culture of on-time deliveries, Frank would go to the delivery bays in New York in the wee hours of the morning to meet the truckers and let them know how important no-excuses on-time delivery was to him. The resulting success was so great that the transportation segment of Perdue, if it were an independent company, would count as one of the larger logistics companies in the country.

CHAPTER TWELVE
INDUSTRIAL ENGINEERING:
EVERYTHING IS IMPORTANT

Frank had the deeply held conviction that *everything is important.* He was into the nuts and bolts of running things, and this certainly gets into the industrial engineering that's part of building and running a plant. Characteristically, Frank made it his business to know a lot about the nuts and bolts.

I know about his nuts-and-bolts approach because I'd sometimes get to accompany him at poultry equipment shows. I saw for myself how much he knew about each booth at these shows.

Visiting the International Poultry Expo in Atlanta each year with him was like attending the show with the world's greatest engineering professor. Whatever the machine that interested him, and he was usually interested in at least one machine at each of the hundreds of booths that we visited, Frank could talk about the device in staggering detail.

He even enjoyed touching the different machines. I don't think he learned anything from resting his hand on the latest transport conveyor roller track; his touching the equipment seemed more like a moment of showing respect that someone had created something so useful and clever.

I remember marveling, as we went from exhibit to exhibit, and talked with rep after rep, hour after hour, that Frank had a truly amazing knowledge about every single machine. He knew what it did, what its weaknesses were, what its tolerances were, what the competition was doing, often who had developed it, and on and on. Both his memory and his range of interest seemed limitless. When he didn't know he'd ask and ask and ask, getting ever-deeper answers.

Since Frank was so into the manufacturing details, it was totally in character that he would take a great interest in the industrial engineering side of things. Frank had a saying that many people remember and that he used frequently, "Get the maximum out of the minimum," and that's what Steve Schwalb, currently Perdue's Vice President of Environmental Sustainability, was tasked with.

An Industrial Engineer's Point of View

Schwalb started in 1982 as a manager of industrial engineering, and he got the job by an unusual route. In 1980, he was living in Pennsylvania but working as a consultant doing an industrial engineering project for Black & Decker in Easton, Maryland. While having an after-work drink at Easton's Holiday Inn, he struck up a conversation with a Perdue associate who told Schwalb, "You would be like a kid in a candy store at Perdue – they really need industrial engineering."

As a result, Schwalb applied for a consulting job with Perdue, and the first time he met Frank was at the Accomac plant in Virginia. The experience wasn't what he was expecting.

"Here I am, a Jewish guy from New York, and I had grown up watching the Perdue commercials. Not only that, my folks were constantly asking if I had met Frank yet and what was he like. So, I see him and I think, 'Oh my God, it's Frank Perdue!'"

Schwalb remembers that Frank had his white lab coat and bump cap on (that's like a hard hat except it's lightweight plastic) and he was inspecting packages of chicken. Schwalb walks over to him and sticks out his hand to shake Frank's. However, as Schwalb quickly discovered, Frank was so focused on whatever he was doing that he didn't relish being interrupted.

INDUSTRIAL ENGINEERING:
EVERYTHING IS IMPORTANT

"Who are you?" Frank demanded.

Schwalb was taken aback by this. There were no pleasantries, just, "Who are you?"

"Steve Schwalb, a consultant with…." is about all Schwalb could manage to get out.

"A consultant? So we have another damn consultant in this place!?"

Schwalb explained that he was reconfiguring the lines for the people who would put chicken parts in trays, making the lines more efficient. This evidently satisfied Frank and it was the end of the encounter.

"That was my first exposure," Schwalb said, "and although I've made it sound like he was gruff – and he was – there was something about Frank and that first encounter that I liked. Actually, it suited me to a tee. As an industrial engineer, I like things straightforward and no nonsense."

Schwalb went on to say, "It was really no different from what he conveyed on TV about being the tough man you could trust to give you the best product possible. Throughout my career at Perdue, it's been very consistent; you never had any doubt what the direction of the company was and what you needed to do to support that."

Schwalb knew he could have worked for other companies that wouldn't have been as demanding, but it also wouldn't have been as fulfilling. "Frank had a way of really motivating you," Schwalb continued. "Looking back on it, working for Perdue was the best career decision I ever made."

Frank often called Schwalb at home with questions relating to Schwalb's work. A funny situation arose owing to the fact that Schwalb is Jewish. "Over the years, my wife Laurie noticed that Frank always called me on Sunday mornings. Typically, Laurie would answer the phone, he'd be charming with her, and then ask if I was there."

INDUSTRIAL ENGINEERING:
EVERYTHING IS IMPORTANT

One day after one of these many, many Sunday phone calls, his wife asked Schwalb, "I wonder why he always calls you on Sunday mornings? What don't you ask him?"

"'I'm not doing that,' I answered.

"'If you don't, I will.'

"So for the sake of marital peace, the next Sunday morning when the call came, I said, 'Frank, you can call me any time, but how come you always call me on Sundays?'

"'You're Jewish and I know you're not going to be in church,' he replied, without missing a beat.

"That was Frank," said Schwalb. "I found it endearing – most of the time. I just knew this was another case of Frank's being as efficient and effective as he could be with his time. He didn't want to deal with a phone call that resulted in a no-answer or a voice mail."

I asked Schwalb if he felt that this intrusion on his personal time was a problem, and Schwalb answered, "There's something satisfying about being challenged to be all you can be all the time. That's what attracted me to Perdue and that's what's kept me here. And then on top of that, you got to see that the efforts Frank drew from you produced results.

"Also, a lot of us felt, 'Here's a guy who genuinely believes in what he's doing, there's incredible potential in this company, and because of his vision, it's going to go places and I want to be a part of it and I didn't want to let Frank down.'"

Schwalb loves his job and would advise anyone starting out in his or her career that you have to love what you're doing to really excel at it. "Regardless of how you approach it, you can't succeed if you don't have some passion or love for what you do. In my case, I'm motivated by thinking, 'The work I do results in feeding people, and making quality food products that people can afford.' I find tremendous pleasure in knowing that I'm doing something good."

FRANK PERDUE'S LESSONS

PAY ATTENTION TO THE "NUTS AND BOLTS." For Frank, everything was important, including the mechanical and engineering side of the business. He regularly attended the poultry equipment shows, and knew an almost uncanny amount about the various machines and their capabilities. He didn't stint on buying the best equipment and he always sought to get "the maximum from the minimum."

CHAPTER THIRTEEN
ACCOUNTING: THE FUNCTIONAL
EQUIVALENT OF AN MRI

Frank had a tremendous head for figures. He liked numbers, and on top of that, quantitative thinking simply appealed to him. He treated numbers the way a doctor would treat an MRI: numbers enabled him to see and understand what was going on deep inside the business, plus numbers were a very quick way of detecting if something was going wrong.

Of course this meant that he had a natural affinity for the accounting department, and as Stan Howeth, the company's Director, Audit Services, once told me, Frank was so good with numbers, so analytical and so detail-minded, that he would have made a good accountant.

A Quick Story about Frank and Math

There was a reason for Frank's comfort level with numbers, but to explain it I need to share something that happened when Frank was 85, maybe half a year before his passing. We were visiting Massachusetts General Hospital to assess how he was handling the Parkinson's disease that was soon to take him.

I remember the situation well. We were seated in deep leather chairs in the doctor's book-lined office, and you could see the Charles River through the office window.

The session began with the doctor showing us some disheartening images taken earlier that day, disheartening because they revealed the extent that Frank's brain had been impacted by Parkinson's. Frank accepted the dismal information stoically. He nodded his head, showing that he understood, but there wasn't any word of complaint or shock. It was as if this was simply a piece of data to be dealt with.

And now came the part that we were there for, tracking how much impairment the Parkinson's had actually caused. The first question the doctor asked Frank was to count backwards from 100 by sevens. Frank did that as fluently as I would have if I were counting forward by twos. No hesitation. And remember, this was a seriously ill person who was only months away from going to his reward.

The next questions were harder, such as listening to a string of numbers and then being asked not only to remember them, but also to repeat the same string backwards. I was expecting to follow along, doing the problems in my head myself.

The trouble was that by the fourth problem, it had gotten too difficult. The questions had become so complicated that I couldn't remember the questions, let alone answer them, and that's in spite of my being a Harvard graduate who likes math. Frank went on for about 20 rounds after I had to drop out.

I was stunned. My jaw was gaping. I couldn't believe anybody could do what I was witnessing Frank do. And to top all this off, he seemed to be answering these totally impossible questions without struggle or even hesitation. True, his voice was weak and slightly raspy from the Parkinson's, but the answers were in every case rapid and fluid.

At the end of the test, I took the doctor aside, out of Frank's hearing and told him, "Doctor, you've been testing the wrong person. I must be the one who's ill because I dropped out after the first few rounds."

The doctor answered that my stopping early was what he'd expect from anyone, and that Frank, in spite of being seriously impaired from the Parkinson's, was performing at an Olympic level. He said Frank's performance was so astounding that he (the doctor) would have given five years of his life to see what Frank was like before he was impaired.

Which brings me to a quick side thought about Frank. He must have had a phenomenal IQ, but you'd never know it because he absolutely, totally never flaunted it. He would talk with everyone at his or her level. He was also one of the more successful men in America, but again, you'd never know it from his house, his clothes, his possessions or any visible status symbol. He was also charitable on a phenomenal scale, not only with his money but also with his time, but he did everything he could to keep it secret. I find it interesting that a man with so much to boast about never, ever boasted.

Frank and Accounting

But anyway, back to the side of the company that most intersected with Frank's head for mathematics. Al Lynch has been an accountant with Perdue since 1967, and today is Senior VP Controller for Perdue AgriBusiness.

"Frank was pretty keen with numbers," said Lynch, "but he was not a micro manager. He was willing to let people run the areas they were responsible for, but he was definitely aware of the details that made the difference, given that it's a business where a few tenths of a cent do make a lot of difference."

Lynch observed that while Frank didn't micromanage, he'd often ask questions. "He was often asking not to get information but to validate it, and checking how much the other person knew."

Stan Howeth, Director of Audit Services, also works in accounting and has been with the company since 1982. As with Lynch, Howeth was struck by Frank's "management by questions" approach. "He asked a lot more questions than you'd expect someone at his level to ask, with the result that he had a much deeper level of knowledge than other folks had."

Howeth noticed that Frank's accounting questions were so penetrating that the presenter would often learn new ways of looking at questions. Frank was continuously thinking of things that the professional accounting people

ACCOUNTING: THE FUNCTIONAL EQUIVALENT OF AN MRI

hadn't considered, and he was unusually knowledgeable about such details as what the cost of every component should be. This knowledge included the hatcheries, the feed mills, the costs of live chickens versus dressed on a per pound basis and a dozen other areas.

He was also very involved with the income side. One of Frank's favorite sayings was, "The job isn't complete until you collect the money."

Like many others in the company, Howeth received his share of middle-of-the-night phone calls. Typically Frank would call Howeth about issues involving payments to a chicken grower for his or her flock of chickens.

"This would be what we call a 'settlement' issue," said Howeth, "and if the producer had concerns about a settlement, Frank would call me to look into all the backup documentation to see what the story was. He wouldn't call the producer back until he himself knew all the facts."

Howeth noted that Frank would try to respond to these kinds of questions as quickly as possible. "He was famous for customer service, but I felt that he also put the same level of effort into providing service for the farmers. He was very customer-producer-farmer oriented."

Frank had every motive to get the payment issue resolved promptly because a good grower could choose to grow for another company. Frank hated to lose a desirable grower.

The way the payment system worked is the growers are paid based on the weight of their finished flock. When a flock of chickens is finished growing and a truck has picked up the birds from the farm, that truck goes to the processing plant where it's put on a scale. The scale weight tells you the gross weight, and then from that you subtract the weight of the truck.

There are many protocols in place to make sure that the weighing is consistent. The truck has to have the same amount of fuel when it is weighed full of chickens and when it is weighed empty; the driver has to be consistently either out of the truck or in it for both weighings; and so on.

During his time with Perdue, Howeth ended up spending many weeks traveling with Frank, accompanying him to the different complexes for the quarterly reviews. They'd usually spend a week on the road, visiting one location, spending the day there, and then driving to the next location, often getting there after midnight or even 1:00 a.m.

Howeth would then meet him the next morning for breakfast at maybe 5:30 a.m. Frank would arrive on time, in coat and tie, having already been out for his morning run.

What really impressed Howeth was that Frank could keep this up day after day for the entire week.

Andrea Williams joined the Company in 1986, starting as a Cost Accountant and is currently Sr. Vice-President, Controller of Perdue Foods LLC. Frank took an interest in Williams' career because he wanted to have more professional women in the company.

According to Williams, "We had many talks through the years, discussing poultry fundamentals and business dynamics. Frank was eager to share his knowledge with those who were eager to learn. I can't imagine there are many Chairmen taking the time to check in on low level accounting staff, but Frank did.

"He told me that he really liked to hire people who had not had everything handed to them – people who had parents who had worked hard to improve themselves and their families' station in life and people who also had worked themselves while they were in school.

ACCOUNTING: THE FUNCTIONAL EQUIVALENT OF AN MRI

FRANK PERDUE'S LESSONS

WATCH THE NUMBERS– Frank paid attention to numbers the way a doctor pays attention to an MRI. For him, numbers were a quick way of understanding what's going on inside the company. He also believed that "The job isn't complete until you collect the money." He visited each facility with his head of Audit Services at least once a quarter to monitor and stay on top of what was going on in the company. He delved into the details of accounting more than CEOs typically do, and he wasn't above talking with new hires about their work and encouraging them in their careers.

CHAPTER FOURTEEN
TRANSITIONING FROM A MEDIUM-SIZE COMPANY TO A VERY LARGE ONE: NOT SMOOTH AND NOT EASY

Although by the mid-1970s Frank knew his part of the chicken industry inside and out, and although there was probably no one in the industry who knew as much as he did about the combined factors of production, advertising, sales, and marketing, even so there were areas where Frank, now in his mid-fifties, was close to deficient.

The skill set that it took to manage a small-to-medium size company was different in concept, character and execution from what it takes to manage a Fortune 500-sized company. The transition was not a smooth one, nor was it easy on any of those involved.

Terry Conway worked for Perdue beginning in December 1970 as Treasurer and CFO, and later became Vice President of Finance. He left in mid-1981 to purchase the Handy Crab Company, but during the time he was with Perdue, he got to witness the kinds of stresses and strains that can keep a small company from growing into a large one.

"In many ways," said Conway, "Frank was quite easy to work for because the guidelines were easy: we had to be the best in every aspect of the company, and the people we worked with on the outside had to be as good as we were on the inside." However, as Conway quickly went on to explain, the story is a lot more complicated than that.

TRANSITIONING FROM A MEDIUM-SIZE COMPANY TO A VERY LARGE ONE: NOT SMOOTH AND NOT EASY

In the 1970s when Conway first joined Perdue Farms, Frank was in his 50s, and in Conway's view, this was a difficult time for him. Frank had to make the business survive and grow, but the business concepts essential for doing so were unfamiliar to him. They were so foreign to Frank that Conway found him "very uncomfortable talking with people who had the kind of experience that I did."

Conway's experience before coming to Perdue included an accounting degree from Notre Dame, a graduate degree from Carnegie Mellon and years of experience in the consulting division of Deloitte & Touche.

"However, my business ideas were not congenial to Frank. I'd make a suggestion and more often than not, his answer might be, 'No, you can't do that,' or, 'I forbid you to do that.'"

Conway took an extraordinary step. "I decided that to survive I had to ignore Frank, to do the right thing, and to be willing to be fired."

It gets even more extreme. "I did some unusual things against his orders, things that had to be done. That was the relationship that we had!"

With his business background, Conway was certain that a lot of things Frank wanted didn't even begin to make sense. For instance, one night Frank called him at 1:00 a.m. saying, "I hate these computers. I want them out of my company; I want you to unplug every one of them and get a truck and get rid of them. *I want them out!*"

When they talked about it the next morning, Conway pointed out that the company payroll was now computerized, and if the company took the computers out, not only would we have to hire and train 20 new people, we'd also have to rent trailers to house the new people.

(As Frank's wife, I have a slightly different interpretation of those words. He loved hyperbole. If I had heard Frank saying them, I would have mentally

145

TRANSITIONING FROM A MEDIUM-SIZE COMPANY TO A VERY LARGE ONE: NOT SMOOTH AND NOT EASY

translated them from Frankish into English, and the results would have been: "These computers are a pain in the neck and at this moment, they're really, really irritating me." End of story. I'd bet money that he didn't mean that he actually wanted the computers removed.)

"Frank had been a yellow-pads-and-pencils kind of a guy," said Conway, "and it took some explaining to make him realize that computers actually save you money and can be more accurate, and they're a good investment."

Conway learned that when he could prove he was right, Frank would quietly retreat. But this kind of contest happened often. Another example that Conway remembers started out as a truly epic battle. The company was expanding and needed another chicken processing complex. However, new complexes were very expensive, difficult to finance, and a new one would take a long time to bring on line.

Frank's wanted to build a new plant so that it would be state of the art and to his specifications. Conway on the other hand wanted to buy an existing complex, knowing that every three or four years there's a downturn and some plants will go out of business. When a big company wants to sell a plant, they usually want to sell it in a hurry, and that can mean some extraordinarily advantageous prices, coupled with the fact that the plant can be rehabbed and up and running relatively quickly.

At exactly this point, Conway learned that Esmark, a big public company, wanted to divest itself of its chicken business, and wanted to do it fast. Without Frank's permission, Conway flew to Chicago and secretly met with the Esmark CEO.

The CEO accepted Conway's offer to buy the complex, which included plants, feed mills and hatcheries, at their depreciated book value under terms that meant Perdue wouldn't be spending additional money for the purchase for the next five years.

TRANSITIONING FROM A MEDIUM-SIZE COMPANY TO A VERY LARGE ONE: NOT SMOOTH AND NOT EASY

The next day Conway, now back in Salisbury, had the unwelcome task of informing Frank; "I just bought five plants from Esmark."

Frank was beyond furious. Angrily he picked up the phone, called the CEO of Esmark, and yelled into the phone, "Conway wasn't authorized to do that. There's no deal!"

According to Conway, "The head of Esmark answered, 'Okay, Frank, we can do that, but it might interest you to know that I just got a call from one of your competitors, and he's offering more.'" Frank immediately changed his mind and Conway was no longer in the doghouse.

"Although Frank later learned a lot about mergers and acquisitions," said Conway, "at the time he didn't understand them, and didn't understand how much we could save by buying at a distress sale and then upgrading to our specifications. It wasn't that he couldn't understand them, but rather that it was so foreign to him that he just hadn't thought about them."

This particular acquisition included the Georgetown processing plant, the Bridgeville feed mill and several hatcheries, all of which proved to be brilliant acquisitions. Right after their purchase, the chicken market recovered from the slump it had been going through and the company was able to pay for the entire purchase in just nine months.

"I've said earlier that it was easy to work for Frank, because of his simply wanting the best, inside or outside the company," continued Conway, "but I sometimes felt that I had to isolate myself from Frank to get things done."

Conway found, in these cases and many others besides, that after the fact, Frank would figure out that it was the right thing to do, and he'd back off. But it was a strange relationship. "I sometimes thought that for Frank, it was as if his whole world was moving out from underneath his feet. It was a new world and he wasn't sure who he could trust, other than Don Mabe, who had the same farming background that he did."

Conway felt that by the time Frank was in his 60s, he had grown into the new reality and was comfortable with what it takes to have a very large company. By then he also had an outside board of directors, and he could bounce things off of them and felt comfortable with them and their experience.

Paul Price, one of the early directors, was impressed that Frank was willing to hire an outside board. From the time Price came on board, Frank's goal was to run Perdue Farms as if it were a publicly owned company. "Given that many owners of privately owned companies don't, he showed great judgment and open-mindedness. He listened to the board and then played it very, very straight."

Viewing all this, Conway summarized it by saying, "It was a big transition, from a small and successful company to a very large and successful company. A lot of people don't make it through that transition, and it's not an easy one, as I got to see firsthand. However, he did it, and it's to his credit."

Conway wasn't alone in finding transitioning to a large company difficult, frustrating, and at times chaotic. One of Frank's flaws was he wasn't good at following chain of command. I got to witness this firsthand many times because I'd hear from people he'd be going around that it was driving them round the bend.

I remember from the management classes I took in the 1960s that almost the first thing you learn when studying administration is the importance of the chain of command. After all, "management is the art of getting things done through others," and there's a lot of academic theory and practical experience that speaks to the importance of operating through the established chain.

TRANSITIONING FROM A MEDIUM-SIZE COMPANY TO A VERY LARGE ONE: NOT SMOOTH AND NOT EASY

Managers and students of management have found over the years that when there's an established hierarchy for reporting problems or communicating with workers, then efficiency, productivity and morale are better. When you break the chain of command and, for example, a worker communicates a problem to his supervisor's manager, the supervisor doesn't have an opportunity to correct the problem.

This not only makes the supervisor look bad, possibly needlessly, but it severely undermines the supervisor's authority. Further, managers, while familiar with higher-level strategies and planning, aren't necessarily prepared to correct operational issues or the day-to-day activities of front-line employees.

There's also the issue of employee morale. Without a clear chain of command, the organization can have an atmosphere of uncertainty or even chaos, which affects the morale of all workers in the organization.

How did Frank feel about all my fancy theories from graduate school? Well … um … he didn't buy them.

Although we talked a lot about issues stemming from his not following the chain of command, especially when I'd hear from other people in the company that Frank was driving them crazy, I didn't feel I could make a really good case for what I believed. After all, the person on the other side of the discussion, that is Frank, had pretty much created a company that at that time employed more than 15,000 people. When he was at a plant and he felt that something needed to be fixed right now, who was I to tug on his sleeve and say, "Wait, Frank, my management class from 25 years ago said, '*Don't do that!*'"

And there was something even bigger involved. The issues that would make him want to interfere and talk with the person who was doing something wrong almost always had to do with quality. It tore at his heart to see a package of chicken going into the distribution system that wasn't perfect. I can still hear him saying, in his pained, slightly high-pitched, squawky voice, "You lose market share one disappointed customer at a time." He didn't want to have a single disappointed customer, let alone hundreds, all because an associate was getting something wrong.

It wasn't in his DNA to wait to talk to someone higher up in management and then be patient until a corrective practice was put in place. This was especially true when he could just talk with the associate right then and there and, as far as he was concerned, fix things.

Frank and I even discussed this exact point: Do you wait until some broad guidelines are issued, even if that takes days, when that might mean countless packages of chicken that Frank didn't want his name on going into the distribution system?

Frank's management style was actually something that family members talked about a lot. We'd often discuss how the personality it takes to found a company (hard-charging, doing what it takes to get the job done, even if it creates a certain amount of chaos) is almost certainly not the same personality that it takes to keep a large company functioning smoothly.

I've often thought that Frank was almost divinely lucky to have a son who had a more process-oriented, rules-sensitive approach than he did. If Jim Perdue had had the same "If I see a problem, I'm going to deal with it, and I'm going to deal with the person who's doing and I'm going to do it right now!" approach that Frank did, I think the company would not have been able to grow. Since Jim took over, Perdue Farms has almost doubled in size, which I take as proof that Jim's personality is exactly the kind needed to keep the business running.

This is a small aside on the subject of leadership style and chain of command, but several times associates would tell me that Frank's going around them

TRANSITIONING FROM A MEDIUM-SIZE COMPANY TO A VERY LARGE ONE: NOT SMOOTH AND NOT EASY

was driving them crazy. There's irony to what I just said because by my talking with them, I was skirting the chain of command principles that I was forever preaching.

My defense? Well, as I often told my dear children, "Do as I say and not as I do!"

Anyway, when people would confide in me that Frank was making life difficult by going around them, I'd tell Frank that there was a problem, but I'd also tell him that I was changing all the details radically enough to disguise the source. When Frank wanted to know who it was who had said whatever it was that I was reporting to him, I'd answer him, "If I told you who it was, or even gave you enough details to make it possible for you to guess, no one would trust me anymore and you wouldn't get the feedback that I know you crave."

Since Frank passionately valued feedback of any sort, this satisfied him and he never pressed me for details that would burn my sources. I admired him for that.

I wouldn't recommend that anyone copy what I just described. I don't think any of it was good management practice. All I can say is, it happened. Lots.

But back to Frank and management theory. To me it's interesting (and actually, I hope it's interesting to you as well), that Frank built the large and successful company that he did without a management degree and by paying no attention to one of the most fundamental principals in all of management.

There were upsides to Frank's approach of jumping in with both feet and talking with whoever was part of a problem, chain of command be darned. It strengthened the culture of quality that he so wanted to instill. Ah, but the downside! Read and enjoy Larry Winslow's story.

TRANSITIONING FROM A MEDIUM-SIZE COMPANY TO A VERY LARGE ONE: NOT SMOOTH AND NOT EASY

Consequences of Not Following the Chain of Command

Winslow was particularly interested in how Frank related to the management concept of chain of command in that it often impacted him and his ability to do his job. Winslow worked for Perdue Farms from 1981 to the time of his retirement in 2004. He started out as the Plant PrePak Manager and finished his career as Vice President of Supply Chain Management. Frank used to call him, "My Plant Guy."

Winslow's previous work experience had been with a very formal company where protocol was emphasized and following the organizational rules was strictly followed. He quickly discovered that Perdue Farms was different. When he had been with Perdue for two months, his secretary rushed into his small office at the plant, her eyes as big as saucers.

"Frank Perdue wants to talk with you!" she said, seemingly hardly able to believe her own words.

"OK, fine, I'll call him." Winslow calmly answered.

"No, you don't understand," she said urgently, acting almost scared. "He's on the phone right now!"

"I can still see her face," remembered Winslow. "It was as if she had gotten a phone call from the heavens. There were about 5,000 men and women working for Perdue at that point, and she could hardly imagine that the Big Boss himself had called *me*."

Winslow could hardly believe it himself. In other companies that he knew of, the CEO would never talk with someone as far down as he was. The call, by the way, was Frank wanting to know how the plant was doing in increasing volume on the prepackaged chicken products. It was the first of many such calls.

TRANSITIONING FROM A MEDIUM-SIZE COMPANY TO A VERY LARGE ONE: NOT SMOOTH AND NOT EASY

Winslow found some pluses to this approach of Frank's talking with anyone at anytime when something concerned him. But as he watched Frank over the years, he also witnessed and even experienced himself that the results could be painfully disruptive.

"For one thing, when he was focusing on something, he'd make it be everyone's priority, even though in the judgment of many or even most of us, that focus meant other priorities wouldn't be addressed. This was a routine occurrence."

In the late 1980s, the top management included Don Mabe, Harry Palmer, Pelham Lawrence and Jim Smallwood. According to Winslow, Frank loved to go around each of them. Winslow can still remember Frank's telling him more than once, "Don't tell Mabe I talked with you."

Worse, according to Winslow, everyone else was doing the same thing. At the time Winslow didn't find this funny, but looking back on it many years later, it was comical.

"It was a love-hate type thing. With all this going around each other, sometimes people couldn't stand each other and the next minute, it's 'This guy is my brother.' It was a really unusual thing how they interacted. They had fought a lot of battles together, so I guess they understood it and they each made it work."

The Culture Tolerated Disagreement and Strong Opinions

For Winslow this meant the people in the company weren't as professional as they should be. But on the other hand, he saw value in having a culture in which people didn't hold in their issues. The culture tolerated really forceful disagreement.

Winslow particularly remembers a day when he and 15 of his colleagues were sitting around a conference table with Frank and Don Mabe. Initially these two were sitting beside each other, facing everyone else at the conference table. But they started to argue, and gradually edged their chairs around until they were completely facing each other, their heads inches apart, and they were yelling at each other. It was an important topic for Frank and he was willing to push hard and Don Mabe was not willing to back down.

As Winslow saw it, the company culture allowed people to be passionate about an issue, and individuals had no problem raising their voices. "It was not the best way to run a large business. In fact, it was more like you would interact in a family basis." This behavior, already described earlier with Jack Tatem and Cornish hens, happened a lot.

The Quality Improvement Process

A major improvement began occurring in 1985. If was one of the major cultural changes that was essential for converting from a small company to a very large one and it had to do with the level at which decisions were made. Before Frank and his son Jim embarked on the Quality Improvement Process (QIP) in 1985, the decision-making and problem-solving tended to be done mostly at the top. However, in 1985, both Jim and Frank began working to have decision-making and problem-solving occur at lower levels, including right down to the level of the hourly associates.

Quoting his father, Jim Perdue said, "Nobody knows more about a job than the person working in his or her own twenty-five square feet. If you have a problem, go to the expert, the person who is doing the work. Have that person sit in on meetings, ask his or her advice."

Jim Perdue believed and still believes that by involving people, and by keeping them informed, "You develop a team, and you have stakeholders rather than workers who only pick up pay checks."

TRANSITIONING FROM A MEDIUM-SIZE COMPANY TO A VERY LARGE ONE: NOT SMOOTH AND NOT EASY

However, changing a corporate culture required a major effort and a major commitment. "It took many years," Jim Perdue said. "Every hourly person got an eight-hour course, and every salaried person got a twelve-hour course, on Quality Management."

Frank himself recognized during this period that with 12,500 associates and eight plants, management had to depend on decisions being made at lower and lower levels. It was a major transition for the company.

Rob Heflin, former Vice President of Human Resources, was heavily involved in this effort. The QIP had a major impact on Heflin's specialty.

As Heflin explains, "Frank was always a voracious reader, and he was tremendously influenced by Phil Crosby's book, *Quality Is Free.*"

According to Heflin, some of the premises that Frank absorbed from *Quality is Free* include the ideas that:

- Quality is much too important to be left solely to the quality control department
- Senior management must commit to training and engaging the workforce to change the culture
- Doing things right the first time adds absolutely nothing to the cost of a product or service.

"Before Crosby," said Heflin, "we had always measured quality, but it had been after the fact, the kind of thing where we'd run production and then measure how much that came out of production didn't meet our standards. Now Frank wanted us to focus on getting out in front of problems, instead of measuring results afterwards. Or in other words, we needed to prevent the defects to begin with. The goal was doing it right the first time."

To help implement this new approach, Frank made it mandatory that all top management attend Phil Crosby's Quality College in Florida. The company sent 50 top people for five days, and then building on that, with the help of consultants, undertook training everyone else.

A Major Change in Attitude

QIP meant a major change in attitude, according to Frank Shipper, a professor of Management at the Perdue School of Business. "Before the Quality Improvement Process, it used to be that writing someone up was a sign of your manhood. Supervisors at Perdue carried pink slips in their pockets and if they saw someone doing something wrong, someone was going to get one of those slips."

However, after the QIP, the approach was positive reinforcement for good things. When you saw someone doing something good, you were to give him or her a reward such as a free lunch pass at the cafeteria.

Incidentally, shortly after instituting the free lunch pass awards, Frank learned that in many, many cases, people weren't turning them in. The recipients were saving the passes as if they were merit badges, displaying them on their lockers or even taking them home and framing them.

Changing the culture from faultfinding to praising good work was a momentously positive factor both for the company and for Frank. For both it reflected an ability to grow and to change.

In nature, the organisms that survive and thrive aren't necessarily the fastest or the smartest (although that may help), but rather the ones that can adapt, and when needed, change. The company and Frank did learn to adapt and change, putting them in that rare and elite group that successfully transitions from a medium-size company to a large one.

TRANSITIONING FROM A MEDIUM-SIZE COMPANY TO A VERY LARGE ONE: NOT SMOOTH AND NOT EASY

FRANK PERDUE'S LESSONS

TO SURVIVE AND THRIVE, BE READY TO CHANGE AND ADAPT – Many companies fail to make the transition from a medium size company to a very large one. Frank was able to make the transition, but it was not smooth. As someone who grew up on a farm and hadn't finished college, Frank wasn't familiar with concepts he might have learned in business school, such as finance and he always had trouble with the management principle of chain of command. Having an experienced board of directors and embracing the principles of the Quality Improvement Process, including pushing decision-making further down in the organization, were essential to making the transition.

CHAPTER FIFTEEN
TURKEYS: THE ONLY THING THEY HAVE IN COMMON WITH CHICKENS IS FEATHERS

During these struggles of growing from a medium-size company to a very large one, people at Perdue were working on extending the brand from chickens into turkeys. This new avenue of growth ought to have meant a huge carryover of knowledge between the two kinds of birds.

It didn't.

As Tom Schaffer, Director of Live Production for Turkeys at our Washington, Indiana complex told me one day, "Back in 1984, we all thought turkeys were just big chickens. We quickly learned that while they both have feathers, that's about all that they have in common."

He has vivid memories of the continuing shock they all experienced when the company began growing turkeys. For instance, for their first ten days, baby turkeys, known as poults, need to be kept in a smaller space than baby chickens. The reason is, unlike a baby chick, poults aren't good at finding food and water, and they don't even know how to move to where it's warm. Whatever they need has to be right nearby, and that means the little poults have to be in a tightly confined space.

There's also a difference in who grows the tom and the hen turkeys. Since toms are grown to 40 pounds, and since they're naturally more aggressive than hen turkeys – sort of like a bull is likely to be more aggressive than a

TURKEYS: THE ONLY THING
THEY HAVE IN COMMON WITH
CHICKENS IS FEATHERS

cow – it's usually someone with considerable upper body strength who chooses to grow the toms. The hen turkeys, maxing out at about 23 pounds, are easier to lift and generally just plain easier to get along with.

One of the perks for growing turkeys for Perdue is the annual Producer Day picnic, when all the turkey growers and their families are invited to an appreciation event. There's usually a big cookout, the company brings in a carnival with rides for the children, and it's generally a nice day for the 250 or so producers who attend with their families. Frank would always attend and sign pictures for them. He wanted us to show up at these events because he wanted the producers to know and feel that they were important to him.

Schaffer first met Frank at one of the Producer Days, and shortly after that, got personally involved with him in a way that wasn't the kind of attention Schaffer was hoping for. It had to do with an awards banquet for the turkey producers.

Schaffer knew that the year before, the company had spent one heck of a lot of money on the first awards banquet. Schaffer hadn't been in charge for the first banquet, but when he looked at what Perdue had paid for the three-course seated dinner for 300, plus an expensive out-of-town speaker, he reasonably enough concluded that here would be an area where he could economize and help the company's bottom line.

He knew there had to be an awards banquet, but to control the cost he reasoned that the company could at least save a substantial amount of money by inviting fewer guests. He decided to limit the awards banquet to the 40 or so growers who had actually won the awards that would be given out.

It was not the right move. When Frank came through the door to the banquet hall that night, his first words to Schaffer were, "Where are all the people?"

TURKEYS: THE ONLY THING
THEY HAVE IN COMMON WITH
CHICKENS IS FEATHERS

Frank often showed his great sense of humor.

Schaffer told him about saving money, but Frank would have none of it. He instructed Schaffer in future years to invite everyone. "The guy who won the Route Award is important," Frank let him know, "but so is everyone else!"

From then on, Schaffer made sure that every year that every producer would be invited. And as usual, until it was medically impossible, Frank would make sure that we always attended, flying from Maryland to Indiana just for the event and returning that night. Frank understood that making this effort underscored the importance he attached to the turkey producers.

Schaffer saw that Frank also made a similar effort with the people in the plants. Frank had many important things he could be doing, but even so, he'd go around the turkey processing plant talking with people. "He'd simply take the time to do it," said Schaffer. "A lot of people in top management in other companies get to thinking they're too important for that kind of thing, but not Frank. This didn't go unnoticed, I can tell you!"

I don't think there's a management course on this, and I wonder if someone has written a book on it, but I think Frank was onto something: management by making people feel important. With the growers and the associates at the plant, not only in Indiana, but actually everywhere, he always went way, way out of his way to show them that they were important to him. It created a reciprocal bond among them.

Still, Frank could be tough, and Schaffer was once the brunt of it. Frank had wanted to visit the turkey breeder farm, but when Schaffer picked him up at his hotel, he saw to his horror that Frank's trousers were torn at the knee.

TURKEYS: THE ONLY THING THEY HAVE IN COMMON WITH CHICKENS IS FEATHERS

Schaffer could see through the gap in the torn fabric that Frank had a badly bleeding gash. Frank had fallen during his usual early morning run.

"We need to get you to the hospital!" Schaffer said urgently, assuming he was saying something obvious.

"No, we'll just stop at a CVS and get some bandages," Frank answered. He didn't want to take time for a hospital visit since it would take time away from his visit to the breeder farm.

Frank and Schaffer arrived at the farm, Frank now wearing several layers of bandages to stop the bleeding. The normal procedure at this point would have been to take a shower before entering the breeder house. It's for bio-security because you don't want to bring in diseases that might harm the turkeys.

However, Frank wasn't eager to take a shower since that would mean getting all his bandages wet. Schaffer scrambled to get Frank some sterile overalls, and then thought everything would be fine.

It wasn't. The next morning Schaffer got a phone call from his boss's boss in Salisbury, Keith Shoemaker. "Schaffer, what the hell did you do? The first thing Frank did when he got back was call me and tell me 'Schaffer didn't make me shower!'"

Schaffer was in trouble, and he knew it.

"I don't care if Jesus Christ Himself shows up, He takes a shower!" Shoemaker yelled at Schaffer.

"Trust me," said Schaffer, "we haven't broken bio-security since. The good thing is, first Frank was right to pay attention to this, and second, he didn't hold a grudge."

TURKEYS: THE ONLY THING THEY HAVE IN COMMON WITH CHICKENS IS FEATHERS

Schaffer has an amusing memory of the first time he took Frank through one of the breeder operations. He knew that Frank was always eager to learn new things, and turkey hens are very different from chicken hens. For one thing, they signal that they're ready for a male's attentions by kind of squatting low to the ground. It's an in-born, instinctive behavior, but Frank couldn't have known this, given that his experience up to this point had been limited to chickens.

"We were going through the turkey house," said Schaffer, "and somehow the presence of tall, moving creatures (namely Frank and me) was confusing to the turkey hens and they began squatting.

"Hey Tom, c'mere," Frank called. "How are they laying?'

"'Pretty good,' I answered as I walked up next to him.

"'But how can you expect them to produce good turkeys when they have such bad legs?' He was looking at the 2,500 hens, many of which were looking at him and squatting.

"'Frank, they don't have bad legs! That's what they do when they signal that they're ready to mate.'

"Frank thought about it a moment and then said, in his wry, joking, off-the-wall voice, 'Wouldn't it be great if you could tell the same thing with people!'"

Selling the Turkeys

Growing the turkeys was one part of Perdue's getting into turkey production, but another crucial part of it was selling the turkeys. Joe Gilmore, who began with Perdue in 1986, spent a good part of his career in turkey sales.

By the way, Gilmore was among the first associates I ever met at Perdue. It was during Frank's and my six-week engagement that I met Gilmore while

TURKEYS: THE ONLY THING
THEY HAVE IN COMMON WITH
CHICKENS IS FEATHERS

accompanying Frank to a marketing meeting in Long Island.

I'm having a little trouble remembering why going with Frank to a marketing meeting in Long Island was part of our courtship. Still, it seemed perfectly natural at the time.

Anyway, Gilmore had a big reason to remember that Long Island meeting. It has nothing to do with meeting me and everything to do with how Frank behaved.

The meeting was about a quality issue. As Gilmore told it, "The customer had a legitimate complaint, because we had recently installed new equipment and were having start-up problems with one of machines for deli meat. The resulting texture of the boneless deli turkey meat was unacceptably soft."

The Perdue team of maybe five people was taken to a small conference room with no windows, dim lighting, and there were about ten people from the customer's side. We were sitting around a conference table, but some were sitting on chairs to the side. An easel was available for Gilmore to use for a presentation.

Gilmore had worked hard on his talk. "We were acknowledging the problem," said Gilmore, "telling how it came about, and what we were doing to make sure that it never, ever happened again. And also, how we'd be making it up to them."

However, Gilmore didn't get to make his case because the customer had hired a consultant, and the guy kept interrupting Gilmore with hostile statements. The consultant seemed bent on making Perdue look as bad as possible, and as far as I could see, the consultant had zero interest in hearing our side, and it seemed as if his whole purpose was to give Gilmore a really hard time.

TURKEYS: THE ONLY THING
THEY HAVE IN COMMON WITH
CHICKENS IS FEATHERS

Wait, I'm being too charitable. I thought the consultant was trying to look important by putting Gilmore down, and the whole performance seemed like a thuggish guy being a bully. I was feeling both embarrassed and angry watching this.

To go back to Gilmore's version of the meeting, "After this went on for awhile, Frank told the customer that he had enough of this. He told the customer that the consultant was messing with his guy and he'd better stop it."

Gilmore was as grateful as a man can be. "I felt as if my field commander was showing that he had my back!"

Thinking back on that event, when Frank showed he wasn't going to let his guy be bullied, Gilmore said, "When I've interviewed job candidates I often pose the question "Tell me about the best boss you ever had?" The consistent answer over a long period of time includes these responses:

"They were competent in their field of work."

"I learned from him or her."

"I trusted him or her."

"They had my back."

"They cared about me."

"They were tough but fair."

Gilmore said, "In other words, the very definition of what it was like to work for or with Frank."

There's a p.s. to this story. Perdue Farms didn't lose the turkey deli business, and the consultant lost his job. The distributor used to tell that story for years, how Frank would defend his employees.

TURKEYS: THE ONLY THING
THEY HAVE IN COMMON WITH
CHICKENS IS FEATHERS

Although Gilmore appreciated that Frank had his back, he knew that there was no doubt that Frank could be a really tough man. "There was a phrase that you'd regularly hear from him whenever there was a problem: 'How long have you known about this and what have you done about it?' It made us know that we weren't working for a slack organization, and the toughness of it and the accountability created an esprit almost like the military."

It's not an accident that Gilmore used a military comparison. He had been a Naval Flight Officer prior to working for Perdue and he was used to a culture of never making excuses, never compromising on facts, and always paying attention to detail. Further, if you don't know an answer, say "I don't know sir, but I will find out."

All this gave him a certain comfort level in adjusting to the Perdue culture. "These things were important to Frank, along with his demands for a strong work ethic."

Frank had a penchant for favoring the underdog, something that turned out to be fortunate for Gilmore. Back in the late 1980s, the turkey and food-service segment of the business (that is, the foods that people would eat outside the home in restaurants and so on) was a relative stepchild in comparison to the chicken sold on the retail side at supermarkets and groceries.

Even so, Frank understood the kind of value that turkey and food service could bring to the company. "'People are spending all this money eating away from home,' Frank would point out, "and we need to make sure it includes Perdue products."

With this on his radar, Frank made sure to give Gilmore the resources needed to grow his side of the business. "He foresaw the changing trend in eating out and understood the need to respond," said Gilmore.

TURKEYS: THE ONLY THING THEY HAVE IN COMMON WITH CHICKENS IS FEATHERS

Gilmore valued the personal side of Frank. "Something that happened over and over again, whenever there were tumultuous times, things that could have affected my morale, I could absolutely count on the fact that he would come by and check on me."

Sometimes Frank would just show up in Gilmore's office. He'd sit in the chair next to Gilmore's desk and ask how he was doing. He's always ask after Gilmore's wife Jennifer and their children, Jordan and Sydney, wanting to know if they were doing OK.

"He always left me with the impression that he cared," said Gilmore.

Like everyone else, Gilmore got some of the infamous middle-of-the-night Frank phone calls. Jennifer, sleeping on the side of the bed where the phone was, would wake up and sleepily pass the phone over to her husband, knowing the call would be from Frank.

The phone calls never began with, "Hey Joe, sorry to be calling you so late!" Instead, Frank's first words were likely to be something like, "I was looking at your numbers and…" Frank acted like there's nothing unusual about this.

Gilmore's reaction to the phone calls was, "That's how Frank was. He had some ways about him that are different and that difference is one of the reasons this company has been so successful. If he needed something from me at 3:00 a.m., as far as I was concerned, he was going to get it."

"Something else about Frank," said Gilmore, "He was always in pursuit of credibility. He didn't want fakes. If you were in this business and you were a phony, you wouldn't last long around Frank Perdue. He was a phony-killer."

Gilmore remembered once when he had to tell Frank about a serious screw up. "Frank," Gilmore said, "I was going to give you all the reasons for this, but the bottom line is I screwed up."

TURKEYS: THE ONLY THING
THEY HAVE IN COMMON WITH
CHICKENS IS FEATHERS

Gilmore loved Frank's reaction. "It was great. He respected and admired everyone who was honest with him, and you knew there would be no retribution. His reaction was, he wanted to know how he could help."

Gilmore enjoyed his time with, as he puts it, "The tough man with a tender heart."

Turkeys and Politics

Pepper Laughon, Chairman Emeritus of Richmond Cold Storage, got to see yet another side to Frank and turkeys. Frank adored Pepper Laughon, admiring his honesty and competence, plus both of them had in common that in a business setting they could be tough as nails, while in social settings they both acted like men whom Central Casting had chosen to play "old school Southern gentlemen."

Laughon's company has been dealing with Perdue since 1986. He and Frank got to know each other when, as Laughon remembered, "Some lobbyist had managed to insert into a federal law that you could claim that your turkeys were fresh, even if they were frozen hard as a rock." This Orwellian law of "frozen equals fresh" put Frank at a competitive disadvantage, given that he had the extra expense of dealing with a perishable product.

Frank asked Laughon for help in getting the law changed, and the two men called on Laughon's local senator. "'You're absolutely right,' the Senator agreed after hearing the case, "and I'll be the sponsor."

However, it didn't work out.

Laughon and Frank waited anxiously for the Senator to swing into action, but nothing happened. Finally the two men talked with the lawmaker, wanting to find out why the delay.

"Even though I thought you were right," the Senator admitted, "I had to trade that vote for something more important."

TURKEYS: THE ONLY THING
THEY HAVE IN COMMON WITH
CHICKENS IS FEATHERS

Eventually the law did get changed, but both men had a problem with, as Laughon puts it, "the total dishonesty of saying that a turkey was fresh even it was frozen so hard that you could use it to pound a nail into a two-by-four."

The experience cemented their relationship because it showed that they operated from the same set of rules. "I enjoy working with people whose work ethics and philosophy are in line with what we do, people who do what they say they're going to do and whom you can depend on," said Laughon. "Life is too short to deal with people who aren't ethical."

The two men also had something else in common. "Frank and I were customer service freaks," Laughon said. "We always wanted answers for our patrons before they thought of the questions or desires. Perfection was a major goal for both of us every minute of every day."

When students ask Laughon for advice, he likes to tell them something that in the end relates to Frank and his success.

"I tell them, your attitude is your altitude. It's your attitude that is going to put you where you end up in life. If your attitude is bad you're going to have a bad life. On the other hand, if your attitude includes integrity and a willingness to work hard and to give back, you're going to have a great life."

FRANK PERDUE'S LESSONS

MAKE PEOPLE FEEL IMPORTANT– Frank would attend grower events, even ones 800 miles away in Washington, Indiana, knowing that this signaled to the growers that they were important to him. He'd also talk with workers on the line and didn't stint on recognition events and family events.

TURKEYS: THE ONLY THING
THEY HAVE IN COMMON WITH
CHICKENS IS FEATHERS

SUPPORT YOUR EMPLOYEES– Frank wouldn't put up with anyone's abusing his employees. One of the ingredients of an ideal boss is he has your back.

CHAPTER SIXTEEN
RESEARCH AND DEVELOPMENT: AN EDGE ON THE COMPETITION

Research and development must have been in Frank's blood. After all, as a child he had watched his father study the poultry magazines and eventually buy $25 leghorn roosters from Texas. Mr. Arthur had figured out that it was worth researching the best breeds and paying extra for them since it meant that the chickens from his hatchery were going to perform better than those of the competition.

Frank saw that it paid off: farmers strongly preferred his father's hatchery's baby chicks and the hatchery grew. Research of the sort he learned from his father suited Frank's personality, and besides, it turned him on intellectually.

Plus, of course, he liked the results. To get those results, he hired geneticists, microbiologists, avian scientists, veterinary scientists, nutritionists and individuals who were expert in the best animal husbandry practices. As Professor George Rubenson from the Perdue School of Business said, "Perdue is an acknowledged industry leader in the use of research and technology."

Frank would often quote the story of an old sea captain who told his son, "My competition copies everything I do, but they can't copy my mind and I leave 'em huffing and puffing a mile and a half behind." For Frank, research and development were the magic keys to leaving competitors "huffing and puffing a mile and a half behind."

RESEARCH AND DEVELOPMENT: AN EDGE ON THE COMPETITION

Research and Development, Birds

Bruce Stewart-Brown has been with Perdue since 1998 and is today Senior Vice President of Food Safety, Quality, and Live Production. He saw Frank as being surprisingly "birdy," meaning that Frank could talk knowledgeably about raising chickens. Stewart-Brown would have expected that someone running such a large company might be exclusively a financial type, as opposed to one who could also be "birdy."

"Frank was very interested in what we were learning and studying on how to raise chickens in the best possible way," said Stewart-Brown. "Frank valued technical expertise and he wanted us to have the tools we needed to study whatever needed to be studied. When he hired Dr. Frank Craig, a professor at North Carolina State, Craig was the first veterinarian hired by a poultry company."

That began a long history of research and a focus on studying how to raise and process chickens in the best possible way. As Stewart-Brown said, "We have farms where we work on making sure the feed is constantly tailored to the evolving chicken breeds. We have labs that have state-of-the-art equipment and qualified experts who are capable and respected by regulators and academicians, as well as customers."

Frank's aim was always to be a year or more ahead of the universities' research. When there was a promising line of research that might take two to three years to test in the land grant colleges, Perdue had (and has) the research facilities to test it and to put it into practice in a third less time.

There was always a lot at stake in the research. Even a small improvement in, for example, feed conversion, can be worth millions of dollars, and the ability to do the research quickly can save big money. Frank knew that spending money on research gave Perdue Farms an edge on the competition

Frank also knew that as a privately owned company, he could invest in research that wouldn't pay off for ten years. Further, he could maintain a high level of research even during downturns in the market. A publicly owned company, having to answer to the stockholders about each quarter's returns, would generally not have the same flexibility.

Research and Development, on the Farm

Jack Brittingham also got a view of Frank's interest in research, but from an on-farm vantage point. Brittingham began with Perdue Farms in February of 1959 and stayed 38 years.

Much of his work over that period was coordinating on-farm experiments. When something looked good on the research farms, Brittingham's job was to test it out on some of the local farms to see if it would work under actual production conditions.

By the way, Frank sometimes talked with me about how things that look great in the laboratory or under research conditions may not work at all under normal on-farm conditions. Frank's approach was to pilot whatever it was on a few farms before recommending it for them all.

One example of something that did make it from laboratory to research farm to sample production farms to industry practice is what we call "tunnel ventilation." In the past, chicken houses were cooled by opening windows. Unfortunately, when you get a summer heat wave, opening windows isn't terribly effective. Heat causes the birds stress, and since a stressed chicken doesn't grow well, a heat wave used to be a major problem for poultry growers.

Brittingham had heard of experiments in other parts of the country for dealing with summer heat in the chicken houses by using evaporative cooling. He and his colleagues began experimenting to see if they could make it work for chicken houses locally.

They began with spraying a mist of water at one end of the chicken house; as it evaporated, it immediately cooled the nearby air. At the other end of the chicken house, the men installed powerful fans that pulled the cooled air through the 400-foot long, 40-foot wide structure. The cooled air being pulled through the 'tunnel' of the chicken house could easily be 10 degrees cooler than the outside air.

It was a clever, inexpensive, energy-efficient and highly effective way of air-conditioning a very large space, and as a pleased Brittingham said, "It turned out that the hotter the weather, the better the ventilation system worked."

By piloting it at various locations, Brittingham and his colleagues were able to prove that it worked beautifully for local farmers. It rapidly became standard practice.

Brittingham enjoyed his time with Frank, but admits that Frank really was a tough man. "I remember once he told me, 'I'd fire my own brother if I had to!' But then he jokingly punched me in the arm and said 'You know I don't have a brother.'"

Getting Into Further Processed

Perdue Farms had always done extensive genetics and animal husbandry research, but in 1995, research efforts were augmented to include "further processed." At Perdue, "further processed" means items such as fully cooked chicken, or breaded chicken, or anything that goes beyond selling uncooked chicken.

Our involvement in further processed, however, was definitely a case of Perdue's coming late to the party. Perdue's chief competitor, Tyson, had already been doing this for years, and it had proven to be a lucrative value-added business for them. In addition, the income from value-added products is more stable, since it's at least somewhat insulated from the vagaries of weather and grain prices.

The reason why we were late was at least in part because we had our own version of value-added. After all, we had the fresh, yellow-skin chicken, and

RESEARCH AND DEVELOPMENT: AN EDGE
ON THE COMPETITION

we had the huge competitive advantage of being close to the large population centers of New York, Philadelphia and Boston. For decades the company hadn't felt the price pressure that would have jolted us into making changes.

However, by 1995, it was clear to all of top management that Perdue needed to get into further-processed operations, and we needed to do it fast. At this point the company hired Dr. Bob Vimini as Director of Research and Development.

Vimini has a doctorate in food science, and his activities included not just helping Perdue get into further processed, but in addition he headed all the R & D, including working with anyone inside the company or out who has expertise in any part of what it takes to improve quality, decrease waste and improve efficiency.

Naturally, all of this was close to Frank's heart. Vimini kept the door to his ten-foot by ten-foot office open, and sometime during the day, he could usually count on Frank's popping in.

Maybe it's because Vimini is a great guy (which he is), but more likely the reason Frank would stop by his office and spend ten or fifteen minutes almost every day talking with him was because Frank really, really liked any part of research. And of course Frank wanted to know about any projects that might leave his competitors "huffing and puffing a mile and a half behind."

When Vimini thinks about those many times with Frank, he remembers that Frank would occasionally quote Ralph Waldo Emerson: "If a man can write a better book, preach a better sermon, or make a better mousetrap than his neighbor, then the world will beat a path to his door, though it be in the woods."

In Vimini's view, Frank embodied the maxim about a better mousetrap, or in this case, a better chicken. Vimini observed that Frank hired more professionals in the technical aspects of producing chicken than any other company, although other companies eventually copied him. "Frank was definitely the first that stressed that area," said Vimini.

When it came to Vimini's work, "Frank had a surprisingly deep knowledge and would ask intelligent questions." But in addition, the daily conversations often included an offer to help if there were any roadblocks from a business standpoint. Frank wanted to make sure Vimini had the resources to get his job done.

Product Evaluation and Taste Testing

Vimini said that during the product evaluations, which Frank would often participate in, Frank would talk about the features of the product that we had to offer in comparison with the competition. The product had to taste good and have good sensory qualities, but it also had to look appealing because consumers also buy with their eyes.

To get the taste and sensory qualities right, Vimini would have blind tastings with 8 to 24 people, and they'd frequently include comparisons between our products and the products of competitors. The tasters often came from Sales and Marketing, since these individuals were more in touch than anyone about what customers want. "In fact," said Vimini, "we worked so closely with them that it's like we were joined at the hip."

But tasters would also include people from Quality Assurance, top management, or simply associates who were recruited for the taste tests. Frank would occasionally be among them, as would I.

For a typical taste testing, they'd have a checklist in everyone's hands with 10 or 20 qualities that they were evaluating. I got to be part of one of the taste testings for evaluating whether people prefer dark meat or white meat. It was fascinating how much effort they put into getting accurate information on this.

There were eight of us testers, and we were asked to sit in separate but adjoining booths in the tasting room. We couldn't see each other and we weren't supposed to talk, and further, we couldn't hear sounds from outside the room so the whole experience was totally about focusing on our task.

I was curious how it would be a fair test since we could have made up our minds ahead of time. If we "knew" we liked white meat, then we might choose that as the tastiest when asked to grade it.

The people who conducted the test got around that problem. They served us cooked chicken in the form of 1-inch ground patties. The cubicles each had a red fluorescent light that entirely masked the color of the chicken meat so even though I looked and looked, I couldn't see any color difference.

Having the chickens in patties meant the mouthfeel was pretty much the same for all three. The patties were lightly and identically seasoned with salt, so that an average person would consider the seasoning hardly noticeable. They weren't completely unseasoned, because that in itself would be distracting.

Anyway, I couldn't tell by sight or mouthfeel or any other way whether I was eating: a) breast meat (that is white meat); b) thigh meat (dark meat); c) or neck meat (the darkest meat of all).

We tasters were then invited to sample each patty and give our opinion of its flavor. I noticed that two of the patties seemed full of flavor and one seemed OK but kind of flat. They didn't tell us which kind we had preferred, but I did learn afterwards that dark meat, particularly neck meat, is the overwhelming favorite of most people when they don't know whether they're eating dark meat or white meat chicken.

Vimini's department determined that the more a muscle moves, the darker the meat will be, and the more desirable the taste. Other things being equal, people prefer thighs, wings and necks if they're going by flavor alone.

RESEARCH AND DEVELOPMENT: AN EDGE ON THE COMPETITION

Even Good Products Don't Always Make It

Taste testing is a critical part of product development, but only a part. Frank was well aware that most new ideas don't work out. If you have a 20 percent success rate with new products, you're doing well.

Things that can go wrong include that maybe the consumer just doesn't accept them, or a national buyer changes its mind, or the cost structure of the product is too high.

One product that Frank really, really liked was a Perdue chicken potpie. It should have been a roaring success because our taste testers said the abundance of perfect fresh chicken chunks along with other premium ingredients were vastly, vastly better than any competing product. Actually, Frank and I got to taste it, and I remember thinking that it was far and away the best chicken potpie I had ever set tooth to. I couldn't wait to buy Perdue chicken potpies at our local grocery store.

The potpies never made it to the market, though, because of how distribution works in the supermarket industry. As Vimini explained it, "Our potpie would have been only one product in this space, and in order to get the supermarket to carry it, we'd need a whole line of pot pies. The same rationale is applicable to other popular chicken products like chicken salad and shredded barbecue chicken."

Speaking of new products that don't make it to market, when Frank was alive, maybe half a dozen times a year someone would write to him, hoping to get royalties for a great chicken recipe, maybe one that had come down in the family and that was popular with everyone who tried it.

The fact is, no matter how excellent an individual's recipe is, it will virtually never work on a commercial scale. If you're developing a recipe that will feed millions of consumers you face an array of constraints and complications that you just don't have when you're cooking for your family or church or club. You need to take into account food safety, plus sourcing and handling the ingredients in a way that their flavors are stable and will taste good after being mass-produced. Another obstacle is you need to be able to produce it a price that is affordable for the consumer.

As Vimini said, "Developing a commercially viable recipe takes our home economists and food scientists an average of six months of formulating and testing. In the case of Perdue Short Cuts®, it took almost three years of unrelenting effort."

(Perdue Short Cuts® are fully cooked chicken and turkey breast products in various styles such as grilled, Italian or honey roasted.)

Like many others, Vimini accompanied Frank on plant visits. "Often we'd be gone for a week at a time. We'd hit as many plants as possible, maybe up to eight of them. The amazing thing is, no matter which of the plants we were visiting, he knew a huge number of people on the production line by name.

"He was great with the hourly associates. He'd remember the last time he had seen them, and he could carry on a conversation with them as if he had been talking with them the day before."

I asked Vimini about whether Frank was as tough as his reputation. "No, not at all, he was inspiring, and I miss him. He expected you to work hard, but as for being tough to work for, no, he was just a nice and compassionate and understanding person."

Vimini has a line from Robert Frost that makes him think of Frank: "Two roads diverged in a wood and I took the least traveled." "Instead of copying what everyone else was doing," said Vimini, "Frank took the trouble to listen to what the consumer wanted and he developed a better chicken. That's what we carry on today, building a better food product. It's not an easy thing to do, but we have a solid heritage and tradition of doing just that."

RESEARCH AND DEVELOPMENT: AN EDGE ON THE COMPETITION

FRANK PERDUE'S LESSONS

STAY ON TOP OF RESEARCH AND DEVELOPMENT— Instead of copying what everyone else was doing, Frank took the trouble to listen to what the consumer wanted and then was willing to fund the research and development efforts that it took to meet those consumer desires. As far as research with the chickens, Frank was surprisingly "birdy," as in he concerned himself with the veterinary issues and knew a lot about the birds and their needs. He valued technical expertise in how to raise chickens in the best possible way and Perdue Farms was the first poultry company to hire a full time veterinarian – and not just any veterinarian, but a full professor from North Carolina State. Frank also invested in research on further processed chicken and was extensively involved in developing new products and testing them.

PILOT IDEAS BEFORE DEPLOYING THEM WIDELY— Frank wasn't content to have theoretical ideas from the researchers but also put considerable emphasis on having test farms to see if what seemed like a good idea in the laboratory would scale well enough to be useful on actual producing farms.

CHAPTER SEVENTEEN
QUALITY: THE ONE ABSOLUTELY NECESSARY INGREDIENT

Frank's emphasis on research and development was not enough by itself to get him the results that he wanted. Like two interlocking sides of a zipper, the research and development side had to mesh with the quality side at every stage. A lot of people put a lot of effort into seeing that research and development was supported by quality. This meant quality control, and again, it was something that was close to Frank's heart.

Steve Berglind, Perdue's Director of Quality Analysis, was a true VIP in Frank's eyes. Berglind was part of the quality team that would make sure that Frank's quality promises were being kept.

Berglind started his career with Perdue in 1985 as the quality control supervisor in Accomac, Virginia. I first met Berglind at a party at our home in Salisbury in 1988, and although I don't remember asking him the following question, he remembered it clearly.

"Isn't it hard," Berglind said I asked him, "to work in quality control for someone who's so demanding?" Berglind was certain, by the way, that I was trying to be sympathetic.

"My answer," said Berglind, was, "No! He may be demanding but I have the good fortune of being on the same side on almost all issues. The truth is, I always found him pleasant to work with."

Berglind saw a lot of Frank. "Occasionally we would drive together the hour and a half or so that it takes to get from Salisbury to the plant in Accomac,

QUALITY: THE ONE ABSOLUTELY NECESSARY INGREDIENT

Virginia. On the way, he would hit me like a machine gun with questions, one after another, and usually he already knew the answers."

The kinds of questions Frank might ask would be about how we were handling a complaint, such as some feathers that hadn't been removed from a bird, or a package that had leaked.

"He'd be asking these questions as if he didn't know the answers," said Berglind, "but later, in the discussion, you could tell that he knew the answers perfectly. He had probably been studying reports from the marketing reps in the field or wherever else he was getting his information."

Berglind found that the conversations always started this way. It was just natural to Frank; it was the way he did things. "It wasn't unpleasant or mean in any way, although I'm sure it could make some people very uncomfortable. However, once he knew that you were up on the answers, the atmosphere would change and the rest of the drive would be congenial and even fun."

The leaky packages that Berglind mentioned a moment ago were a big issue for quality control in the early days. It was a huge and continuing concern for Frank. For Berglind, solving this problem meant updating all the plant machinery. It also meant a different way of over-wrapping the chicken, using a different film, and a beaded seal around the edges that when heated to the right temperature is leak-proof.

Berglind has a favorite memory of Frank at the Accomac plant. It's a large plant, with maybe 1,200 associates working there. One day back in the 1980s, the company instituted a policy that everyone at the plant had to wear a hair net. People wore 'bump caps' anyway, which look like a construction worker's helmet, but they're plastic and much lighter. Anyway, Frank comes in wearing his white lab coat, like everyone else, and his white bump cap.

However, Frank was bald and already wearing a bump cap, so it probably didn't occur to him that he needed a hair net. However, when Margaret

QUALITY: THE ONE ABSOLUTELY NECESSARY INGREDIENT

Wessels, the associate in charge of making sure everyone wore a hairnet, saw Frank about to enter into the area where chickens are processed, she barred the door and wouldn't allow Frank to come in unless he was wearing a hairnet.

"She was trembling," Berglind remembered, but Frank reassured her, telling her, "If it's the right thing to do, it's the right thing for everyone."

Frank spent a lot of time in the plants, especially since he was a believer in "management by walking around." One day Frank was looking around for a quality control person, and couldn't find one. He or she might have been there, but since everyone in the plant wears a white coat and bump cap, Frank couldn't find the person. By the time he got back to the office, this had grown in his mind into a major issue.

Arthur "Mr. Arthur" Perdue and son Frank reviewing plans for a feedmill.

Berglind recalls how Frank solved this. "As a result of that one incident, every quality control person now wears a bright red lab coat and bump cap. That way the 15 to 30 quality control people in each plant stand out like firemen, and it's obvious who to go to for a complaint."

A Rating System for Quality

Frank only once in his career nominated anyone for the annual Perdue Farms Excellence Awards. These are given in several categories and can be given to individuals or teams. The only nomination for an Excellence Award that

QUALITY: THE ONE ABSOLUTELY
NECESSARY INGREDIENT

Frank ever made was the one given for a project Berglind undertook to make it easier to compare how different plants were doing in relation to quality.

Before Berglind's idea, each plant had its own rating system, and while one plant might have 250 points as the highest they could earn for quality, another might have a scale that only went to 180 points.

Having incompatible rating systems was a headache for Frank, given that he was a deep believer in Peter Drucker's "You can't manage what you can't measure." Berglind created a 100-point scale, so everyone could compare how the different plants were doing.

"The way it worked was everyone started out with 100," Berglind said, "and then they'd have to subtract points for such things as having some birds not having all the feathers removed, or having a bone found in a boneless breast, or bruising, or skin that was torn or barked, or – and this was something that was very important to him – not having trimmed the fat sufficiently from the chickens."

This latter was crucial for Frank because his advertising at the time included the slightly naughty but highly memorable slogan, "I took it all off." In the ad, Frank was referring to fat, not his clothes. Berglind needed to make sure that we really were trimming all the fat from Perdue chickens.

In Frank's last couple of years, he'd stop by Berglind's office and reminisce. The two men would talk about how, long ago, things didn't have to be written down, and that when you shook someone's hand, there was trust, and if you bought 100 pounds of corn you didn't have to worry about its being a full 100 pounds, and it might even be a little more because they'd throw in some extra.

When Berglind looks back on his time with Frank, he thinks there's a lesson for young people. "My advice is, the most important thing you can ever deliver to your customers is a reason to come back. My wife and I have been to Olive Garden 200 times because they give me a reason to come back.

With other restaurants, we only go once. Perdue Farms would never be the company we are today if we just depended on first time customers."

Frank Could Be Demanding

Sandy Bishop is the Perdue Director of Food Safety and Quality, Fresh Operations. She began working for Perdue Farms in 1983. When interviewing people for this book, the first 40 people out of the 134 on my list were almost uniform in saying how great Frank was to work with. I'm ready to believe that every one of them was sincere, but I could also imagine that they wouldn't be in a hurry to tell Frank's widow about the rough spots.

In later interviews, starting with Bishop, I began deliberately asking people to talk with me about where Frank got his reputation for being demanding. In the case of Bishop's story, I believe that what you're about to read is accurate (actually, I know it is because I asked her to check it and correct it), but it's not a 360-degree reflection of Bishop's entire attitude. Rather, it's her response to my asking what it was about Frank that gave him the reputation for being tough.

She told me that the first time she really talked with Frank was when he was doing a walkabout, checking up on things at the Salisbury Plant. He told her that he didn't like the look of some of the birds that were coming into the plant.

"Who is the service man who's working with the growers on these birds?" he demanded. "Have you talked with him about this?"

"I haven't interacted with anyone on the live side, Mr. Perdue," Bishop answered "I've only worked with the people in the plant."

"Well the guy who had your job before, Alan Culver, would have known every one out in the field."

This sounds really harsh, but Bishop's reaction was, "Frank was right. There are many situations in the plant that are impacted by what's going on with

QUALITY: THE ONE ABSOLUTELY
NECESSARY INGREDIENT

the farmers who grow the chickens, and as I soon learned, many times to solve issues in the plant, you've got to have the folks who are working with the people who grow the chickens be in the boat with you."

She also came to see that her job wasn't just about food safety and food quality in the plant, it was about everything that impacted food safety and food quality everywhere.

"Another time when I experienced that Frank could be a demanding boss was at the plant in Lewiston," she continued. "Perdue fresh chickens are supposed to be fresh, not frozen, but one day when he was doing a walkabout, he found that the chicken in the tray packs that were coming out of the cooler had a crust of ice on them. They weren't frozen all the way through, but the chicken was hard to the touch.

"This was completely unacceptable to Frank. He absolutely made sure that everyone in the Lewiston Plant knew that Perdue sold fresh chicken, not frozen chicken."

Bishop's job was to find out what had gone wrong. This was tricky because you need the coolers really cold because of food safety and shelf life, but not so cold that the chicken freezes. Chicken doesn't freeze at 32 degrees, which reminds me of something Frank told me: "Water is the only substance that freezes at exactly 32 degrees," so it's not as simple as making sure that the cooler is above 32 degrees. Actually, you'd like to have the cooler be exactly 28 degrees because chicken won't freeze at 28 degrees as long as there's proper air circulation.

Bishop spent the next three days in the cooler, trying to figure out which of the air baffles hadn't been positioned correctly, causing the cooling to be too cold in some areas. In the end, she got it right so that none of the product would be shipped partially frozen.

Bishop felt that Frank had an impact that was felt by everyone. He'd often come to the plant, and he made sure that everyone knew that he or she was responsible for quality. If the quality data from the regular meetings were not what they should be, the people in operations would be held accountable.

All in all, Bishop appreciated that Frank was tough and demanding. "This foundation of 'Quality first and foremost and that everyone is responsible' was the block that I built my career on. It's a valuable lesson for young folks entering business."

Quality Extends to the Wording on the Packages

Roger Lipinski started with Perdue in 1984 as part of the product development effort. His story on getting packaging right involves me, and he still blames me for all of it. What follows is his story, but since I'm the author, I get to tell you my side first. What you're about to read happened in the late 1980s.

One Tuesday, I knew I had to be out at midday and that Frank would be working at home. I left him with some *Perdue Done It!* chicken tenders for lunch, something I could count on Frank's liking. However, Frank, for all his super intelligence and generally savvy approach to the world, had up to that point never learned to use our microwave oven. He hadn't needed to, it didn't interest him and he just hadn't bothered with it.

Knowing all this, I typed out detailed directions for him about what buttons you press to make it work and, in particular, how to set the timing. I scotch-taped the directions onto the front panel of the microwave in our kitchen, and left the house expecting that all would go well.

It didn't, and for the following reason. I had given Frank the timing directions from the tenders package.

Frank popped two tenders in the oven, used the timing that I had written out for him, and, then what passes for a catastrophe happened in the Perdue household: *the resulting chicken was tough!*

186

QUALITY: THE ONE ABSOLUTELY
NECESSARY INGREDIENT

The correct timing in a microwave depends on the weight and size of the items that you're cooking, so while the timing would have worked for four pieces, it dried out and toughened the two tenders that Frank wanted to eat. And now back to Lipinski's story.

"Frank calls me on a Tuesday," said Lipinski, "and the tough *Perdue Done It!* tenders meant he was one unhappy camper."

By Thursday, Lipinski was 100 miles away in Wilmington, Delaware at DuPont's microwave testing facility. There he was, standing in front of banks and banks of different brands of microwave ovens, including various models of each different brand. He was testing almost countless samples of Per*due Done It!* under different microwave conditions.

To make sure the testing was accurate, he had brought with him a $25,000 Instron machine that scientifically measures tenderness. His goal was to learn all he could about the results you get microwaving tenders with different times, different wattages and different numbers of tenders.

As a result of all this testing, Perdue packaging people re-wrote the directions on the wrapping film for all future packages of *Perdue Done It!*. The new directions called attention to the fact that microwaves vary, and then said how many minutes to set the microwave for, depending on the number of tenders.

What impressed Lipinski most was that "Within two weeks of Frank's having eaten a tough tender, the new wrapping film with the more accurate directions had been printed and all the packages with the tenders that were being sold had the new directions. That, by the way, meant discarding all the old packaging film."

Lipinski is pretty sure that most companies wouldn't have been this agile. "For a safety issue, other companies could act quickly, but this was a quality issue and an eating experience issue. We spent a lot of money and a lot of time to get it right."

QUALITY: THE ONE ABSOLUTELY
NECESSARY INGREDIENT

Lipinski had many experiences with Frank's putting quality first, and one that particularly struck him was using peanut oil for cooking the chicken nuggets. We no longer use peanut oil today, but back in the 1980s, peanut was the oil of choice because it didn't break down easily when heated, it had a neutral taste, and generally, people just plain liked it.

However, Perdue Farms is also in the soybean oil business and we produce millions of gallons of it a year. It would have been much more economical for Perdue Farms to cook its nuggets in an oil that we were already making rather than buy peanut oil on the outside.

Even more of a problem, Frank had invested a lot in the soybean oil refinery. As Lipinski takes up the story, "It's a good business for us today, but back then he was throwing money in and not getting money back out."

One day early on, he and Frank were in the plant that makes chicken nuggets and Frank asked, "Are you using Perdue oil?"

"No, I've been working with the guru of oil at the Perdue oil refinery, and the problem is, the soybean oils didn't taste quite as good as the peanut oil."

"Frank looked at me and, said, 'Well, get it right!'"

Lipinski waited as it took a whole year for the soybean oil refinery to figure out how to refine the soybean oil to the state of purity that would be needed to produce good-tasting nuggets. Getting it right meant replacing equipment with better and more expensive equipment, and it meant a lot of trial and error. "Month after month." Lipinski remembered, "our refiners would send us barrel after barrel of oil, and it was never quite good enough."

However, in all that time there was never any pressure from Frank to use his own oil. "You don't see that a lot anywhere else," said Lipinski. "That's true commitment to doing the right thing. Frank knew that we could make the nuggets slightly better with somebody else's oil, so that's what we did."

In the end, the decision to hold off on using Perdue oil until they had upgraded it to the quality that Frank wanted turned out to have a major payoff for the company. "Frank wanted the best oil in the industry, and he was smart enough to put two and two together: that if it wasn't good enough for us, it wasn't good for others either."

Getting it right turned out to be an excellent business decision. By the time Perdue's soybean oil was good enough for Frank, it was so good that it began winning awards, and the company became the preferred supplier for many other food companies. Today we produce more than 75 million gallons of it a year and supply roughly 70 different customers. They use it in snack foods, salad dressings, sauces, margarines and cookies, among other products.

Lipinski knows a little about where Frank got his predisposition to be willing to spend money on the right equipment. "Frank was a big reader, and one of the books he talked about a lot was the story of how, founder of Carnegie Steel. Carnegie became great in the steel industry because he was always state-of-the art when producing his steel."

Carnegie could produce the best steel for the best price because he had the best equipment. If he put in a furnace to make steel and two years later there was a better furnace, he'd discard the old furnace and put in the new one.

"Like Carnegie, Frank's philosophy was even if you bought something two years ago, if something better became available, he would never say, 'Keep this because we just spent $200,000 on it.'"

Subliminal Signaling

Randy Day is today President of Perdue Foods, but part of his career, which began in 1980, included replacing the head of Quality Assurance, Alan Culver, when Culver retired. Replacing Culver was a momentous, if not traumatic, event in the company's life because Culver had been on the job for an entire generation, and up to then had been the company's only head of Quality Assurance.

Day knew he had big shoes to fill, and at this point Frank did something that showed great insight and that was also truly helpful to Day. It was in 1992, but Day didn't understand what was going on until Frank explained it to him.

"Frank began a habit of visiting every plant in the company with me every quarter," said Day. "One day he asked, 'Do you know why I do this?'"

Day didn't know.

"I want people to know that if you say it's so, that it's the same as if I'm saying it."

For Day, "It was one heck of a lot of support."

Frank was good at understanding subliminal signaling. He understood that for Day to replace someone who was almost an icon in the company, people needed to know that Frank was behind him.

FRANK PERDUE'S LESSONS

RESEARCH AND DEVELOPMENT NEEDS TO BE BACKED BY QUALITY CONTROL– Frank was willing to invest large amounts of time and money and new equipment to solve quality problems such as leaky packages. He also believed in the Drucker saying, "You can't manage what you can't measure," and he placed a high value on ways of measuring quality more effectively. Having the quality control people wear red lab coats and red bump caps might seem simplistic, but now people in the plants could immediately find one of them when there was a quality issue.

INSISTING ON HIGH QUALITY CAN BRING MARKETPLACE SUCCESS– He was willing to endure for an entire year the cost and inconvenience of using peanut oil bought from outside vendors for his nuggets, even though he was a cooking oil producer. He didn't use any of his own soybean oil until the refiners had figured out how to produce oil with characteristics that made it as good as peanut oil, with the result that he now had a huge new market for his soybean by-product, oil.

RECOGNIZE THE POWER OF SUBLIMINAL MESSAGES– Frank helped his new quality control chief with a subliminal message: by accompanying him to quality meetings, people would realize in the future that when the man spoke, he was speaking for Frank.

CHAPTER EIGHTEEN
SELLING INTERNATIONALLY: GEOPOLITICAL AWARENESS MEANS GLOBAL OPPORTUNITY

Part of becoming a large company meant having international markets. Frank began looking into this in the 1980s, and as a result, today we sell chicken and also grain in more than 100 countries. Some chicken companies have lost their shirts as part of the learning curve for getting into international sales. Perdue, in contrast, has consistently done well during its international expansion.

Considering that Frank Perdue didn't finish college and spent his childhood on a farm, he had a remarkable degree of geopolitical awareness. Dr. Brian Polkinghorn, Distinguished Professor of Conflict Analysis and Dispute Resolution at Salisbury University, got to witness Frank's geopolitical savvy when attending a party at our home.

There were probably 100 people at this particular event, but knowing about Professor Polkinghorn's experience and knowledge of Africa, Frank made it a point to talk with him.

For starters, Frank was interested in South Africa. Polkinghorn was surprised by the sophistication of Frank's questions about the country.

"What fascinated me was he knew what he was talking about. He was super intelligent, and he asked one good question after another. It felt sort of like I was defending a doctoral thesis. It wasn't an interrogation, but the questions were so insightful."

SELLING INTERNATIONALLY: GEOPOLITICAL AWARENESS MEANS GLOBAL OPPORTUNITY

This was back around 2001, and the kinds of questions Frank was asking included wanting to know Polkinghorn's opinion of how stable the government was, was the supply system a hub and spoke system, and he particularly wanted to learn everything he could about the country's infrastructure.

From there, according to Polkinghorn, Frank, without skipping a beat, moved on to discussing Zimbabwe. He was wondering if you'd wake up one day and find your business padlocked and you'd be lucky to get out alive. "He was right to worry about Zimbabwe," said Polkinghorn. "When I was there later, the inflation rate was eleven million percent a year. The things that had concerned him years earlier had happened."

Next the conversation moved on to talking about Botswana, and how Botswana had a culture of doing things by the books, and how it was a culture that was at least relatively free of bribes and stealing. Frank was aware that in Botswana, you were probably not going to face goons with baseball bats. However, he also knew that there were still challenges back then, such as if you wanted to get a driver's license, it could take a couple of months, and business could move at a slow pace.

Polkinghorn never forgot the experience of hearing Frank talk so knowledgeably about topics that you might guess would be far removed from selling chickens.

Frank Could Focus on the Crux of an Issue

Carlos Ayala is the Perdue Vice President for International, and in the interest of full disclosure, I should quickly mention that he is my son by my previous marriage. He's worked for Perdue since having a summer job at age 16 cleaning hatchery waste.

Ayala sees Frank as having an amazing ability to zero in on what was important. "Some people are inherently great artists. Others are great mathematicians. Well, Frank, he had the ability to first identify and then focus in on the crux of an issue."

For Ayala, a great example of this was chicken paws ("paw" is poultry industry word for chicken foot). "Most people don't know this, but if you're in China and you serve someone a nice big boneless breast filet, they would be insulted. If instead you gave them a foot of the chicken, they would be honored. And the bigger the paw, the better."

Frank understood the cultural importance of large paws in China. He knew that Perdue's *Oven Stuffer® Roaster*, which is a really big chicken, had the biggest feet in the industry, and this meant the roaster paws had the potential for being remarkably popular in China. Back in the early 90s, Perdue started processing chicken paws and exporting them to China.

"Today," said Ayala, "that paw business is generating tens of millions of dollars in revenue to the company and nearly 130 jobs in the process. It's now the most profitable item we export, and somehow Frank, more than 20 years ago, was able to grasp the importance of them."

Ayala found Frank to be remarkably fair and trustworthy. "There was no bias, one way or the other, with Frank. People knew exactly where they stood and in today's world where people are afraid to hurt someone's feelings, it was surprising the degree to which Frank would be almost Spock-like (as in *Star Trek*) with regard to feedback: If something was good, he'd let you know; if something was bad, he'd let you know."

Ayala believes that this generated a huge amount of loyalty and it created a filter, where people who were comfortable being held accountable stayed, and those that didn't...well, they didn't last long. "What a great filter to have!" Ayala observed.

SELLING INTERNATIONALLY: GEOPOLITICAL AWARENESS MEANS GLOBAL OPPORTUNITY

FRANK PERDUE'S LESSONS

CULTIVATE GEOPOLITICAL AWARENESS– While many chicken companies lost money on their international ventures, Perdue has had a record of doing well year after year. Part of this was Frank's considerable geopolitical awareness. In addition to his own studies, he'd ask penetrating questions of experts,

BE FORWARD-LOOKING– In the early 1980s, he not only understood the value of becoming an international company, he also was sensitive to the fact that different nationalities place different values on different parts of the chicken. In the case of China, Frank foresaw more than 20 years ago that chicken paws would be a major export, and today paws are responsible for more than 100 jobs and millions of dollars in revenue.

CHAPTER NINETEEN
PHILANTHROPY: FRANK'S
ENTREPRENEURIAL APPROACH

Frank was always philanthropic, but generally, he kept his donations anonymous. His usual gifts were given with the requirement that the recipient was not to tell anyone.

I first learned of his unwillingness to talk about his donations when, within days of our getting married, he made what I considered a major gift to the Girl Scouts. As a former Girl Scout myself, I was eager to broadcast the news to anyone and everyone. I was bursting with pride and thinking about what a wonderful thing he had done for an organization that helps girls "build courage, confidence, and character."

I mentioned to the late Chris Whaley, who handled Perdue public relations, that this would surely result in wonderful PR for the company. Whaley quickly clued me in. Frank wouldn't want it and he preferred to keep quiet about all his donations.

Frank Endows the Perdue School of Business

Anonymous giving was generally his pattern, but there were three noteworthy exceptions that I was to witness. The first began in 1985, when the late Thom Bellavance, President of Salisbury State College (now Salisbury University), talked Frank into endowing a business school. For Bellavance, the part about founding a business school was a fairly easy sell; Frank valued education and he particularly liked the idea that students could learn things that it had taken him years or decades to understand.

PHILANTHROPY: FRANK'S ENTREPRENEURIAL APPROACH

The harder part was getting Frank to agree to having the business school named after him. Frank didn't want this and resisted it strongly. He and I talked about this, and I know that he didn't like anything to do with "self-aggrandizement." However, Bellavance persuaded Frank that if he allowed the school to be named Perdue, that the brand itself would help attract students and faculty, and perhaps even more important, a public gift of this sort would signal to other potential donors that investing in education in our region was a good thing to do.

Liz Bellavance, Thom's widow, saw the beginning of this enterprise. When she and her husband arrived at Salisbury State College in 1980, state funding for the college was decreasing, and Bellavance wanted to compensate for this by attracting private funding.

Bellavance immediately thought of Frank as a possible sponsor for a school of business. "In addition to Frank's connection with the school and national image in the chicken business," said Liz Bellavance, "Thom admired Frank's standards for excellence."

However, after Bellavance approached him and before agreeing to it, Frank, in characteristic manner, investigated Bellavance's history at previous educational institutions. Frank wanted to make sure that Bellavance was capable of creating a business school and that he intended to stay at Salisbury to see it through.

Getting this information was wise. It's not enough just to write a check and hope for the best. Business schools do occasionally fail, and Frank wanted to make sure that his wasn't one of them.

The $10 million that Frank donated to make the Perdue School of Business possible had a multiplier effect. "With Frank's gift," said Liz Bellavance, "three other endowments followed: the Schools of Science; Liberal Arts, and Education. Salisbury is the only state institution in the country to accomplish such a feat. Thom always credited Frank's making the first gift with enabling the subsequent gifts to happen."

An Entrepreneurial Gift to Salisbury University

Tim Mescon also has an opinion on Frank and educational philanthropy. Mescon has been researching entrepreneurship for the past 35 years, and since he often interacted with Frank on business school matters, he got to study Frank up close and personal. Interestingly, he feels that few people actually know just how entrepreneurial Frank was.

According to Mescon, when Frank made his $10 million gift to Salisbury University, he was the first substantial donor in the history of the institution. This gift incorporated one of the best aspects of entrepreneurialism: it created more entrepreneurialism.

In this case, once Frank had made his gift, it quickly inspired additional donations. In the years that followed, local entrepreneurs gave a total of $100 million. Frank's impact, however, went beyond the dollars involved.

"I got my first inkling of what made Frank tick when I learned about Frank's role in recruiting me and the other faculty members at the Perdue School," said Mescon. Frank was so detail-minded that in the mid-1980s, he actually made a personal visit to the Wharton School of Business to talk with faculty and administration, getting their assessment of what makes a great business school professor."

Mescon was impressed that Frank, who didn't finish college himself, left with a great deal of knowledge about how the faculty system works. Even better, he had in his hands a collection of recommendations for possible hires for the newly formed Perdue School of Business.

"Frank was willing to do what it took to ensure that the school he had endowed would prosper. How many people who make large donations get as deep into the weeds as Frank did? After all, it would have been much easier and less time-consuming simply to write a check and be done with it."

PHILANTHROPY: FRANK'S ENTREPRENEURIAL APPROACH

Janet Dudley-Eshbach is the current president of Salisbury University, and like Bellavance and Mescon, she also got witness Frank's hands-on approach. He was one of those on the University's search committee to interview her for the job back in the spring of 2000.

"I was nervous about meeting him," admitted Dudley-Eshbach. "He was legendary, but for me it wasn't because of chickens; it was because in many ways he was considered the founder of Salisbury University."

Dudley-Eshbach knew that Salisbury University had been a teacher's college when it began in 1925, and that Frank Perdue had changed everything when he endowed the Business School in 1985. As a result of his gift, and the three additional endowments that it inspired, Salisbury University became the only comprehensive public university in the nation with four endowed schools. "He set an extraordinary precedent that has created untold value for Salisbury University and for the region," said Dudley-Eshbach.

"I mentioned that I was nervous when I first met him," she continues, "but I soon found that he was likable and accessible. It was heartwarming that he totally embraced having a woman as president, and I didn't see a sexist bone in his body. He was incredibly supportive."

Dudley-Eshbach is proud that the Perdue School itself serves a large audience beyond the University. Its outreach helps people who want to start their own businesses, and it's responsible for the largest number of startups of any academic institution in Maryland. "The Perdue School of Business is an economic engine for the entire Eastern Shore," she said, "and it's a center for entrepreneurship for our region."

Dr. Bob Wood, former Dean of the Perdue School of Business, considers Frank something of a hero. "When Frank founded the Perdue School of Business, he had a vision of giving students the tools that they would need to make it easier for them than it had been for him. The business school was to be a shortcut to success."

PHILANTHROPY: FRANK'S
ENTREPRENEURIAL APPROACH

Following that vision, Wood and his colleagues make sure that the students' overall experience includes more than just sitting in a classroom. Whether it's writing skills, presentation skills, or experience working in the real world, or studying or working in such countries as China, Argentina, France, or Germany, the students are given experience as well as academic knowledge. For proof that it worked, there are 20,000 business schools in the world and only 716 are, like Perdue, accredited. "As a school founded in 1986, we're still young, but we already have a national reputation," said Wood.

"Frank was both inspirational and practical, he was good at both. He had an aura, when he walked into a room that you just knew he was a leader. It was a gift, like Mozart could compose music or Patton could win battles."

Memo Diriker has been Professor of Business and Marketing at the Perdue School of Business since 1988, and his current research focuses on the "Three Es: Effectiveness, Efficiency, and Evidence." During the last 25 years, Professor Diriker often thought of the techniques and innovations of the man whose work he occasionally analyzes in his classroom.

Diriker noticed that Frank really enjoyed being around students. "He used to invite all the Perdue Scholars to a buffet dinner at his home each year. It was an awesome feeling for these 20 to 30 students to be able to talk with the man who had the ideas for some of the marketing they're studying in their textbooks."

One of Diriker's favorite memories happened at one of the dinners. The format of these dinners was there would be a buffet, and at the end of the dinner, Frank would get up and talk for a few minutes. According to Diriker, "In the beginning, he would look like a tired executive, tall but slightly stooped under the burdens of running a multi-billion dollar enterprise. But, when he started to talk about the business and the industry, he would come alive! He would transform before their eyes from a senior executive to the energetic entrepreneur that he really was."

PHILANTHROPY: FRANK'S ENTREPRENEURIAL APPROACH

The students would have a chance to ask him questions, and this would energize him even more. "You could see the sparkles in his eyes from the very back of the room," said Diriker. "He was totally engaged in this and obviously enjoyed interacting with the students."

At one point, one of the students asked him a question about teamwork. "His answer," said Diriker, "is one that I often repeat in my classrooms because he was able to get across in a simple sentence something they all need to know about leadership. Frank answered, 'Teamwork is very important as long as you understand when the day is done, someone has to make the decision.'"

Frank Supported United Way

Endowing the Perdue School of Business was one of Frank's most visible philanthropic efforts, but he was also a major behind-the-scenes supporter of United Way. Frank was a huge admirer of United Way and I can remember at the yearly parties we used to give for the organization, the absolute delight he'd take in seeing the increases each year in the amounts contributed.

Kathleen Momme, the Executive Director in Salisbury, appreciated Frank's efforts. "We don't have the records from back in the 1970s, but I believe Frank was the first to make possible employee campaigns for United Way of the Lower Eastern Shore. If he wasn't the first, (although I think very likely he was), he had to be among the first three employers to do this."

What Frank started, or was part of starting, has now grown to 238 local organizations that support United Way of the Lower Eastern Shore. "His pioneering efforts," said Momme, have made an incalculable difference in our community. It was groundbreaking and tremendously important."

Kathleen was also impressed that Frank helped 19 local charities to create endowments. He liked the idea of endowments, knowing that when a charity had a permanent funding mechanism, more time can be spent on delivering services and less on raising money.

PHILANTHROPY: FRANK'S ENTREPRENEURIAL APPROACH

The endowment efforts were in partnership with the Kresge Foundation, and the way it worked was if an agency could raise one dollar toward an endowment, Kresge would match one-third of that dollar, and Perdue would match two-thirds of it. The effort raised $12 million in endowments in perpetuity for local charities.

How many people have philanthropic efforts that do so much so creatively to help their local communities?

"Something else that Frank did," added Momme, "he would open his home to members of the Anchor Society, that is, individuals who contributed more than $500 that year. People enjoyed visiting his house and getting to know a person who was otherwise just an icon to them. They found that he was fun and some of them enjoyed saying, 'I played ping pong with Frank Perdue.' The year Frank began the tradition of inviting United Way Anchor Society donors to his home, membership in the society was 168 members. Five years later it was 460 members."

Frank and the Delmarva Shorebirds

In 1995, Frank did something else that benefitted the local community, even though it may not look like traditional philanthropy. When he donated the land and built a minor league baseball stadium, and then the next year when he brought the Delmarva Shorebirds to the area, he made possible inexpensive family entertainment that could benefit everyone.

It's hard to measure how much this did for the local community, but I got a clue from our then-local Sheriff, Hunter Nelms. Sheriff Nelms said that the community feeling and wholesome small town values that went with the Shorebirds games actually had an impact on law enforcement and made his job easier.

As was Frank's pattern, he didn't just sign a check and expect the baseball project to materialize. While still planning the project, he called the then-President of Salisbury University, Thom Bellavance, to ask for a couple of faculty members to help with a feasibility study.

The study was to evaluate how building a minor league baseball stadium in Salisbury would be a success. Professor Memo Diriker was one of the ones assigned to look into it. However, according to Diriker, the initial investigations made the project look dubious.

"When Frank heard this," said Diriker, "he pulled me aside and stated, 'You're a smart man, I didn't ask the question, 'Is it feasible?' I asked you how to make it feasible.' It turned out that not only could it be made feasible, but the Arthur W. Perdue stadium regularly beat all attendance records for the South Atlantic League."

Frank's motive in building the local stadium and bringing the Delmarva Shorebirds to the area was largely that he wanted to provide affordable local entertainment to the region. However, that didn't keep him from using his business expertise in all aspects of it.

Selling the Shorebirds

Joseph D. Salerno has an inside view on how Frank handled the business side of the Shorebirds and two additional teams he wound up co-owning. Salerno was CFO and Board member of Integro Inc., and CFO of Marsh Inc., as well as Mercer Consulting Group. Salerno has himself been involved in buying and selling minor league baseball teams, so he was well aware of what Frank was up to when in the year 2000, Frank wanted to sell three of them.

Salerno's point of view was particularly interesting to me since I had been privy to what was going on from our side. Frank, now in his 80s, was in declining health, and he knew that his son Jim didn't want to take over the teams. That meant Frank wanted to sell the three franchises and he wanted to sell them fast.

Frank quietly put the Delmarva Shorebirds, the Bowie Baysox and the Frederick Keys up for sale. When I heard Frank discussing this with others, I

PHILANTHROPY: FRANK'S ENTREPRENEURIAL APPROACH

was worried that we were dealing from a position of weakness – after all, declining health and an absolute need to sell aren't the best cards to be holding when doing a deal. I was worried that we'd be rolled. I think most people in Frank's position would have been rolled. That's not, however, what happened. Read on.

According to Salerno, "Frank's business success in selling the three minor league baseball teams that he and his partners owned is almost legendary. It's something people are still talking about 15 years later. If you are buying or selling a baseball team today and you study the comparable sales, you will be told to throw out Frank's transaction because it was such an outlier."

Salerno explains that when someone decides to sell a minor league team, you'll see a price range among comparable sales of plus or minus 10%. Frank negotiated a sale that was 50% above what you would have expected based on comparable sales.

According to Salerno, here's how it happened. Frank knew that Comcast wanted to create a sports division, so he knew that they were motivated to buy. He also calculated that the geographic location was good for Comcast since they were based in nearby Philadelphia.

Frank also knew that Comcast knew that another package of baseball teams in the area probably wouldn't come up for at least another ten years. "Having calculated all this" said Salerno, "he in essence created an approach that for the minor leagues is unique as to methodology and price."

Frank created a sealed bid auction. Says Salerno, it was a high-risk operation for Frank because he could have come up with nothing. Most people in his situation would simply have negotiated with the various potential buyers, and if one didn't meet the price, you move on to the next. That's the safe way because you are in control and you're not going to lose your shirt.

However, a characteristic of Frank was that, like a poker player, he was comfortable with calculating the odds and then taking a gamble based on those odds. "He had a tremendous instinct for business," said Salerno, "plus he had studied where Comcast was coming from and had assessed how badly Comcast was likely to want the teams."

The gamble paid off. He was able to get a price that was 50% above what the expected price would have been. "He was a superb businessman," said Salerno, "even when it was something far outside of his usual area of expertise."

FRANK PERDUE'S LESSONS

HAVE AN ENTREPRENEURIAL APPROACH TO PHILANTHROPY– In community philanthropy, he donated in ways that would create more donations, whether it was in the 1970s being an example of company-wide support for United Way, or creating matching funds for permanent endowments for 19 local charities. In the case of Salisbury University, his initial endowment of $10 million to found a business school elicited a total of $100 million in endowments. His philanthropy extended to non-traditional outlets. Donating a baseball stadium may not seem like your average philanthropy, but the motive was to provide affordable local entertainment.

IT'S NOT ENOUGH JUST TO WRITE A CHECK– Once he had agreed to found a business school, he didn't just write a check. Instead, he studied how business schools worked and personally was involved in interviewing and recruiting faculty.

For him, the Perdue's school's aim was to teach students the skills that would make them a success in making still others a success.

CHAPTER TWENTY
LOYALTY: HOW TO NURTURE IT

Frank was able to create immense loyalty among the people who worked for him, and large numbers of employees stayed with him for their entire careers. Years after he passed on, I still come across former employees who treasured their time working with him. Given that he could be demanding, cantankerous, inconsiderate of people's personal time, plus a great vast hoard of other characteristics that made for a tough and difficult man, why did so many brilliant and competent people stay with him for life?

I have a quick answer from Carol Breslau. Her late husband, Robert, worked for Perdue for 30 years, and Carol Breslau often witnessed Frank's habit of calling her husband at all hours of the day or night.

"Would you mind telling me," I asked her one day, pretty much out of the blue, "just why somebody didn't assassinate Frank for his middle-of-the-night phone calls?"

Carol Breslau has a sense of humor and was fine with that question. "They didn't assassinate Frank because Frank was just being Frank. Bob and I used to laugh about the calls, and Bob and I would ask each other in amazement, 'When does he ever sleep?'

"The fact is they had a lot of fun together. Now that I'm thinking about those middle of the night phone calls, I'm sure they're both up in Heaven laughing about them."

LOYALTY: HOW TO NURTURE IT

Frank Was Extraordinarily Loyal to the People Who Worked with Him

That was the short answer. A longer one was that difficult as Frank could be, he was able to generate unusual levels of commitment and loyalty. I think this came about because loyalty is a two-way street, and Frank was extraordinarily loyal to the people who worked with him.

He was actually more loyal to his associates than most people would or even could know. On weekends, when other people might be watching TV or playing golf, Frank would be visiting associates in the hospital. Elaine Barnes would give us a list of hospitalized Perdue workers and we'd visit them. Also, I don't think I can count how many funerals we attended, but we always went. For him, attending a funeral meant showing respect for the deceased and being a comfort for the family. He didn't miss funerals even when it meant chartering a plane to be there.

He also spent time visiting retired employees, and he clearly felt that his loyalty to the retirees didn't end just because the associate was no longer receiving a paycheck. To him, associates, whatever their level, and whether they were retired or not, were like family.

He also made a practice of always attending the safety celebrations that the different plants had. When a plant had achieved a million man-hours with no accidents, Frank would attend even if it meant that to be present for the night shift's award, he'd have to get up at 2:00 a.m. and drive an hour to be there for a 3:00 a.m. ceremony.

I didn't need to ask why he did it. I knew that if there was life in his body he would. He understood that it meant something to the people who had achieved something, to have him there, appreciating their accomplishment. There was no way he was going to disappoint them.

While I'm talking about loyalty, and how it was a two-way street, I have to talk about what it was like going through a plant with Frank. He knew an incredible number of the associates. We'd go through and he'd introduce them to me by name, and often he'd know some offbeat fact about them, such as how many years an associate had worked with no sick days, or how many children she had. I loved the infinite respect he showed to each person. There was never the faintest trace of distance or lording it over them. It was more like, "We're all a team and we each have our role, and I very much respect your role."

A Goal: Entertaining All the Perdue Associates in Our Home

Further, Frank had an additional way of showing the associates that they were important to him. He had a goal of entertaining in our home every person who worked for Perdue. That meant once a week, 100 or so associates would come for a buffet dinner, and often Frank would serve the associates himself from behind the buffet line. At the end of the evening, he would thank the truckers or sanitation workers or whoever our guests were that night, saying that he knew the company would never be what it is today without them.

Personally, I think this attitude meant the world to our guests. Actually, I know it did because often they'd tell me so. In later years, after Frank's passing, I several times attended funerals of Perdue associates and during the viewing, family members would tell me that one of the most exciting things that had happened in the deceased's life was being entertained in Frank's home.

Supporting Perdue Reservists

Frank always had soft spot in his heart for any Perdue associates who were either members of the National Guard or Reserves. He showed this in many ways. During Desert Storm, 82 Perdue associates were deployed overseas and Frank would write letters to every one of them every month.

He started the correspondence by sending them each a DVD player along with a year's supply of batteries. Then, each month we would send them packages of gifts, often with current movies and magazines. We'd also send things like chocolate bars, although we knew not to send them in summer because in some areas where troops were deployed, the temperatures would reach over 120 degrees and the chocolate would melt. At Frank's request, I also found addresses for their wives and sweethearts, and we'd send them gifts as well.

We heard from the associates how much these letters and gifts meant, including that they created "bragging rights" when soldiers could show their fellow soldiers that Frank Perdue, the head of the company, had written to them.

Once an associate wrote to Frank saying he knew that Frank had said that while deployed, he would keep not only his job, but all his seniority, all his accrued vacation time and that Frank would make up any difference in pay, "But," asked the soldier, "what happens if the war lasts a long time? What if it lasts longer than three years?"

Frank wrote back, "You can count on your job and everything that goes with it even if the war lasts 20 years. If it's longer than that, we'll have to talk about it!"

As the individual told me, "You don't forget a thing like that!"

Brian Lipinski, like his brother Roger, has been with Perdue for most of his career, and he's another person with a deep personal understanding of why people were willing to stay with Perdue for life. Brian started in 1987, three years later than Roger, as a line supervisor in the plant that made fully cooked chicken in Bridgewater, Virginia. Today he's the Senior Packaging Engineer at Perdue Headquarters.

The first time I got to know Brian Lipinski was when he was deployed to Iraq for Operation Iraqi Freedom in 2003 and 2004. Frank went all out to support the Perdue Reservists whenever they were deployed overseas. Brian Lipinski was one of the Reservists stationed in the Iraqi theater.

Before Christmas in 2003, Frank asked me to query each of the Perdue Reservists about what they'd like to have us mail them for a Christmas gift. I asked each soldier to pick something in the $100 range.

LOYALTY: HOW TO NURTURE IT

One of the answers really caught Frank's attention. First Sergeant Lipinski, who was deployed as a member of the military police, said he would love to see a couple of Radio Shack walk-about two-way radios under his tree.

Lipinski went on to explain that since communications were very limited in the large operating area, the battery-operated walk-about radios were an essential line of communication. The Radio Shack walk-abouts worked well, and when "a situation" developed and you needed someone or something, it could be life-threatening not to be able to call for backup.

Frank, with reasoning that I thought was typical of him, said that if it could be life-saving for Brian in his MP job, then it would almost certainly be just as important for all the other 100 MPs in Brian's unit.

Frank and I went to the local mall's Radio Shack and bought a walkie-talkie for each of them. But that wasn't all. Frank also calculated how many batteries the walkie-talkies would need in order to be useful for a year. We bought the batteries too, and then, when you put all the walk-abouts and all the batteries together, there were so many items that it took Frank, me, my son Carlos, and the store manager to lug them all to Frank's car. We mailed them off to Iraq the next day.

Lipinski has been with Perdue for 27 years and he said it's the character of the organization that keeps a person there for so long. "I was chatting with Owen Schweers recently (he's the former Director of Packaging) and we were agreeing that the people who stay are people who want to contribute, as opposed to just having something that you add to your resume. We stay because we know we're making a positive difference."

Lipinski noted that if you look at the ID cards that all associates wear, the owner may be middle-aged or older, but often the photograph on the card is of a much younger person, or even just the face of a kid. People simply stay with Perdue.

Brian Lipinski had something else he wanted to say. It had to do with the end of his deployment in Iraq.

LOYALTY: HOW TO NURTURE IT

"I invited Frank to our homecoming event. I knew you both were sincere about your support, but perhaps Frank would have more important things to do. I was very, very wrong. It became a huge event and a cherished memory for me that you both showed up for our welcome home ceremony. It wasn't around the corner; it was in Western Maryland, a ten-hour round trip. It was unbelievable.

"I still remember my Army General wanting to get a picture with Frank. People just couldn't believe that Frank had done this. Even six or eight months later, I'd meet people from my unit who were still talking about Frank's having taken the time. It gave everyone such a sense of pride, that such a prominent figure in the community would care enough to show up."

Spending Time with Associates

While it's true that Frank could be tough and demanding, and it's also true that I've heard people call him a tyrant, an autocrat and worse, on the other hand he had a gift for being able to talk with anyone, and the ability to make everyone feel important. In addition, he was an egalitarian. He didn't care whether you were a duchess or a ditch digger; he would treat you with equal respect. Having good relationships with the people who worked in the plants was all-important to him.

Lorenzo Beach who currently manages a large unit of our plant in Georgetown, Delaware, managed the Salisbury Plant while Frank was still alive. By the way, Beach was the second African American plant manager at Perdue. (Andrew Dorn was the first.)

Beach saw a lot of Frank because Frank stopped by the Salisbury Plant several times a week for lunch at the plant's cafeteria. Frank could have eaten in nice restaurants, including ones that were nearer the Perdue headquarters building five miles away, but I know that he enjoyed the hustle and bustle and the feeling of energy you get when visiting a plant.

Beach told me, when we met at the local MacDonald's to talk about Frank, "I can still see him, standing in the food line at the cafeteria. To my surprise, he always got the same thing: he'd get a chicken breast and a small diet Pepsi in a Styrofoam cup. No vegetable, nothing else. I never saw him eat anything else."

The Salisbury Plant cafeteria holds about 200 people and Frank almost always sat at one of the tables in the middle of the room. Sometimes associates would join him and he'd talk with them, but usually, he'd sit with Beach.

"The first thing he'd do," said Beach, "was ask how different associates were doing, and he'd ask about them by name, such as (and I'm mentioning real people), Milton, Norman, Lola or Delsie."

Beach felt that Frank was really good at talking with anyone, at whatever level, and he loved walking through the plant, talking with people. "Even in his last half year of his life, when he was so weak that I had to stand beside him to make sure he wasn't going to fall, he still liked to go through and visit with the hourly workers."

Beach appreciated that someone as famous and prestigious as Frank would stop and talk with an hourly worker, and take an interest in him or her, even if the person were a new hire. "Frank had a great memory for details of a person's life. If I had just introduced him to an hourly associate who was a new hire, he'd also ask how the new hire was making out and was he or she being treated well."

"When I look back on my career, I feel that Perdue has offered me more than I ever thought I would have. It gets back to what Frank told me right at the beginning, 'If you work hard, do a good day's work, and are honest, you're going to do well.' I feel that I did, and things did work out well."

Lester Gray started as a flock supervisor in North Carolina in 1983, and today is Senior Vice President for Operations. When Gray had been with the company five years, his dad passed away, and a few days later, at 7:30 a.m. on a Sunday, he got a totally unexpected call.

"I was eight layers underneath Frank, and I don't even know how he knew that my dad had passed away." Still, when Gray picked up the phone, he heard the squeaky easily recognizable voice saying, "Lester, I just heard that your dad passed away and I wanted to talk with you about it."

The two men spent an hour and a half, swapping stories. "He told me about how important Mr. Arthur had been to him, and he encouraged me to talk about how much my father had meant to me."

People who are new to Perdue often asked Gray if Frank was really as hard as people said he was, and Gray's answer was "Yes, he was phenomenally driven and hard-driving." But Gray remembered how much time Frank spent with him when he lost his father and concluded, "It takes a tough man to make a tender chicken, but it was a tender man who ran Perdue Farms."

Charlie Carpenter is the Perdue Director of Breeders and Hatcheries, and he also has some observations on why people stay loyal. "Frank always took an interest in the individual and the individual's family. He made you feel a part of the family. When I first started work there, he introduced me as 'The newest members of the Perdue family,' and I still remember how it made me feel."

Carpenter appreciated that Frank made you know that *you* were an important part of the company. "He had an incredible way of doing that, making you feel that you, your job and your family mattered not only to the company but to him personally."

Frank would always ask after Carpenter's wife, Marsha, and their two sons, but that was only a small part of it. "When our first son was born, it turned out that he had jaundice. When Frank learned about it, he called me back a couple of hours later and I found out that Frank now knew more about jaundice than I did! He had taken the trouble to make phone calls to his medical friends, and he had some reassuring answers about what we were up against. You just don't forget something like that."

LOYALTY: HOW TO NURTURE IT

Lisa Moyer isn't a Perdue associate, but her husband is. She and her family also got to experience that Frank cared. Her husband Jack Moyer has worked for Perdue for 34 years, and is currently a Maintenance Supervisor in Salisbury. He's also a hero. In addition to working for Perdue Farms, he's a volunteer firefighter.

Back on September 1, 2002 (a date Lisa is unlikely to forget), her life and her family's life changed. Her husband was among sixteen emergency workers who were injured responding to a gas leak in a residential home when a catastrophic propane explosion took the life of a utility worker on the scene. Six volunteer firefighters including Moyer were seriously injured. Moyer suffered severe burns to his arms and face and spent a week at the Johns Hopkins Bayview Burn Center and four months recovering.

Christmas that year could have been a difficult one for the Moyer family. However, just before the holiday, a huge package of presents arrived, not only for her and her husband, but for children Kenton, Shannon and John as well. In the package were letters and notes from Frank and Jim and other family members, and all were expressing concern, caring and support for the family at this difficult time.

For her, this package was momentous. It showed that Frank and all his family cared, and it demonstrated as nothing else could that her husband was more to the company than someone who simply earned a paycheck. She was greatly touched that the Perdues cared enough about just one of the Perdue Farms 19,000 associates to do this.

That, by the way, is to me one of the true pluses of being a family-owned company. I guarantee that Frank and every family member who wrote to the Moyer family really cared, and that every letter and gift was from the heart. We decided that year that instead of exchanging gifts with each other, we would instead do something to try to make Christmas a little better for the Moyers. In a large publicly owned company, would, or even could, the stockholders feel the same level of concern and caring for an injured associate and his or her family?

LOYALTY: HOW TO NURTURE IT

Kirk Daugherty is another person who understands why people felt loyal to Frank. Daugherty has been in law enforcement for his entire career, and is currently Chief of Police in Snow Hill, Maryland. When Frank was no longer able to drive, which included his last five years, Kirk took over the job. He was part driver, part bodyguard, and for the most part, an agreeable and entertaining friend when Frank had to be on the road. In that role, Daugherty saw Frank in many roles.

"I got to see a side of Frank that most people wouldn't know," Daugherty began. "If a good worker was having a rough time financially, Frank, without telling anyone, would quietly help him out. I know story after story about the people who worked for him whom he helped, but he wouldn't talk about it. He wanted you to give 100 percent, but he'd be there for you if you needed it. With him, loyalty always went both ways."

Daugherty was impressed that Frank was always respectful of people's time, including Daugherty's. "In all my years with him, he never kept me waiting. If I was supposed to pick him up at, for example, 7:30 a.m., he'd be coming out the door at 7:30 a.m."

Daugherty started out as an employee, but as time went on, he felt that they were friends. There came a time fairly early on when he didn't even think of it as being a job. And Frank certainly didn't treat him as just a driver. Frank would always be in the front passenger seat as opposed to sitting in the back, which would have been the usual arrangement for most people with a driver.

"When we'd go on trips," Daugherty noticed, "he was always careful to make sure that all my expenses were covered. Most successful people might not have an understanding about what money means to people with a more average income, but Frank didn't forget where he had come from and had empathy for people who were in a different situation from him."

Carlos Ayala, one of Frank's two stepsons, and now Vice President for International, has an additional observation on Frank and loyalty. "I believe Frank's one extravagance was cars. I remember he had just bought a new

Mercedes S600, and I was told to go pick up one of his daughters at the airport, using his car. On the way, I was hit on the side by someone. The car was really messed up and I was ready to look for a new job.

"It was evening and I walked into his house a bit … um … nervous. I can remember the details, even though it must have been 20 years ago. Frank was in the kitchen, taking a cup of hot chocolate out of the microwave, as I explained that I had just wrecked his new car.

"To my surprise, Frank wasn't in the least bit upset. He asked if anybody was hurt and I explained that no, everyone was fine, and then he said something to the effect of 'Don't worry about it then. As long as nobody was hurt, it doesn't matter.' The same guy who would insist on flying coach was the same person who was fine with his brand new car being wrecked, as long as nobody was hurt. That was Frank. With an attitude like that, who wouldn't be loyal?"

Going Above and Beyond in Human Relations

We've been talking about loyalty to the Perdue associates, but Frank also created loyalty in the community. Andy Booth, from AWB Engineers in Salisbury, remembers several examples of Frank's almost incomparable considerateness. Frank would frequently do things that made people feel important, valued and appreciated.

The background of the story you're about to read is that Frank had a condo apartment in Ocean City, Maryland that we used constantly for entertaining. However, when we first bought it at a bankruptcy sale around 1998, it needed a lot of work to make it habitable. The former owner had been both a drug addict and an alcoholic, and he had trashed the place beyond belief.

There were maybe 20 workmen involved in the renovation of this true "fixer-upper," including the cleaning crew, the electricians, plumbers, painters and so on. After months of working on the place, they had transformed it into a gorgeous showpiece just right for hosting Perdue associates, customers, chicken growers, grain farmers, authors and charity events.

LOYALTY: HOW TO NURTURE IT

Booth remembered that Frank invited everyone who worked on the renovation to a "Completion Party," and this included Booth, who as the engineer, had made sure that even though the condominium initially appeared to be something out of a Stephen King novel, that the foundations were firm and the place could be restored.

The Completion Party was a first-class event, with the same hors d'oeuvres and beverages that we would have served for customers or top management. In Booth's opinion, "Frank went above and beyond since his guests that night weren't expecting it and he'd probably never see most of them again. It was a gracious thing to do. However, I wasn't able to attend the party."

The reason was that a few days earlier, Booth had been in an airplane crash and at the time of the Completion Party, Booth was a patient at the Shock Trauma Hospital in Baltimore with a broken back. Frank learned about this and arranged for an 11" by 17" get-well card in a leatherette presentation frame, and had all of the guests sign it to wish him a speedy recovery.

"That gesture meant a lot to me," said Booth. "It revealed a quality person who went out of his way to care about the needs of others. It wasn't his job to care about someone who hadn't interacted with him much at all, but he did it anyway."

Ron Alessi is another who fondly remembers the kind of behavior that inspires loyalty. Alessi is a local businessman in Salisbury who knew Frank for 30 years. Their interactions did not involve business, but instead were related to various community philanthropies, including the Salisbury Zoo.

"There was a party for the Friends of the Zoo," Alessi recalled. "It was at your home and it was something you guys did every year. It impressed me that Frank was right there, talking with everyone."

That particular evening, more people came than expected and there weren't enough seats in the living room, even though the room holds 150. Alessi remembers that Frank saw the problem and invited the 15 people who didn't have seats to come upstairs to the family room and then, when Frank looked around and saw that there still weren't enough chairs for the 15 people, he went around the house looking for more chairs until he had made sure that everyone had a seat.

"What struck me particularly" said Alessi, "is he didn't tell someone else to find the chairs. He did it himself. It showed how caring he was. He was concerned about their being comfortable. He was very considerate."

There are many skills it takes to be an entrepreneur, but I'm going to put high on the list the ability to create loyalty. There may be entrepreneurs who are successful even while being jerks, but I think being a loyal and caring employer was what kept Frank's associates with him year after year.

FRANK PERDUE'S LESSONS

LOALTY IS A TWO-WAY STREET– Frank inspired loyalty in part because he was extraordinarily loyal to the people who worked for him. He went out of his way to have new hires feel that they were part of the Perdue family. He'd take the time to talk with associates who had lost a parent, or to research health information when an associate had an ill child. He'd get up at 2:00 a.m. if necessary to attend night-shift safety celebrations He'd visit associates in the hospital, he'd call on retired associates, and for the sake of their families, he'd attend the funerals of associates.

TREAT ABSOLUTELY EVERYONE WITH RESPECT– He took the trouble to learn the names, and often personal facts, about a huge number of associates on the line, and when talking with them, which he often did, his approach wasn't boss-employee, but rather, "fellow team member." To show the associates that they were important to him, he had a goal of having everyone who worked for him be a guest at our home for dinner. For years, we would have 100 associates a week over for dinner, and at the end of the evening, he would thank them for making Perdue the success that it is.

CHAPTER TWENTY-ONE
LEADERSHIP STYLE: YES, HE REALLY WAS A TOUGH MAN

It takes leadership to build an organization from two people to 19,000, and to expand from a single hatchery to a meat and grain company that sells its products to more than 100 different countries. What were the leadership qualities that made this possible?

I actually asked Frank this question, and although he had no enthusiasm for talking about his own leadership qualities—he dismissed his accomplishments, saying he had been in the right place at the right time—he did give some opinions on leadership in general.

Frank felt that energy was one of the essential qualities of a successful leader, and that it would be rare to find a successful leader who was lazy. He also felt that integrity was all-important, because long term, people want to deal with people they can respect and trust. He understood the importance of leading by example, and I remember him once saying, "A fish rots from the head down," which I take to mean that if the head of a company cuts corners, that this will be the culture of the entire company.

He was extremely aware of the importance of a company's having a strong culture. He once told me that a strong culture, one where people believe in what they're doing, means "people are willing to work hard for something higher and more important than just ego or money."

Frank also talked about how values are at the heart of a culture, and part of a leader's job includes creating the culture. I have a note from years ago with his saying, "If a culture is weak, people have limited motivation and they work only for money. When values are strong the culture is strong and people are excited to work there."

I wish I had gotten him to talk more on the ingredients of leadership, but I didn't. He wasn't terribly introspective anyway, and also, I think there was a modesty about him that explains why it was hard to get him talking on the subject of why he was outstanding. As a sentient human being, he had to know he was exceptional, but he was temperamentally unwilling to wallow in it.

I didn't get as much firsthand information on his opinions of his own leadership style as I wish I had, but I did ask others. I started with Don Mabe, since Mabe had worked for the company beginning in 1957 and he was probably the person closest to Frank in all those years.

Frank Encouraged Different Viewpoints

Don Mabe and Frank had an interesting relationship. Since they both grew up on farms, they both seemed to speak the same language, and Frank had a huge amount of respect for Mabe's intelligence, hard work creativity and wisdom. They could almost have been brothers. In fact, since they were both only children, I've sometimes wondered if they weren't relating to each other like the brothers they each never had.

On the other hand, I used to think of the two of them as Athens and Sparta. Back in ancient Greece, it happened that Athens and Sparta fought each other, even though they had more in common with each other than with many of the countries that surrounded them. Like Athens and Sparta, Frank and Mabe had epic battles, and I can even remember a discussion among some lawyers that the biggest liability of the whole company was that Frank and Mabe could get so angry with each other.

LEADERSHIP STYLE: YES, HE REALLY
WAS A TOUGH MAN

My own opinion is that the lawyers got it wrong. Maybe they knew about Frank and Mabe yelling and screaming at each other at board meetings, but what they didn't know is, an hour later, Mabe, his wife Flo and Frank and I would be having dinner together, happily laughing, consuming adult beverages, and sharing stories and memories as if nothing had ever happened.

Frank and Don W. Mabe, CEO of Perdue Farms, 1988-91. Don began his career with Perdue Farms in 1957.

Neither of the two men took any of their disagreements personally and neither held a grudge. For them it was apparently normal and routine that if they disagreed, they would express it forcefully.

(For the record, Frank's style with me was completely different. People used to tell me that I must be one tough cookie to be able to stand up to Frank Perdue. Actually it didn't take any toughness on my part, which is good because I don't have any. At home, he was gentle and considerate. In fact, I can't remember Frank's even raising his voice with me. He had a tremendous ability to calibrate his responses to the people he was dealing with.)

In spite of a lifetime of arguing with each other, even including some bellowing and hollering, Mabe knew how to take Frank. He found the relationship satisfactory and told me, "We had a great relationship but we'd disagree at times. It was a contained kind of fighting and never personal."

They actually had lots to fight over because on the issue of spending, Mabe and Frank were yin and yang. Frank was focused on growing the company and gaining market share, while Mabe was often more practical about what these efforts would cost. Another continuing issue was chain of command. As Mabe told me, "He didn't understand chain of command. I had been in the military and I knew not to go around people. Frank didn't get this."

Still, Mabe liked the relationship. "People would often ask me how it was to work for Frank. I'd always answer them, 'I didn't work for him. I worked with him.'"

Which, by the way, was another major ingredient in Frank's leadership style. Many, many people told me the same thing: they felt they were working with Frank, not for him. Frank and Mabe might fight, but Frank's leadership style encouraged different opinions, and people were free to express their dissent as forcefully as they wanted given that they were all working toward the same goal. I think it's a key element in Frank's success that he allowed people to feel safe to disagree with him.

Frank Saw Both the Forest and the Trees

Like Don Mabe, Bob Turley also had a president-of-the-company's point of view on Frank and leadership. He started out with Perdue in 1987 in Quality Assurance, became a complex manager, and from 1993 to 2004 was Perdue Farms' President.

"Some people said he was demanding," said Turley, "but his attitude was (and I often heard him say this), 'People like being on a winning team, and all the long hours and challenges are worthwhile when you're playing on the wining team.'"

Turley felt that Frank was tough, but fair, and if you got the job done, he rewarded you. "What I appreciated the most was you could always speak your mind, and he wouldn't hold it against you or carry a grudge."

Turley was impressed that for Frank, no detail was too small. "Most people who run companies get deeply involved in only two or three things, but

LEADERSHIP STYLE: YES, HE REALLY
WAS A TOUGH MAN

Frank was involved in everything. I don't know a single thing Frank was not involved in. It didn't matter what it was, if he was thinking about it, he was passionate about it."

Turley noticed that although Frank made it his business to learn all aspects of the company, he nevertheless had great vision. "He was a leader who could see both the trees and the forest. Most people can't do that. He was unique."

Vision and values were at the heart of Frank's drive to make Perdue Farms a leader in the industry.

However, that wasn't what Turley found most unique about Frank's leadership style. "He always knew what the customers wanted, and a lot of that was because he was out there listening. One of his greatest statements was, 'To be successful we must develop products and services for the consumers before they realize it is something they want.'"

"Frank was able to do this on a regular basis." In pretty much all of Turley's evaluation of Frank's leadership style, one thing emerges: Frank was gifted at getting information. He allowed people to speak their minds, he was willing to be detail-minded yet could look at the big picture, and "he was out there listening."

He Was Gifted at Getting Information

Randy Day felt that some of Frank's leadership success came from his humility. "I never felt that he thought, 'I'm the smartest guy in the room and I don't need you.' Instead, when he'd come into the room, I felt as if he was thinking, 'There's a lot of brainpower in this room, let's use it! I want everyone's ideas.'

LEADERSHIP STYLE: YES, HE REALLY WAS A TOUGH MAN

"One of the ways he worked with us and would lead us is he didn't come in and say, 'I want you to do this,' but rather it was 'These are the results I want!'" For Day, this ability to tap into and use the insights and abilities of others was a large ingredient in Frank's leadership style.

Eileen Burza was the Senior VP of Finance and Chief Financial Officer from 2001 until her retirement in 2013. She's still with Perdue, however, as she was appointed to the Perdue Board of Directors immediately after her retirement.

Burza was the most senior female executive at Perdue Farms. That made her something of a pioneer, since historically the meat industry hasn't exactly been a magnet for top-level executive women. Personally and as a woman, I was beyond delighted to see how much people respected her. She earned that respect through an attractive combination of competence, confidence, and collegiality.

Frank Could Be Flexible

Burza got to see an important ingredient in Frank's management success: flexibility. The year she started with Perdue, there were heated discussions within the company's sales and marketing groups about whether we should get into the frozen chicken market. The problem was the company had been in business for more than 80 years by then, and part of the Perdue Farms identity was, "Our chickens are always fresh, they've never been frozen."

"You might expect that Frank would be firmly on the side of staying with the approach that had built the company," said Burza. "But instead, and more so than many of the people who worked for him, he was open to change. Or put differently, he knew that if the market was moving, we needed to move with it."

She saw the essence of this when she, along with 15 other members of top management, were in the Perdue Farms boardroom, sitting around the large mahogany conference table. It was a windowless room, so all the focus was

LEADERSHIP STYLE: YES, HE REALLY WAS A TOUGH MAN

on what was going on around the table.

The topic was whether to abandon the company's 80-year identity of being the fresh chicken company. Burza already knew that some who were present felt that the topic was so delicate and controversial that they were uncomfortable even bringing up the subject. Messing with the company's identity in front of the founder would, you might expect, be a ticklish thing to do. There was a lot riding on the discussion. Emotions were strong, opinions differed, and the stakes were high. The participants must have been worried about how Frank would react to this.

Frank was getting hard of hearing, and as the discussion proceeded, he leaned over to Burza, who was sitting next to him, asked what was being said.

"They're discussing whether we should keep to our tradition of selling only fresh chicken, or should we follow the market and sell frozen chicken," Burza told him.

Frank looked at her, a puzzled look on his face. "If it is what the customer wants, and we can make money doing it, then why are we discussing it?" he asked.

Burza was deeply impressed at how flexible and non-dogmatic he was over something that had been part of the core identity of the company, and by extension, his identity. "He understood that product attributes need to change as the consumer changes, and he was never stuck in his ways. He wouldn't compromise on quality, but if the world is going to change, he was flexible enough to change with it. It was impressive for someone in his 80s."

When Frank was no longer driving, Burza would have lunch with him every few weeks. She'd drive him to one or the other of his two favorite restaurants, Brew River and Goin' Nuts Cafe.

"At these lunches, which almost always included his favorite fried oysters and applesauce, I got to see firsthand an interesting pattern in how he got

225

information."

Each time they would start lunch with his asking several standard questions such as, "How is Vernon?" (her husband) or some other personal items, almost as if he had a mental checklist of social questions he should ask. "And then zap! He'd be all business and would start asking questions about the company.

"What was different about his questions was he was always drawing you out, but he wasn't giving you his opinions. I know of CEOs or managers who let you know what answers they're looking for." Frank didn't do that.

"He'd ask your opinions on things that interested him, such as the amount of debt we were carrying, or ways of paying it off, or whether we should change to a different breed, but you never really knew where he stood on these things. You knew he'd be asking many other people the same kinds of questions. For him it was the research that he did before coming to his own conclusions."

In Burza's case, he'd ask questions relating to finance, and he showed that he had a gut-level business sense about it. "He understood the math, but he could see beyond the math to what was really going on."

Part of leadership involves image, and Burza noticed how Frank presented himself. "Frank was always well dressed. I remember he had several pairs of dark custom-made pants which people wouldn't have known were custom made, except you could tell if you looked for the handmade button holes. They were always nicely pressed, his shirts were crisply starched, and he liked striped shirts, particularly Façonnable ones. Sometimes he'd wear a tie and sometimes not. Typically he wouldn't be wearing a jacket, except in winter he'd wear a black zippered jacket with his baseball team's logo sewn on it." She felt that Frank always projected a professional, business-like, competent and appropriate look.

226

LEADERSHIP STYLE: YES, HE REALLY WAS A TOUGH MAN

For Burza, Frank's leadership style involved awesome flexibility, impressive information-gathering skills, and although she didn't express it this way herself, she might have seen something of Frank in Sherlock Holmes' statement that, "It is a capital mistake to theorize before one has data. Insensibly one begins to twist facts to suit theories, instead of theories to suit facts." Frank acquired a lot of data before making his decisions. And finally, Frank made sure, in his dress, to project the image of a well-dressed competent executive.

The Difficult Job of Letting Go

As Frank approached his 80s, he had to face one of the most difficult yet important jobs of a leader: handing over the reins to his successor. There were times during this period when I'd look at Frank and think of Sherlock Holmes, although this time in a different context from Holmes's fact-finding that I mentioned a moment ago. The fictional detective used to say that when he was forced to be idle because he wasn't working on a case, his mind was "like a racing engine, tearing itself to pieces because it is not connected up with the work for which it was built."

Frank and Jim had a deep love for each other, but as Frank tried to pull back and let his son run the company, his mind turned into Holmes' racing engine, tearing itself to bits from lack of activity.

Still, to Frank's credit, he recognized his problems with pulling back. In fact, he had a lot of self-awareness when it came to the issue. He and I would sometimes talk about elite athletes who hung on past their expiration date. Frank occasionally mentioned the sad case of Sugar Ray Leonard, who could have ended his career in the ring as a champion, but instead tried over and over again for the comeback that never quite came.

Frank didn't want to be like Sugar Ray Leonard, and intellectually he knew that it was essential that he pull back. Still, knowing in your head can still mean a struggle in your heart.

LEADERSHIP STYLE: YES, HE REALLY
WAS A TOUGH MAN

Mike Roberts was President of Poultry and Food Products during Frank's last three years, and he witnessed the tension for Frank between wanting to be deeply involved in the company while at the same time wanting to support his son Jim's role as Chairman of the Board.

Roberts came in the later part of 2002. As he said, "Frank was in his 80s by then and he didn't view himself as leading the company any more, but he would attend meetings. He didn't speak up much but instead would listen intently to what Jim and the others were saying."

I know that Frank had made up his mind not to insert himself too much into board discussions since he didn't want to undermine his son. However, as Roberts said, he still had an intense interest in what was going on, and had opinions as well.

"He would come around and ask me questions after the meetings and his questions gave an insight on his thinking. For instance, Frank felt that if the time-strapped consumer wanted fully cooked, then we would be fools not to provide it. However, he also felt that as a late entry, we would need to have a superior product if we were to make it in the market place."

Roberts got to observe Frank's doing something that is seriously difficult for a leader: he watched Frank pull back and barely participate in meetings, knowing that it was his successor whose job it now was to run the show.

Debbie Kelly has been a member of Perdue's Board of Directors since 1996. I remember Frank and Jim both discussing that they very much wanted a female board member, and I remember their enthusiasm when they found Kelly.

Kelly recognized that Frank and Jim were very different people. "I joined the board after Frank had passed the leadership torch to Jim. Jim is more collegial, not that he doesn't have strong opinions about some things. That's what's needed today in a company as large and complex as Perdue has become.

228

LEADERSHIP STYLE: YES, HE REALLY WAS A TOUGH MAN

"One person can't do it all. The kind of person whom it took to start the company, including differentiating the product and building a brand, is different from what's needed in a company that is operating in a large mature market."

Kelly gives Frank a lot of credit for being able to turn things over to his son. One of the most important aspects of leadership is managing succession and in cases when this is not handled well, the company is at risk. Many companies do not survive the transition, and it's easy to read in the Wall Street Journal or the New York Times cases of families and companies that fall apart because the founder didn't accept the need to let go.

For Frank, this letting go was emotionally arduous, but as a leader, he was able to discern the necessity, and he forced himself to do what he knew was right for his son, the associates, and the company.

FRANK PERDUE'S LESSONS

DEVELOP A STRONG AND POSITIVE CULTURE– Frank put immense effort into developing a strong culture, knowing that when people believe in what a company is doing, they're working for something higher and more important than only money or only ego. People often said they were working with Frank, not for him.

ALLOW DISSENTING VIEWS, STRONGLY EXPRESSED– Part of the Perdue culture included permission to express ideas strongly. Frank didn't hold it against you for disagreeing with him, and you could get him to change his mind

FACILITATING SUCCESSION IS DIFFICULT, BUT WITH GOOD WILL, CAN BE DONE SUCCESSFULLY– For Frank, turning over the reins to his son was emotionally difficult, but he was tremendously self-aware of the problem and worked to make the transition as smooth as he could. The process wasn't seamless, but in the end, it was successful.

CHAPTER TWENTY-TWO
THE PERSONAL SIDE: WHAT WAS
FRANK REALLY LIKE?

So far you've been reading about Frank as a businessman, employer and philanthropist, but there was a vast personal side to him that contributed to his success.

I got a clue about one part of this personal side the day after we had returned from our honeymoon. It had to do with what was important to him. I was waiting for Frank in his headquarters office and noticed that Elaine Barnes had lined up on his desk probably 20 fancy-looking invitations, all of them to amazing parties in Washington and New York. Because he was world-famous by then, he was invited everywhere.

The engraved invitations, often on thick cardboard stock with gilt edges, came from people with famous names and were to parties that I think many people would die to attend. Barnes told me that he got that many equally impressive invitations every week. Curious about these amazing invitations, I asked Frank about them.

What Was Important to Frank

We discussed whether attending these kinds of parties was something he wanted to do. The answer was a definitive no, they weren't important to him. What was important was being close to his family, his church, and his community.

THE PERSONAL SIDE: WHAT WAS
FRANK REALLY LIKE?

The result of this conversation was not only did we skip all those invitations, but instead, we ended up being the people to issue invitations. However, instead of entertaining the rich and famous, we entertained people who were far more important to him, the Perdue associates. Since Perdue employed something approaching 20,000 at the time, that meant plenty of entertaining. It also happened to be a perfect fit for my personality and upbringing, since I grew up in the hospitality industry and *love* entertaining.

I think Frank's major goal in entertaining was to express appreciation and also to have the individual guest feel important and valued. At the end of each party, he would speak briefly, thanking our guests – his employees – and telling them that he knew the company would never have become what it was today without them. Then he'd answer questions, so for example a truck driver or a sanitation associate could ask the founder of Perdue Farms about whatever was on his or her mind.

We invited people in groups of 100, most often associates who knew each other, such as the secretaries, or computer experts, and we did this on the theory that for at least some people, it would be intimidating to be invited to the home of the head of the company. We figured that if guests came with people they knew, they'd be more comfortable.

It's incongruous, but Frank, who was basically a shy man, absolutely adored having the house full of people. He used to tell me that he loved seeing the house come alive, filled with animated guests having fun.

He was a gracious host and often would serve his guests from the buffet line. He was good at going around and shaking everyone's hand and, for that moment, giving each person his whole attention, making the person feel important. In fact, that was one of Frank's gifts, being able to talk with anyone at his or her level, whether a worker on the line of a processing plant or the president of the United States. I've seen him relate to both with equal grace, ease and sincerity.

THE PERSONAL SIDE: WHAT WAS FRANK REALLY LIKE?

I have a favorite memory of these parties. One evening, I noticed an African American couple off in the corner of the room, not mingling or participating in the animation and bustle and fun of that night's party. I went up to them, wanting to find out what was wrong.

"My wife works for Perdue sanitation," the husband told me, "but I don't. I work for the city Department of Sanitation. If I try to tell the guys who work with me I had dinner at Frank Perdue's home, they'll never believe me."

My Polaroid to the rescue! I grabbed it from my office, which was next door to the living room where that party was taking place, and then looked for Frank. Predictably, he was in the center of a large crowd of people, shaking hands and making each person feel important. I interrupted the scene and in a low voice, explained the sanitation man's problem.

Frank instantly got it, and grinning like a fellow conspirator, left the twenty or so people who had been surrounding him and walked to the corner of the room where the couple was. He warmly shook hands with the man, and then, as I prepared to take the picture, Frank put his arm around him as if they were old buddies. I quickly snapped their picture. A minute later, Frank was autographing the photo with the Sharpie pen he always carried in his shirt pocket.

I watched Frank write, "To Mike, it was great having dinner with you last night, Frank."

The couple beamed.

Frank Was an Egalitarian

That story captures something important about Frank. The important thing was that everyone was important to him. Wayland Hicks, former Executive Vice President at Xerox, CEO of Nextel and also CEO of United Rentals, North America, was on the Perdue Farms Board of Directors from 1992 until his retirement in 2014. During his more than two decades of watching

THE PERSONAL SIDE: WHAT WAS FRANK REALLY LIKE?

Frank in action, one aspect of Frank's personality particularly struck him: Frank never put himself over the people who worked for him.

"My sense is Frank was a very humble human being," said Hicks. "He wanted to give people a feeling that he wasn't above them. He seemed to act on the principle that all human beings are God's creation and everyone is worthy of respect."

Hicks saw this in both Frank and Jim. "When the two would walk through a plant, both of them would talk with the associates, they both knew the names of many of them, and you could see a caring on the part of both father and son."

Hicks remembered another example of Frank's egalitarianism. "Once I got on a plane with him and realized that he was going coach. As I was changing my ticket to be with him, I was thinking, 'Here's a guy who's a household name, and yet he's flying coach.'"

Hicks wondered why Frank would fly coach and then came up with the answer that, "Frank didn't want people to think of him as different from anyone else. But still, how many people do you know who have achieved so much in life who would think that way and behave that way? I don't think there's any employee in the company who would have begrudged his going first class."

Hicks felt Frank's office was another example of his not putting himself above others. "By this time Frank had passed the baton to Jim, and Jim, now the CEO, was occupying Frank's old office. Jim had done nothing to change the office and as we entered it and I looked around, it struck me that it was surprisingly humble. There was nothing about it that showed that this was the office of the chief executive of a billion-dollar company.

THE PERSONAL SIDE: WHAT WAS FRANK REALLY LIKE?

"For one thing, it was small. I noticed that it had room for his desk and chair, and there were two additional chairs for visitors, plus an assortment of file cabinets, but the office wouldn't have fit more furniture without being crowded.

"I looked over at the walls, which were made of inexpensive, unpretentious pine wood. The desk itself was solid, handsome and serviceable, but it was almost certainly from the 1940s and the carpet may have come from the same era.

"And then something else struck me about the office. I saw something built into one of the walls, something about the length and shape of a door, but it wasn't a door. I pointed to it, asking Jim what it was.

"'It's a pull-down wall bed,' Jim explained. 'In the past, my dad used to go home, have dinner, and when dinner was finished, he'd go back and work until the wee hours, and then pull down the wall bed, and catch a few hours' sleep. After that, he'd go back home to have breakfast with the family and clean up before starting the new day.'"

It's as if everything about Frank was consistent with his being humble and hardworking. He was also a frugal man. He didn't mind spending $10 million on an advertising program, but in his personal life, he preferred to live way, way below his means. When Perdue Farms made money, instead of spending it on himself, he reinvested it in the business.

He used to say that when you have money in the bank, it means that you're able to take advantage of opportunities when they arise. Saving money both provides you with freedom of action and prevents a lot of worry.

As far as I could observe, he seemed completely immune to the pleasures of acquisition. Our home on Woodland Road was an example. Our neighbors across the street were retired teachers, and on one side of us was a guy who ran a local vending machine company, and on the other, a guy who was partners in several local grain elevators. It wasn't exactly Millionaire's Row.

THE PERSONAL SIDE: WHAT WAS
FRANK REALLY LIKE?

In fact, one of my favorite stories about our Woodland Road home comes from Owen Schweers, the Perdue Director of Packaging. As Schweers tells it, Frank had decided to bring in a big supplier for a visit to Salisbury. Schweers and the supplier were to meet Frank at his home.

Schweers was driving and as they came to our house, his VIP passenger started laughing heartily. "Okay, that's a good one!" he chortled. "But you're not going to get me on this. I know Frank Perdue wouldn't live in that little ranch house!"

"No, this is Frank's house, " Schweers insisted, pulling his car up to the front door.

"*Sure, right,*" said the supplier, still laughing.

They parked next to our front door, and Frank, having heard the car in the driveway, opened the door, ready to greet his guests.

"Oh my God," whispered the supplier. "This really is Mr. Perdue's house!"

Frank could have lived in a mansion but he chose not to. Although to be accurate, I should point out that the house was much bigger than it appeared from the road. We had a sizable basement configured for entertaining large groups of guests.

Frank Wasn't a Fan of Conspicuous Consumption

Frank didn't own racehorses or yachts, and although he did have a Mercedes, he kept the first one for 25 years and only gave it up when finding the replacement parts became too difficult. He kept his second Mercedes for more than a decade until his passing.

He bought quality clothes, but he took care of them, and as for shoes, if we're talking dress shoes as opposed to athletic shoes, he bought three pairs in 17 years. I know this because each year I'd wonder how long he could keep this up, the not getting around to buying new shoes.

THE PERSONAL SIDE: WHAT WAS
FRANK REALLY LIKE?

The fact is, he'd wear his shoes until they had holes in them, I'd have them resoled, and he'd just kept on wearing them until there were more holes and we went through the cycle of another cobbler visit. I bet we had the highest cobbler bill in Maryland.

A favorite memory I have of Frank and shoes happened during our wedding in July of 1988. Frank was looking spiffy in a to-die-for handsome Ermenegildo Zegna dark suit, Paul Stewart white shirt, and an Hermes tie. Still, there was something very, very wrong with this picture.

You wouldn't have seen this under almost any other circumstance than Frank Perdue's own wedding, but here's what happened. There came a point in the ceremony when we both were kneeling in front of the altar at the church where we were married.

I didn't even see what I'm about to describe, but a lot of our guests did. I only know about it for sure because the wedding photographer gleefully took a bunch of pictures of it and loved displaying them to all who would look. Including me.

Frank Perdue, the famous captain of industry, had *an inch and a half hole* in the sole of one of his shoes and a smaller hole in the other.

Once we were married, I made sure that he no longer wore shoes with holes, but I cherish this memory because it shows that buying new shoes wasn't a priority for Frank. How many businessmen or women who were as successful as he was wear their shoes until they have holes in them?

This brings me to a favorite memory from my son by my previous marriage, Zé Ayala. We were all in the parking lot of the Coq d'Or restaurant in Philadelphia, and Frank saw a shiny new penny on the ground. Frank bent down, picked it up and held it aloft with a flourish. "He seemed as pleased," marveled Zé, "as I would have been finding a $10 bill!"

236

THE PERSONAL SIDE: WHAT WAS FRANK REALLY LIKE?

Another area where we didn't squander money was air travel. We never traveled first class until he was in his 80s, and then only after his doctor said it was medically necessary during the many overseas business flights when we were visiting overseas customers.

I think he had several motives for traveling economy up to then. For one thing, if he traveled economy, it meant that top management was also going to fly economy, and that helped with his overall ethic for the company of not spending money on consumption, and instead spending it on investment.

I'm also certain that he enjoyed talking with people in economy class. If you only travel first class, you're going to get out of touch with the rest of the world real fast. And then, a final reason is I think he actually enjoyed leading a somewhat more down-to-earth life when given the chance.

Frank also really enjoyed using the subways. When we'd be calling on customers in any part of Manhattan, we could have come in a chauffeur-driven limousine, but in fact, we'd go there by subway. He knew the New York subway system perfectly, so obviously he had used it a lot. For that matter, if we were in London, Paris, Tokyo, Moscow or Beijing, we'd also use their subways. We used to love to attend the Wimbledon tennis matches, and while his peers would be arriving in their chauffeur-driven Rolls Royces, Frank and I would be having a great time coming there using the "Tube."

I'm thinking of another thing that wealthy individuals spend money on, and that's art. Although he did buy works of art, these were most likely to be in the high $1,000 range, or occasionally, in the $10,000 range, but never in the million-dollar range. Whatever art Frank bought, it would be from unknown artists and it would be displayed in our home simply and solely because we both loved it. On second thought, it wasn't only because we loved it; another reason is Frank liked helping little-known artists.

Something else, he did buy top-quality, brand-name, expensive clothes. He recognized that he was the walking embodiment of his brand, and I remember many visits to the Paul Stewart store on Madison Avenue. Also, I don't believe he ever left the store without having some alterations. He cared about the fit, and his manner of dress, while never flashy, seemed to broadcast taste and quality.

This may sound to you like he was extravagant on clothes, but you wouldn't easily guess the care he took of them. I told you earlier I thought that we were likely to have had the highest cobbler bill in Maryland, but I'm also ready to bet that we had one of the higher re-weaving bills in all of New York.

If, for example, the knees of a pair of trousers were wearing thin, my job was to mail the trousers to Alice Zotta in New York. She specialized in invisible re-weaving. If I remember right, even a small project might run $50, but since it meant that an expensive suit would last another couple of years, going to the trouble of having the thin spots rewoven made a lot of sense.

He didn't spend money on himself, but at restaurants, he was always the one to grab the check and he gave phenomenal amounts to charity. When I once asked him why he spent so little on himself, he had a very matter-of-fact answer: First, he didn't want more, and second, he was happy with what he had.

He was an almost Legendary Charmer

Frank may have been humble and frugal, but he was also known for his personal charm. Even though he's been gone for almost a decade, a week doesn't go by when I don't meet someone who remembers even a brief interaction with him, and they don't just remember him, they remember him with the greatest pleasure.

In my experience, normal people don't get that response from other people. We might meet a movie star and remember him or her, but usually we don't remember the meeting as being especially personally delightful. With Frank Perdue, I think just about everyone I meet who mentions him from social situations remembers him with pleasure.

So how did Frank get to be remembered by people he interacted with even for a moment? I'll tell you one thing it wasn't. Frank was a naturally shy person, so being effusive and tremendously outgoing wasn't part of his magnetism.

The thing that I noticed first about Frank is when he was speaking to someone, he gave the person his total, full, undivided attention. I used to call it his, "At this moment, you're the only person in my world" look. It had to be flattering to the person on the receiving end, and it had to make him or her feel important. There was never any looking over the person's shoulder to see who else he could be talking with. When he was talking with you, you had his full attention, whether you were a person working on the line in a processing plant or president of the United States.

Cindy Downes from my office remembers to this day how, when he was listening to her, he'd support his chin in the palm of one hand and then rest the elbow of that hand in the palm of the other hand. It was a characteristic gesture when he was giving something his full attention and it made her feel that nothing else mattered to him except what she was saying. When Frank was listening to you, you knew he was *listening*.

He might ask questions about what you said, but in general, he would be talking less than 10 percent of the time and listening to you the rest. While you were the center of his attention, you probably felt wonderful.

Another ingredient in charm is being appreciative. Surprisingly, Frank was not effusive in praising people. His compliments were legendarily sparse, and I've heard people say that a compliment from Frank Perdue was so rare and extraordinary that it would cure cancer. But maybe just because he used praise so sparingly, when he did praise someone, they might remember it the rest of their lives. His compliments had particular impact, probably more than they would have if he used words lightly.

THE PERSONAL SIDE: WHAT WAS FRANK REALLY LIKE?

Also, his compliments were different from flattery; they didn't have an agenda behind them; they weren't a means of achieving something; rather they came from his core; they were a reflection of what he valued and what he stood for. If a compliment came your way, you probably felt ten feet tall and remembered it for life. Every time you thought of it, you felt wonderful.

Frank had another way of creating extraordinary rapport, but to explain it, let me illustrate it by jumping backwards to a late 19th century story that involves British Prime Ministers William Gladstone and Benjamin Disraeli. A lady who had been a dinner partner for each of them was asked which of the two prime ministers she preferred. She answered, "Disraeli. When I talk with Gladstone, I feel that I'm talking with the cleverest person in England. But when I talk with Disraeli, he makes me feel that *I'm* the cleverest person in England!" Disraeli had the gift of making his dinner partner feel wonderful.

Frank had the soul of a Disraeli. He excelled at making others feel important and valuable. He didn't boast about himself, instead he sought out things in the other to make him or her feel important and that would make himself appear less important.

As an example, he suggested that I refrain from talking about trips abroad or fancy parties if I was in the presence of anyone who wouldn't have done these things. His reason? If I talked about them, it might make the other person feel less important.

He also believed that one of the secrets to developing rapport, whether face-to-face or during a speech, was never to boast but instead to be self-deprecating. Or put differently, that humility is attractive and arrogance puts people off.

Although he was conscious of what he was doing in being self-deprecating, it was also sincere. He didn't consider himself above anyone. When we entertained at our home, he would treat a sanitation worker with the same

240

respect as he would a duchess. (Maybe even with a little more, because he really, really respected anyone who worked.)

Something else about Frank and personal magnetism: he wasn't a complainer. I can remember times when he was experiencing back pain yet he was careful to hide his back brace under his suit as he'd go off to, say, an award ceremony at one of the plants. Given the pain he was in, he would have been entitled to complain or ask for sympathy. He didn't because he wasn't there to steal the focus for himself and his problem.

Far from complaining, he was endlessly upbeat. He was often smiling, ready with a quip or a joke or a hilarious pun. He fits the old saying that "the most attractive raiment of all is the cloak of good humor."

Frank had another characteristic that people found attractive. Although I'm sure in a business situation he must have been the ultimate poker player, in social situations, he seemed to me to be almost guileless. You felt you were dealing with a genuine person, not one who was programmed or scripted or putting on a mask. He wasn't acting a part; he truly was who he appeared to be.

I can think of something else that people found attractive. He could talk with you on just about any subject that interested you. I remember watching in awe as he talked with the Librarian of Congress about literature, and then a few days later, he was talking with the docent of a museum in the island of Nevis, where Alexander Hamilton was born, about some of the lesser-known aspects of Hamilton's life. And right after that, he was talking with a friend's young son about baseball.

Frank's long-time friend Judge Alfred Truitt was particularly impressed by the wide range of topics Frank could discuss. "Frank had an insatiable appetite for knowledge on a wide range of subjects and his search for answers made him a voracious reader. Sometimes I'd get a call from him at 2:00 a.m. and he'd call just because something had shot through his mind. He didn't think about the time he was calling and assumed that everyone else only needs two hours of sleep a night."

I'm not sure the late night phone calls count as charming, but Truitt told me he enjoyed the conversations because they were about things that interested them both. Since Truitt is a judge, Frank was apt to call him about the crime novels he had just been reading. "The call could be about his having just read something or other and he wanted to know what I thought about it. He read Scott Turow, John Grisham, Mario Puzo – that kind of stuff appealed to him. I'm positive he was reading business books all the time too, but that's not what he talked about with me."

Frank and Family

Frank's family that all-important to him. When we'd be on a long car drive, which would happen several times a week, we'd always be talking about his children and grandchildren, naming each one and discussing what they were up to.

Getting together for Thanksgiving with his children, grandchildren and great grandchildren was one of the delights of his life. He also arranged for a family trip every year with all of them, and he'd write heartfelt notes to all of them on their birthdays.

Frank's Ethical Will

Something else that I thought was incredibly special, he knew he was going to leave his family material things, but he wanted to leave them values as well. The result was his *Ethical Will*.

What you're about to read is something he and I spent many days on. We'd talk about the values he felt were most important, and then I, acting as his secretary, would write down what he had said. He'd read them, revise them, and then add more.

THE PERSONAL SIDE: WHAT WAS FRANK REALLY LIKE?

Here's the end result:

Dear Children, Grandchildren and Family Members (present or future):

I want little more than your long-term happiness. To be happy you need character and self-respect and these come from following your highest values. To be happy, consider the following:

1. Be honest always.
2. Be a person whom others are justified in trusting.
3. If you say you will do something, do it.
4. You don't have to be the best, but you should be the best you can be.
5. Treat all people with courtesy and respect, no exceptions.
6. Remember that the way to be happy is to think of what you can do for others. The way to be miserable is to think about what people should be doing for you.
7. Be part of something bigger than your own self. That something can be family, pursuit of knowledge, the environment, or whatever you choose.
8. Remember that hard work is satisfying and fulfilling.
9. Nurture the ability to laugh and have fun
10. Have respect for those who have gone before; learn from their weaknesses and build on their strengths.

He wanted to have this read at his funeral, and he got his wish. During the service, the grandchildren got up, faced the 2000 mourners, and then took turns with each grandchild reading one of the recommendations. It was incredibly moving, to hear his words and thoughts coming from the mouths of young people.

THE PERSONAL SIDE: WHAT WAS FRANK REALLY LIKE?

I've always felt that Frank was the man who had it all; he was not only a successful business man, and community participant, he was also an adoring parent and grandparent. On top of that, he was also true romantic.

Frank as a Romantic

I was impressed that Frank, as a captain of industry and a tough man, had a romantic side. He'd always send me two dozen red roses at Valentine's, and something that really impressed, touched moved and delighted me, he'd include with the roses some wonderful little handwritten love message, always in French.

I have a favorite memory about this side of Frank. He was a passionate tennis fan and we'd go to Wimbledon each year for the matches. One year, as we walked to the Tube on our way to get to where the matches were being played, we passed a store window with the most enchanting china pattern. It was gold and green, and had beautiful birds painted on it.

I could see it on our dining room table during a dinner party, along with gorgeous white linens and tall candles. They were so beautiful I yearned for them, so of course I began hinting that they'd be nice to have. Each time we walked by them, which was maybe six times because we were there a week, I'd hint and hint for all I was worth.

"Aren't those just beautiful?" I'd say, tugging at his sleeve and pointing at the plates. Or another day, "Oh look, they're still there – wouldn't they look beautiful in our home?"

Nothing seemed to register.

We were leaving London on Sunday morning, and on Saturday I knew the shop closed at 6:00 p.m. That Saturday evening, I watched with a heavy heart as 6:00 p.m. came and went and the store was now closed. No more chance of getting the lovely china.

THE PERSONAL SIDE: WHAT WAS
FRANK REALLY LIKE?

A half an hour or so later, Frank suggested we go out for dinner. We got in a cab, and soon the cab pulled up at a restaurant that was just next door to the shop with the china. I felt a twinge of minor sadness, to be so near the china that I thought was so beautiful, now with no possibility of ever buying it.

We got out of the cab and were heading toward the restaurant, but then I stopped in my tracks. There was a small light inside the closed china store. I took a few steps closer and could now see through the window of the darkened store that someone was standing inside holding high a candelabra with three lit candles. In the other hand, butler-style, he was holding a tray with a champagne bottle and three glasses.

At this point Frank said, all casualness, "Oh look, the store you liked is still open, want to go in?"

As we entered the store, he was beaming like a little boy. He had arranged for the store to be open and the champagne to be ready for us. The proprietor set the candelabra down, and poured champagne for all of us. As we sipped champagne, Frank invited me to buy any china I liked.

The china I liked turned out to be Lynn Chase Winter Birds, and it cost roughly three times more than I had ever spent on china. When I saw the price, I was shocked. Frank asked me how many place settings I'd like, and because the price was so much more than I was expecting, I thought I should be modest in my request. "Four would be *wonderful,*" I said from the heart.

Frank turned to the store manager and said, "The lady would like twelve. Please ship them to this address."

Well, that was his romantic side. He also had a nostalgic side to him. He never, ever forgot his agricultural roots.

I remember his last months when walking had become difficult for him, one of his great pleasures in life was for me to drive him to the port on the Wicomico River. We'd just sit in the car, watching as the 1,500-ton grain

THE PERSONAL SIDE: WHAT WAS
FRANK REALLY LIKE?

barges were being unloaded, the grain headed for the feed mill in Salisbury.

I got what he was feeling because at one point in my career, I was a rice grower, and there's something almost magical about how soil, sunlight, water and seeds combine to produce this incredible abundance. Together we'd sit there watching barges, tugboats, the grain-filled trucks, and we'd also get to watch the ducks, geese and crows, not to mention the "LBJs" that were flocking there to eat any grain that had spilled.

By the way, are you wondering what kind of bird an LBJ is? It's the name we used for birds that we couldn't identify: they were "little brown jobs."

Frank's Last Hours

Since this is my last chapter, perhaps it's a time to tell about Frank's last hours and last words. They weren't exactly words, though in my mind, they count as words. But first, for this story to make sense to you, please understand that Jim's and Frank's relationship always involved teasing and ribbing each other. It's just how they were with each other. Jim's way of saying goodbye to his father was exactly in keeping with how he had interacted with his father all his life.

At the time, as far as the family and the hospice nurse knew, Frank was in a deep coma, lying utterly still. Jim Perdue came to say good-bye to his father, and leaning over Frank's bed, said, in the exact joking, teasing kind of nanner-nanner-nanner voice he would have used when Frank was well, "Dad, the company is doing better today than it did when you were running it!"

Deep as Frank's coma was, he somehow heard and understood. He responded with a surprisingly loud and enthusiastic, "Ho! Ho! Ho!"

I loved it that Frank went out surrounded by people who loved him and that his last "words" were laughter.

THE PERSONAL SIDE: WHAT WAS
FRANK REALLY LIKE?

Final Thoughts

I've given a lot of thought to what I should say at the end of this biography. Maybe the best is just a cri *de coeur* about what I really thought of him. For me it was the privilege of a lifetime to spend time with someone who was not just a successful man, but also a profoundly good one. The reason I wrote this book is the hope that some of the ideas that came from such a man might be helpful to you, not just in business, but in life.

EPILOGUE: JIM PERDUE'S REFLECTIONS ON HIS FATHER AND ON PERDUE FARMS

People have used many terms to describe my Dad: entrepreneurial, tough, driven, detail minded, customer-intimate, fair, honest and many more. These traits of Frank Parsons Perdue come to life in the many anecdotes and stories of many associates chronicled in this book and summarized after each chapter.

But what will always be most remembered about Frank Perdue is the fact that he gave life to the values of the company that Arthur W. Perdue established in 1920. And he then reinforced those values so that it was "crystal clear" what was important to Perdue Farms. Many people call this a company's culture. He established a culture that people liked and, as a result, Perdue is a company with an extraordinary number of loyal and long-term associates.

The values from which Perdue Farms derives its strength today include Quality, Integrity, Trust, Frugality, Hard Work and Teamwork. Perdue's stated vision is "to be the most trusted name in food and agricultural products." When consumers talk about Perdue, trust and quality are the two values they describe as unique to Perdue. Trust was reinforced by the fact the Frank Perdue, through his advertising, personally promised the quality of his products. He was also the first to offer a "money-back guarantee."

Customer intimacy and integrity are strong values that are imbedded in the idea that the customer is always right and always "say what you do and do what you say" with a customer, associate or producer.

249

EPILOGUE

The values of the company, which were established by Arthur Perdue and reinforced by Frank Perdue, will not change. We may change our business model or our mission, but the 95-year-old values will always be how the company will run.

The voice and face of Perdue Chickens greeted millions of people weekly in their living rooms.

Frank was a "hands-on" manager of Perdue Farms.

Three generations of American agricultural industry leaders
Frank Perdue, Arthur Perdue and Jim Perdue.

Chicken frankfurters were another Perdue innovation. Even though they did not become popular in the U.S., the company exports millions of pounds of them every year.

Three Birds at Orioles Park, Baltimore, Maryland.

Mitzi and Frank on Holiday.

Frank and wife/author Mitzi Perdue during a Library of Congress trip to Spain. Frank and Mitzi were married in 1988.

Frank often joked that he, "looked like a chicken."

ABOUT THE AUTHOR

Mitzi Perdue holds a bachelor's degree in government from Harvard University and a master's in public administration from the George Washington University. For two decades she was a syndicated columnist, first for Capitol News, writing about food and agriculture, and then for Scripps Howard, writing about the environment. She has a lifelong interest in business and success, having watched how her father, Ernest Henderson, along with his business partner, Robert Moore, founded and built the Sheraton Hotel chain. She was a commissioner on the U.S. National Commission on Libraries and Information Science and a past president of American Agri-Women, the oldest and largest American farm women's organization. She spent decades growing rice in California, and when Frank and Mitzi met, they decided that chicken and rice go well together.

www.mitziperdue.com

QUOTES FROM FRANK PERDUE

- *Baseball is correlated to business; the Yankees do not win most of the time by accident. Winning is never an accident; it's a matter of getting the best players to play and turning them loose.*

- *You can go to the worst operator there is and find something in his operation that's better than you are.*

- *Do things right, treat people right, be honest in your dealings, and the business will grow; it will grow because you did things right, not because you wish it was big.*

- *You've got to have the courage to make decisions and that means you're going to make mistakes.*

- *Find out what the customer wants and then make it better.*

- *A business that doesn't change is a business that is going to die.*

- *If the quality is there, the consumer will want it, buy it and pay for it.*

- *There is no substitute for high quality. Quality is the one absolutely necessary ingredient of all the most successful companies in the world.*

- *Don't tell me what's right about my product. Tell me what's wrong because that's the only way I can make it better.*

- *It is surprising how often the things that make you happy can also make you successful.*